AF412572

Georgia O'Keeffe and the Camera

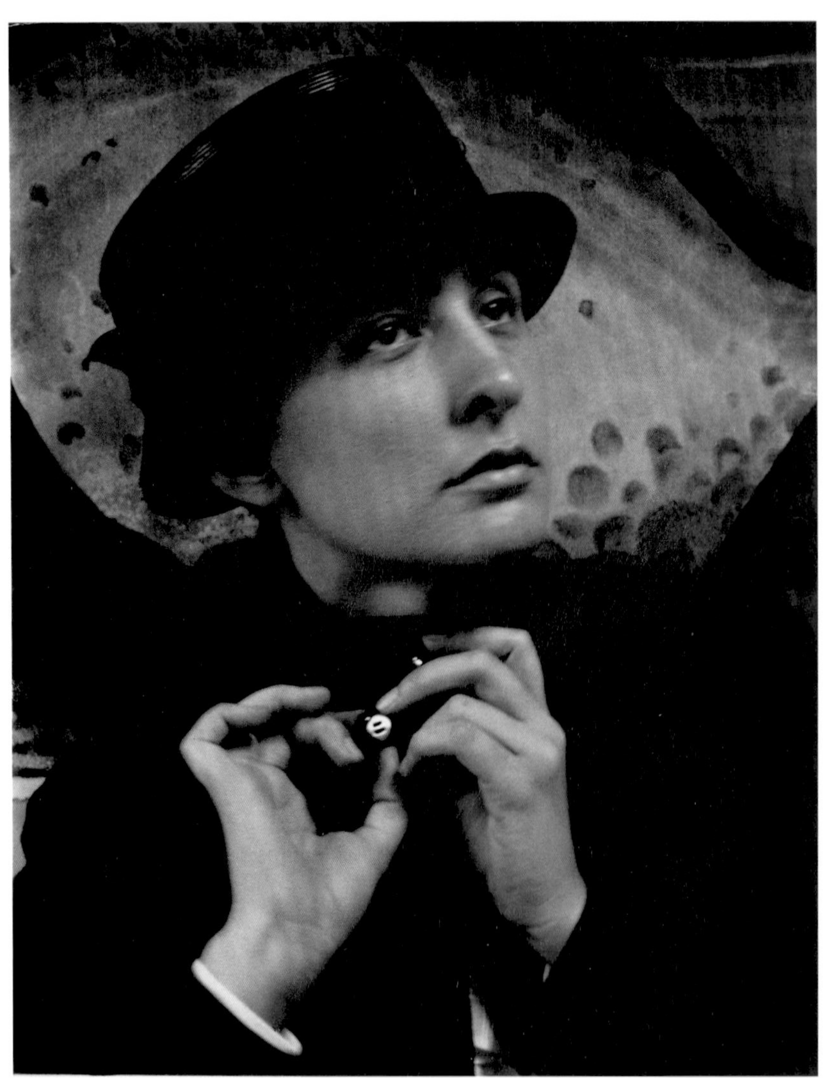

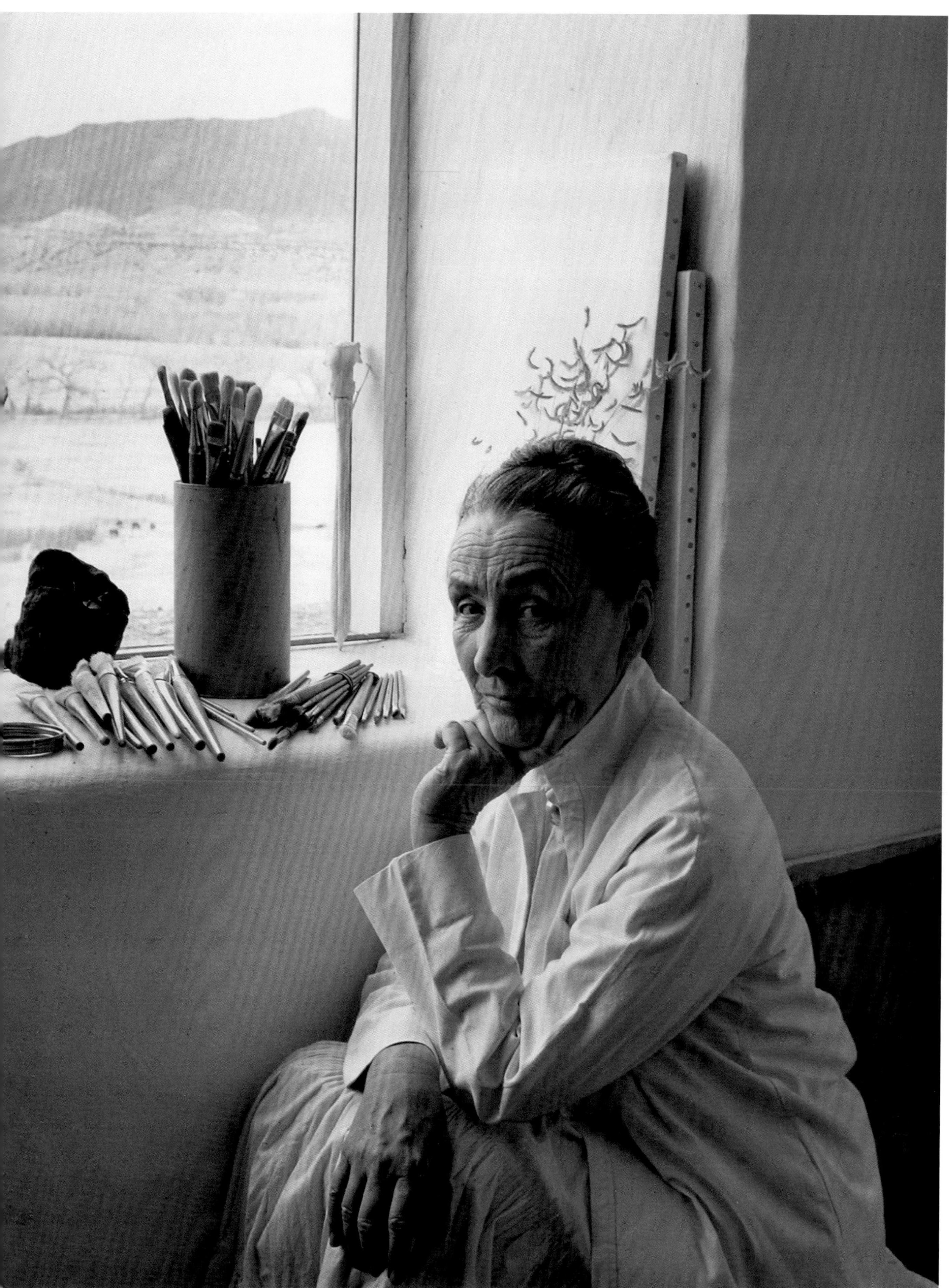

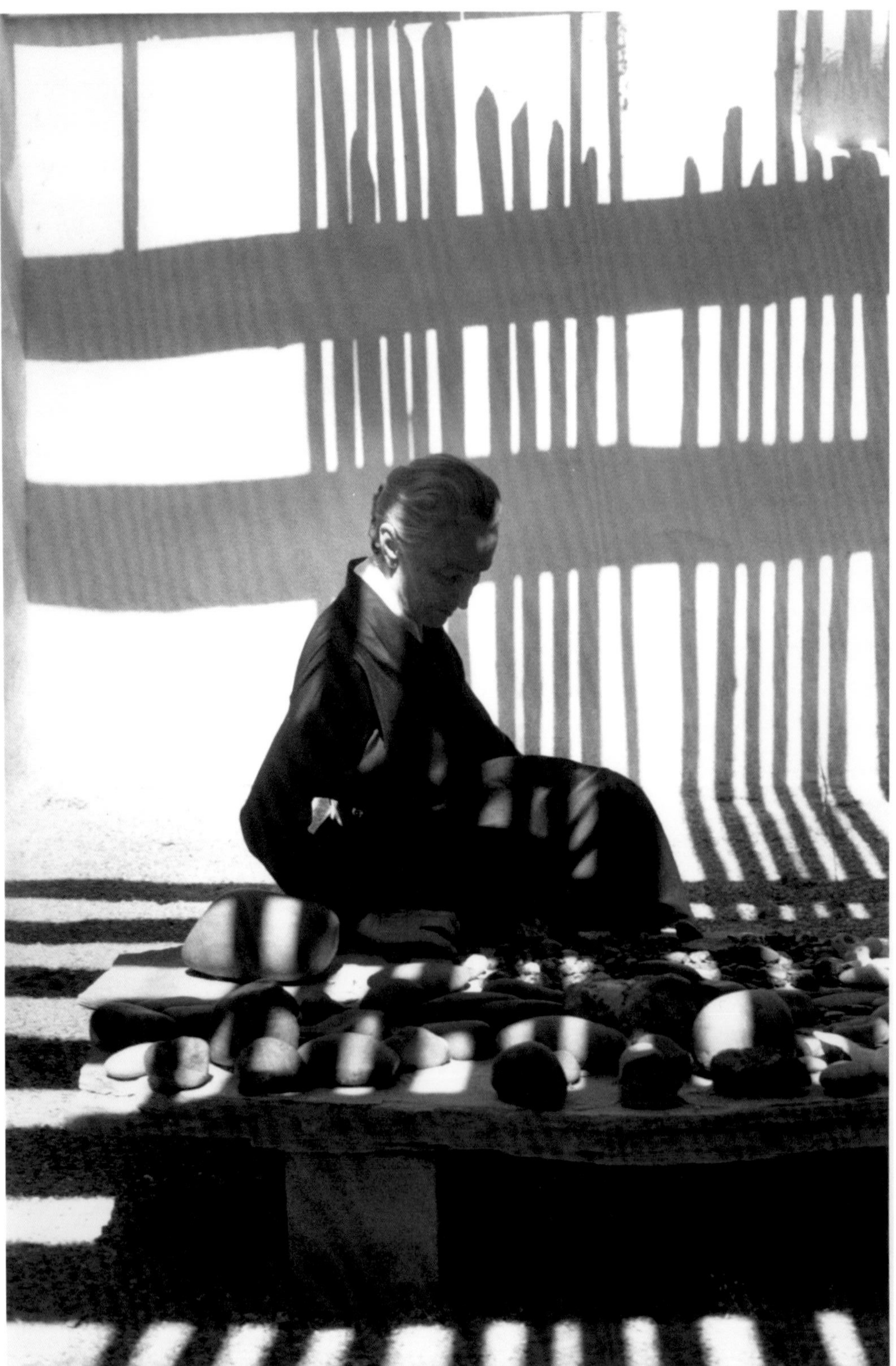

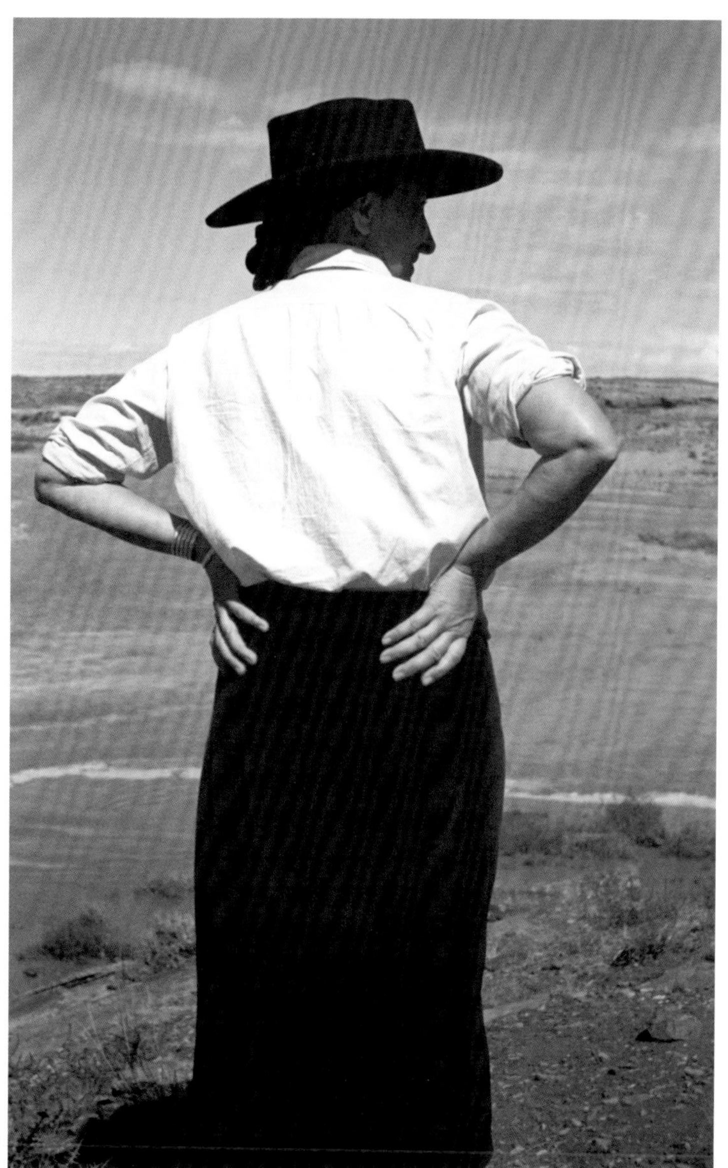

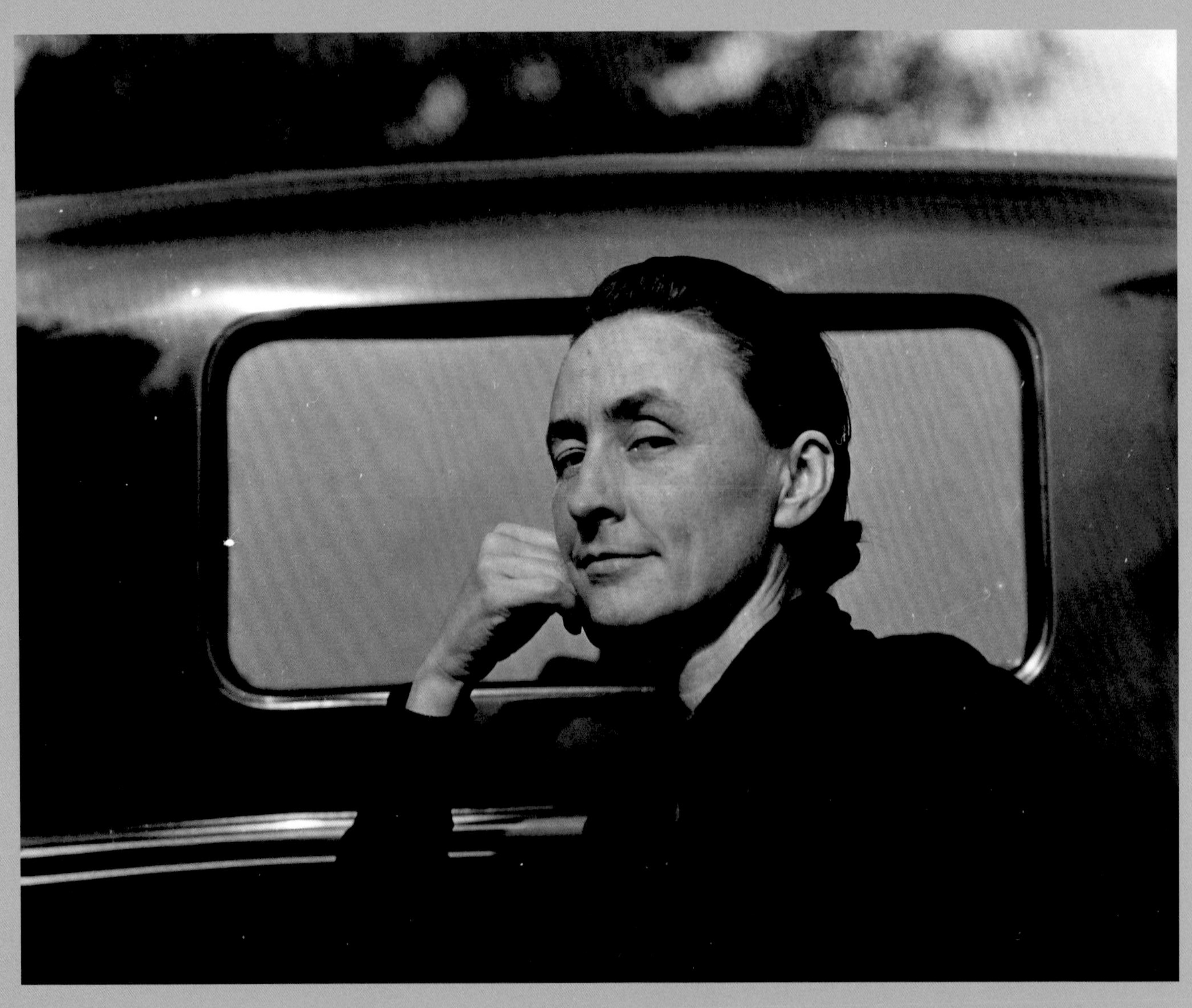

SUSAN DANLY   WITH AN INTRODUCTION BY BARBARA BUHLER LYNES

Georgia O'Keeffe and the Camera *The Art of Identity*

YALE UNIVERSITY PRESS, NEW HAVEN AND LONDON

IN ASSOCIATION WITH THE PORTLAND MUSEUM OF ART, MAINE

Presentation of the exhibition
at the Portland Museum of Art
was funded with support
from Scott and Isabelle Black,
Bank of America, and The Bear
Bookshop, Marlboro, Vermont.

Copyright © 2008 by Yale
University and the Trustees of
the Portland Museum of Art,
Maine. All rights reserved.

This book may not be reproduced, in whole or in part,
including illustrations, in any
form (beyond that copying
permitted by Sections 107 and
108 of the U.S. Copyright Law
and except by reviewers for
the public press), without
written permission from the
publishers.

Designed by Margaret Bauer,
Washington, D.C.

Set in Sabon and Cronos.
Printed in China by Oceanic
Graphic Printing, Inc.

Illustrations

Cover: fig. 50; page ii: fig. 14;
page iii, fig. 53; page iv: John
Loengard, *Rock Collection,
Abiquiu,* 1966 (printed later),
14 15/16 × 10 1/16 in. (37.9 ×
25.5 cm), Gelatin silver print,
National Portrait Gallery,
Smithsonian Institution;
acquired through the generosity
of Pat and John Rosenwald,
NPG.2004.81; page v: fig. 8;
page vi: fig. 5; page x: fig. 59
(detail)

*Library of Congress
Cataloging-in-Publication
Data*

Danly, Susan.
Georgia O'Keeffe and the
camera: the art of identity /
Susan Danly; with an
introduction by Barbara
Buhler Lynes.
    p.   cm.
Exhibition catalog.
Includes bibliographical
references and index.

ISBN 978-0-300-12682-2
(clothbound: alk. paper)
ISBN 978-0-916857-48-6
(paperbound: alk. paper)

1. O'Keeffe, Georgia, 1887–
1986—Portraits—Exhibitions.
2. Art and photography—
United States—Exhibitions.
3. Portrait photography—
United States—Exhibitions.
I. Portland Museum of Art.
II. Title.

ND237.O5A4 2008b
759.13—dc22   2007052375

A catalogue record for this
book is available from the
British Library.

The paper in this book meets
the guidelines for permanence
and durability of the Com-
mittee on Production Guidelines for Book Longevity
of the Council on Library
Resources.

10 9 8 7 6 5 4 3 2 1

Contents

xi   **Directors' Foreword**
DANIEL E. O'LEARY AND GEORGE G. KING

xii   **List of Lenders**

xiii   **Acknowledgments**

1   **Introduction**
BARBARA BUHLER LYNES

7   **"Miss O'Keeffe"—Photography and Fame**
SUSAN DANLY

42   **Plates**

106   **O'Keeffe Chronology**

110   **Exhibition Checklist**

116   **Selected Bibliography**

119   **Index**

122   **Illustration Credits**

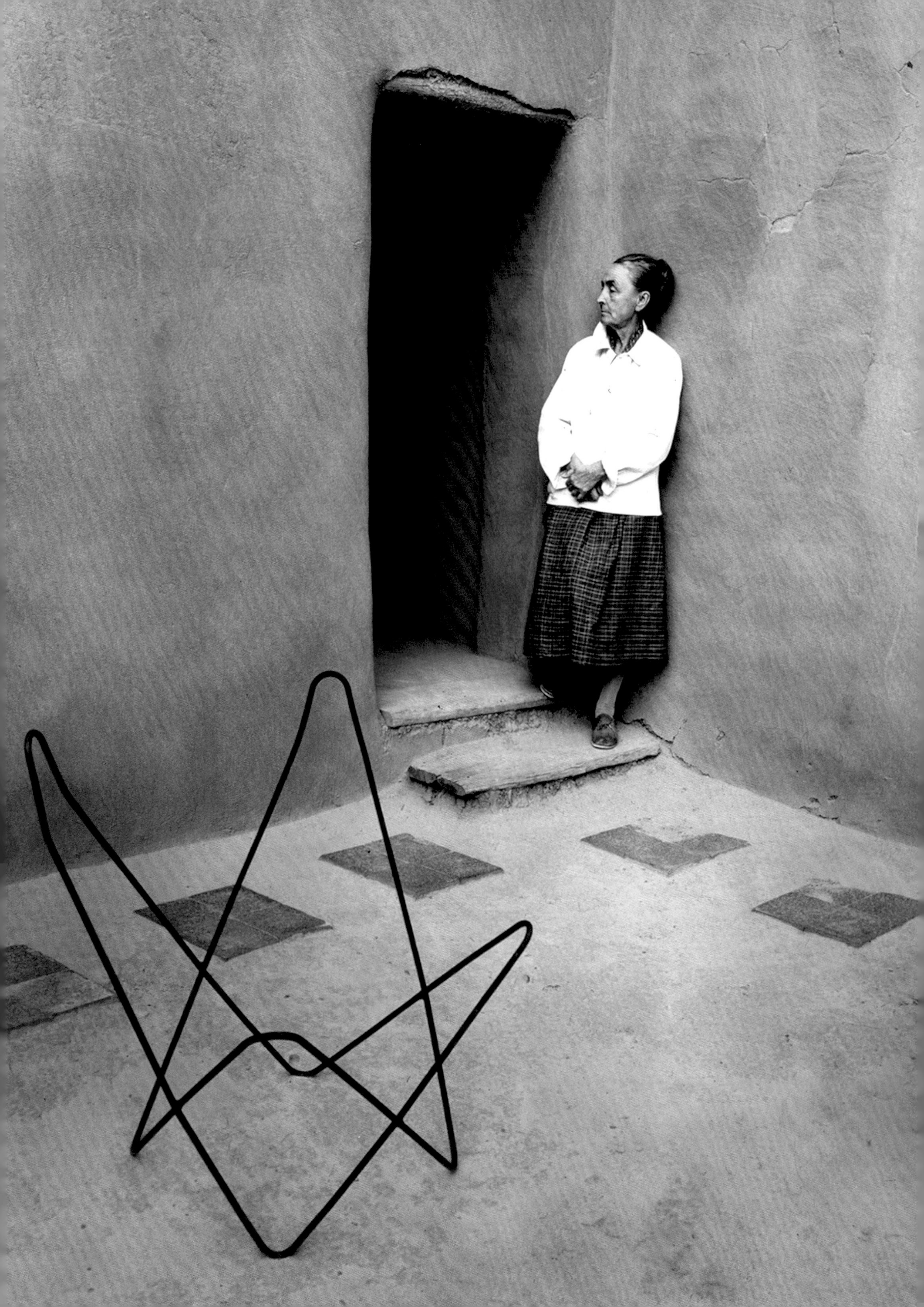

Directors' Foreword

The Portland Museum of Art and the Georgia O'Keeffe Museum are especially pleased to collaborate in organizing the traveling exhibition *Georgia O'Keeffe and the Camera: The Art of Identity*. The works on view examine for the first time the complex relationship between developments in O'Keeffe's art and photographs made of the artist and her houses in New Mexico over the course of her long career. This pairing of paintings and photographs establishes two opposing public images of the artist. The first was set forth in the 1910s by New York photographer Alfred Stieglitz, and the second, crafted by O'Keeffe herself, developed particularly after 1929, when she began working part of every year in New Mexico. Together these views of O'Keeffe and her art help us understand the nature of her long-lasting artistic reputation.

We wish to acknowledge the outstanding work of the exhibition's co-organizers: Susan Danly, Curator of Graphics, Photography, and Contemporary Art, Portland Museum of Art, and Barbara Buhler Lynes, Curator, Georgia O'Keeffe Museum; and Emily Fisher Landau Director, Georgia O'Keeffe Museum Research Center. They have successfully assembled a wide range of drawings, watercolors, paintings, and sculpture by O'Keeffe to consider in association with images of O'Keeffe by such well-known photographers as Ansel Adams, Eliot Porter, Todd Webb, Irving Penn, Arnold Newman, and Yousuf Karsh. Lynes's introduction and Danly's essay for the catalogue that accompanies the exhibition explore the growth of O'Keeffe's fame within the framework of the popular press and the role that photography played in making her work known to a broad public audience.

Presentation of the exhibition at the Portland Museum of Art was funded with very generous support from Scott and Isabelle Black, Bank of America, and The Bear Bookshop, Marlboro, Vermont. At the Georgia O'Keeffe Museum support was provided in part by a generous grant from The Burnett Foundation. Additional funding for the exhibition and related programming at the Georgia O'Keeffe Museum was received from The Annenberg Foundation, Kerr Foundation, JP Morgan Chase Foundation, the Kaiserman-Robinson Family, William Randolph Hearst Foundation, New Mexico Arts (a division of the Department of Cultural Affairs), Santa Fe Arts Commission and 1% Lodgers Tax, New Mexico Tourism Department, and the Members of the Georgia O'Keeffe Museum.

DANIEL E. O'LEARY
Director, Portland Museum of Art, Maine

GEORGE G. KING
Director, Georgia O'Keeffe Museum

Lenders

Amon Carter Museum

Beinecke Rare Book and Manuscript Library, Yale University

Center for Creative Photography, University of Arizona

Corcoran Gallery of Art

Eiteljorg Museum of American Indians and Western Art

Evans Gallery, Portland, Maine

Georgia O'Keeffe Museum

The J. Paul Getty Museum

Balthazar Korab, Ltd.

The Metropolitan Museum of Art

National Portrait Gallery

The Pennsylvania Academy of the Fine Arts

Philadelphia Museum of Art

Portland Museum of Art, Maine

Princeton University Art Museum

Stark Museum of Art

The Andy Warhol Museum

and private collectors

Acknowledgments

As with any collaborative museum venture, success depends on the efforts of numerous staff members and trustees. First and foremost, I would like to thank Barbara Buhler Lynes, Curator, Georgia O'Keeffe Museum, and Emily Fisher Landau Director, Georgia O'Keeffe Museum Research Center, not only for the depth of her knowledge about Georgia O'Keeffe, but also for her willingness to share the rich resources of the Museum and its Research Center. Eumie Imm-Stroukoff, Librarian and Assistant Director at the Research Center, Museum Assistant Curator Heather Hole, and Museum Registrar Judy Chiba Smith also assisted in organizing the exhibition.

The exhibition would not have been possible without the generous assistance of and loans from many institutions and private collectors. The Portland Museum of Art would like to thank the following individuals who helped further the public's appreciation of the art of Georgia O'Keeffe and the photographers who knew her: Martha Sandweiss, Amherst College; John Rohrbach, Amon Carter Museum; Patricia C. Willis, Beinecke Rare Book and Manuscript Library, Yale University; Sarah Cash, Corcoran Gallery of Art; Leslie Calmes, Marcia Tiede, and Amy Rule, Center for Creative Photography, University of Arizona; Suzan Campbell, the Eiteljorg Museum of American Indians and Western Art; Betsy Evans Hunt, Evans Gallery; Weston Naef and Paul Martineau, The J. Paul Getty Museum; Balthazar Korab; Malcolm Daniel, The Metropolitan Museum of Art; Frank Goodyear, Jr., National Portrait Gallery; Ashley Carey, the Philadelphia Museum of Art; Joel Smith, Princeton University Art Museum; Sarah Boehme, Stark Museum of Art; and Heather Kowalski, The Andy Warhol Museum.

The Portland Museum of Art is especially grateful to Mead Brownell for her assistance with research on David McAlpin and Ansel Adams and to the staff of the Art Library at Wellesley College for access to their resources. Michelle Komie, Laura Jones Dooley, Mary Mayer, John Long, and Margaret Bauer at Yale University Press are to be credited for the production of this handsome catalogue. The exhibition and catalogue are the result of efforts by my colleagues at the Portland Museum of Art, particularly Director Daniel O'Leary; the staff of the Curatorial Department, Erin Damon, Tom Denenberg, Jessica Routhier, and Sage Lewis; Registrars Lauren Silverson and Ellie Vuilleumier; Preparators Stuart Hunter, Kris Kenow, and Greg Welch; Public Relations Director Kristen Levesque; Graphic Designers Karin Lundgren and Teresa Lagrange; and Amber Degn in the Development Office.

SUSAN DANLY
Curator of Graphics, Photography, and Contemporary Art
Portland Museum of Art, Maine

Introduction Barbara Buhler Lynes

No artist has been photographed from the beginning to the end of a career as frequently and consistently as Georgia O'Keeffe (1887–1986). She was first photographed in 1917 by world-famous photographer Alfred Stieglitz (1864–1946) when she traveled to New York to see the solo show of her work he organized that year (fig. 1). After she moved to New York in 1918, Stieglitz continued photographing O'Keeffe until 1937, when the seventy-three-year-old avatar of American modernist photography finally put his camera down. By then he had made more than 350 photographs of the artist, who became his wife in 1924.

Even before Stieglitz's death, Ansel Adams and Arnold Newman had made O'Keeffe a subject in their work, and she was photographed in subsequent decades by these and other important American photographers until the end of her life. Because so many of these images, made over an almost seventy-year period, have been and continue to be reproduced in newspapers and popular magazines, O'Keeffe at any age is easily recognized by the public.[1]

Long before Stieglitz began photographing O'Keeffe, he wanted to create a specific kind of portrait. As O'Keeffe put it: "His idea of a portrait was not just one picture. His dream was to start with a child at birth and photograph that child in all of its activities as it grew to be a person and on throughout its adult life. As a portrait it would be a photographic diary."[2] He had initiated his experiment when his daughter, Katherine, was born in 1898, but his first wife, Emmeline, put a stop to the project, claiming that he "was spoiling the child's fun and making her self-conscious."[3] Although Stieglitz was never able to realize his concept completely, the composite portrait of O'Keeffe that he produced over a twenty-year period has become one of the most celebrated achievements of his career.

There is no question that O'Keeffe understood what Stieglitz wanted to accomplish and that she was committed to helping him realize his conception, but the degree of her complicity in the creation of Stieglitz's

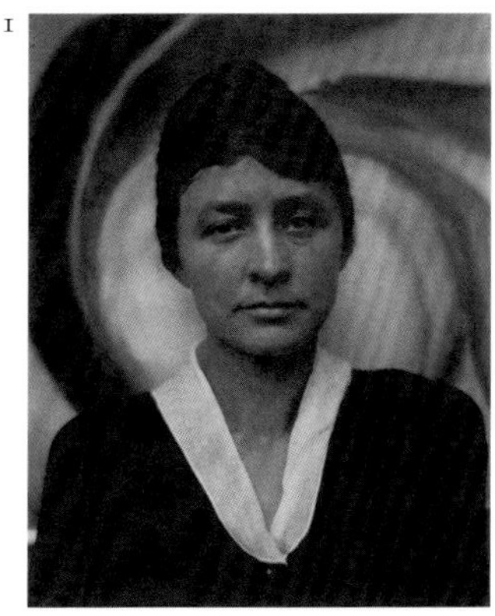

composite portrait has long been discussed. Some suggest that O'Keeffe
was a highly active participant to the point that the composite portrait was
a collaborative effort. Others argue that Stieglitz was in total control of
his model, posing her precisely as he wanted to meet his objectives.

Neither O'Keeffe nor Stieglitz wrote or spoke directly about this
issue, although O'Keeffe pointed out the difficulty of holding poses for
Stieglitz in the introduction she wrote for the catalogue of the exhibition of
the composite portrait held at The Metropolitan Museum of Art in 1978.
She stated: "For those slower glass negatives I would have to be still for
three or four minutes. That is hard—you blink when you shouldn't—your
mouth twitches—your ear itches or some other spot itches. Your arms
and hands get tired, and you can't stay still. I was often spoiling a photograph because I couldn't help moving—and a great deal of fuss was
made about it."[4]

Although O'Keeffe and Stieglitz were silent on this issue, another of
his models of the 1910s and 1920s was not—his niece and O'Keeffe's close
friend Georgia Engelhard Cromwell. In describing his working methods,
Engelhard stated: "Frankly my recollections of posing for Alfred were a
minor version of hell....He was terribly intense and exacting—and everything about the pose had to be just so down to the position of your thumb-
nail....There was no conversation except rather barked commands to
do this or that with your hands, your head…and he could get quite upset
and a bit gruff if you didn't instantly comply."[5] And in 1977 she wrote:
"He portrayed the sitter as he saw him, not as the sitter wished to appear."[6]

The O'Keeffe of Stieglitz's photographs from the 1910s and
1920s—especially those that present O'Keeffe in the nude or partially
clothed and often positioned before one of her recently completed and
innovative abstract works—is depicted as a highly sensual, seemingly
naive, vulnerable force of nature (fig. 2). Stieglitz's exhibition of many of
these images in 1921 created a sensation in New York, not only because
they were startlingly sharply focused, "straight photographs" of the nude
female form, but also because they confirmed the then-scandalous love

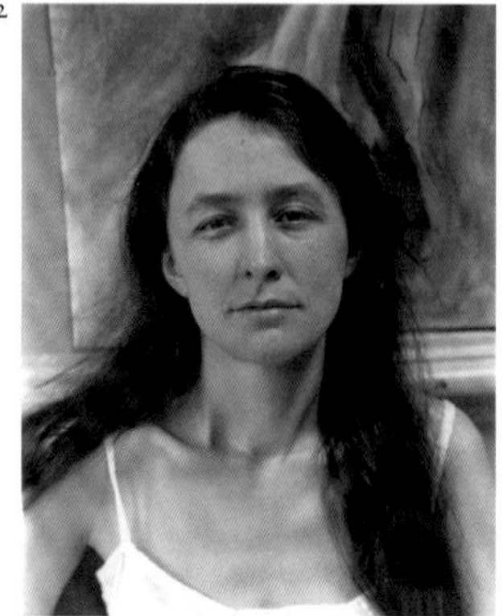

affair between the thirty-four-year-old O'Keeffe and the fifty-seven-year-old married guru of the New York art community. As art critic Henry McBride later put it: "It made a stir. Mona Lisa got but one portrait of herself worth talking about. O'Keeffe got a hundred. It put her at once on the map. Everybody knew the name. She became what is known as a newspaper personality."[7] Moreover, Stieglitz's photographs forged a public image of O'Keeffe as a sexually liberated, modern woman, and this image functioned as a visual equivalent for his ardent and ongoing promotion of O'Keeffe's art as a manifestation of her sexuality.[8]

O'Keeffe objected from the beginning to articles about her that described her as anything but a serious, hard-working, thoughtful artist. But she was most bothered by the sexualized interpretations of her art that dominated the criticism, especially with respect to the retrospective exhibition of her work that Stieglitz organized in 1923. Yet, at this time, she was not in a position to challenge Stieglitz. Although she realized that the critics had taken their cue from him, he was one of the New York art community's most prominent art authorities, and his support was responsible for her burgeoning career and thus her increasing financial independence. Also, having lived with Stieglitz since 1918, O'Keeffe knew well enough that neither she nor anyone else could change his opinion.

Yet O'Keeffe effected various silent strategies to counter what she considered misconceptions of herself and her work, such as shifting the emphasis in her imagery away from abstraction. She felt that her decidedly innovative abstract works, whose sources were indeterminate, had been responsible for generating Freudian interpretations (fig. 3). Although abstraction would remain the basis of her subsequent work, by the end of the 1920s, she had successfully identified herself as a painter of recognizable forms for which she remains best known today (fig. 4).

But her success in moving critics away from Freudian interpretations of her work by increasingly depicting recognizable forms was limited. That is, her representational depictions of natural forms, especially her large-format paintings of the centers of flowers, were seen as female sexual

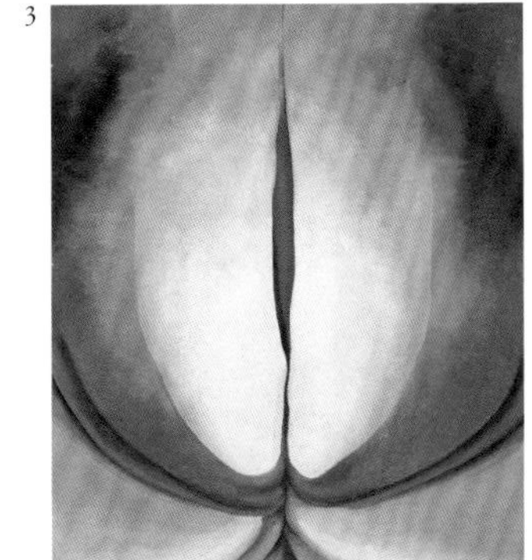

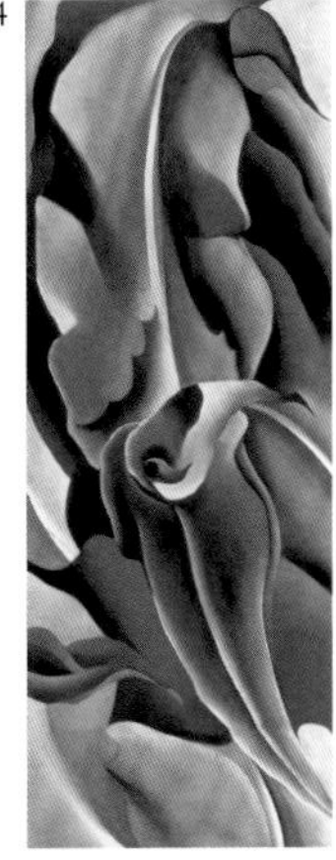

forms even though most flowers are considered to be androgynous, containing both male and female parts. However, in Stieglitz's photographs of the mid-to-late 1920s—such as *Georgia O'Keeffe—After Return from New Mexico,* 1929 (fig. 5), taken at Lake George, New York, after O'Keeffe had spent the first of many summers painting in New Mexico—O'Keeffe appears as self-assured, independent: anything but the vulnerable, sexual creature of his early portraits.

It seems that O'Keeffe had either come to play a more assertive role in Stieglitz's composite portrait or that she had gained and projected the kind of self-confidence that these later photographs assert. Certainly, she demonstrated another degree of assertiveness in the 1930s, after she had gained financial independence through the sale of her work. She publicly denied the validity of Stieglitz's ideas about her work by denouncing Freudian interpretations of it.[9]

Whatever the case, it seems that O'Keeffe had learned how photography could assist in the art of establishing a public identity. This is especially evident after 1949, when she moved to New Mexico, three years after Stieglitz's death, and began allowing herself to be photographed by numerous professional photographers. Having learned the art of promotion through photography from a master, she increasingly relied on the medium to establish her public image as a hard-working, no-nonsense pioneer and individualist whose commitment to her work had allowed her to realize the American dream of self-fulfillment. The success of her effort in this regard is best measured by the fact that the public image she created effectively overtook the one presented in Stieglitz's early portraits of her.

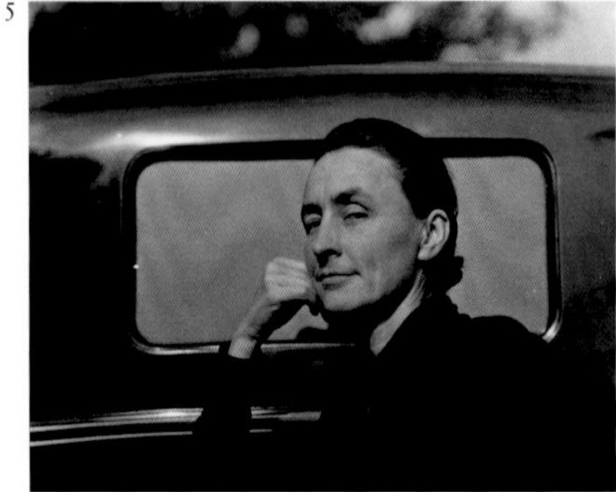

Notes

1. Photography has played an equally important role in popularizing her art. Even as her work has been exhibited regularly in this country since the 1920s and is currently on view to a public increasingly hungry for experiencing it at the Georgia O'Keeffe Museum, photographs of it have been reproduced not only in the media since the 1920s but also, in the past several decades, through a thriving industry that reproduces it on calendars, note cards, postcards, and posters.

2. See Georgia O'Keeffe, "Introduction," in *Georgia O'Keeffe: A Portrait by Alfred Stieglitz* (New York: The Metropolitan Museum of Art and Viking Press, 1978), n.p.

3. See Nancy Newhall, *From Adams to Stieglitz: Pioneers of Modern Photography* (Millerton, N.Y.: Aperture, 1989), 128.

4. O'Keeffe, *O'Keeffe: A Portrait,* n.p.

5. Georgia Englehard Cromwell to William Iness Homer, December 15, 1977, in William Iness Homer Archive, Georgia O'Keeffe Museum Research Center, Santa Fe, New Mexico.

6. Ibid.

7. Henry McBride, "O'Keeffe at the Museum," *New York Sun,* May 18, 1946, 9.

8. For a discussion of the critical reception of O'Keeffe's art in the 1910s and 1920s, see Barbara Buhler Lynes, *O'Keeffe, Stieglitz, and the Critics, 1916–1929* (Ann Arbor, Mich.: UMI Research Press, 1989; 2nd ed., Chicago: University of Chicago Press, 1991).

9. See Georgia O'Keeffe, Statement, in *Fifty Recent Paintings, by Georgia O'Keeffe.* Exhibition catalogue, The Intimate Gallery (New York, February 11–April 3, 1926), reprinted in Barbara Buhler Lynes, *Georgia O'Keeffe: Catalogue Raisonné,* 2 vols. (New Haven and London: Yale University Press, in association with the National Gallery of Art, Washington, D.C., and the Georgia O'Keeffe Foundation, Abiquiu, N.Mex., 1999), 2:1099.

"Miss O'Keeffe"—Photography and Fame   SUSAN DANLY

When Georgia O'Keeffe first showed her work in New York in 1916 at Alfred Stieglitz's avant-garde 291 gallery, she was virtually unknown as an artist. By the time of her death, some seventy years later, she was one of the most famous people in America (fig. 6). Photography played an essential role in establishing her reputation, promoting her career, and creating her public persona. From the beginning, O'Keeffe's professional and personal life were inexorably entwined with the needs and desires of Alfred Stieglitz, who over the course of almost thirty years became her artistic mentor, commercial dealer, portraitist, lover, and, later, husband (fig. 7). The numerous O'Keeffe biographies that have appeared since her death dissect their complex artistic, business, and sexual relationships.[1] And although any discussion of O'Keeffe and photography necessarily begins with Stieglitz in New York, the artist's concerted efforts to develop and maintain friendships with other photographers later in her career, after she moved to New Mexico (fig. 8), are also important. By looking at how her art and personal life were illustrated and discussed in the popular press, we gain insight not only into the details of a carefully crafted public persona but also into the ways she consciously redefined her art after 1930. Photographs of O'Keeffe alone in the rugged New Mexico landscape, of her traditional adobe homes at Ghost Ranch and Abiquiu, and of her as a venerable older woman convey strength, independence, and a strong will (fig. 9).

Photographers and Friends: From Sexual Object to Venerated Artist

During the mid-1910s, O'Keeffe was an art student at Columbia Teachers College in New York and often visited Alfred Stieglitz's famed gallery of modern art, the Little Galleries of the Photo-Secession (later called simply 291 after its Fifth Avenue address).[2] She was frequently accompanied by

6
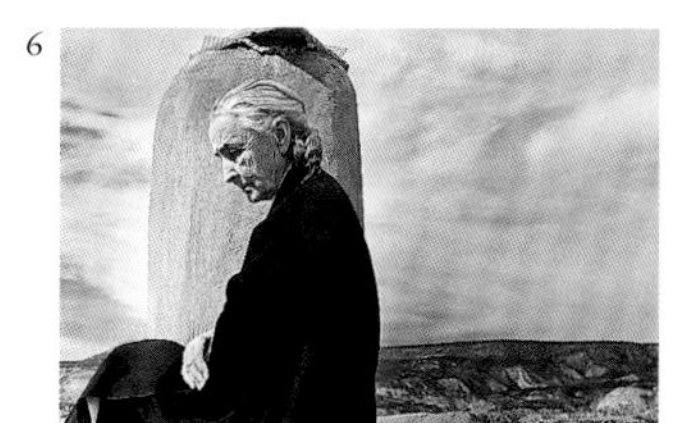

7
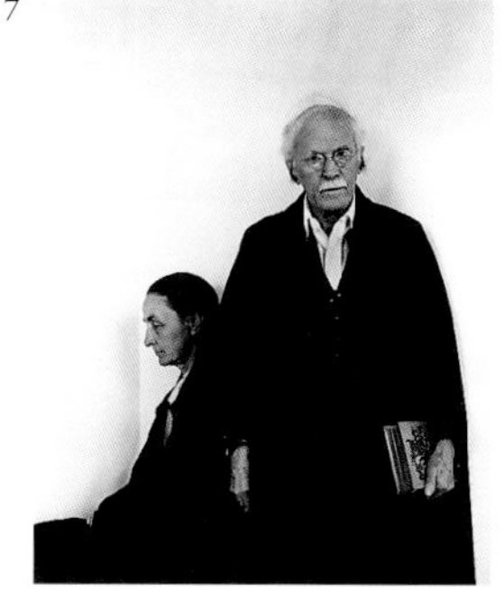

8
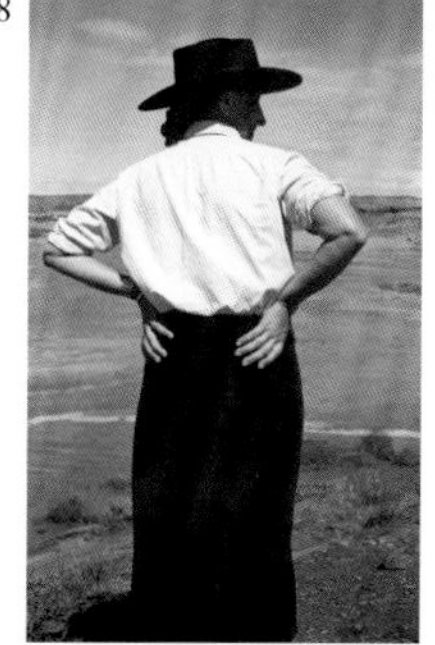

9
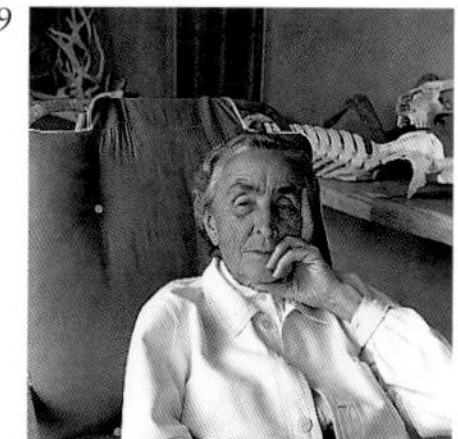

her friend and fellow art student Anita Pollitzer, who engaged Stieglitz in conversations about modern art, though O'Keeffe remained reticent. Without O'Keeffe's knowledge, Pollitzer showed the artist's recent charcoal drawings to Stieglitz, and the two were introduced in 1916. Stieglitz was immediately captivated by her work and included some of her drawings in a group exhibition that year. He also began to show her the work of other artists in his gallery, to send her copies of his avant-garde art magazine *Camera Work,* and to organize exhibitions of her art.

O'Keeffe's first solo exhibition at 291 was in 1917. By then, she was teaching at West Texas State Normal College in Canyon. After classes ended in late spring, she traveled back east to visit friends. As she freely admitted to Pollitzer, though, it was really Stieglitz she wanted to see.[3] She arrived in New York shortly after the exhibition had closed, but Stieglitz obligingly rehung it for her. The show had featured abstract watercolors and charcoal drawings she had made in South Carolina and watercolors and oils of the west Texas landscape. Stieglitz also documented the installation for O'Keeffe in an album of eight images that he later sent to her in Texas (fig. 10). His installation echoed the spareness of her abstract imagery; he had hung the works as far apart as possible in the small gallery space. Stieglitz's photographs emphasize the simple lines of the wood molding, the tonal variation of the burlap wall covering and fabric below the chair rail, and the elemental contrast of light and dark, especially in her charcoal drawings.

One of the most compelling images in the album is Stieglitz's photograph featuring an O'Keeffe charcoal and an abstract sculpture, a small plaster somewhat reminiscent of Auguste Rodin's work (fig. 11). Stieglitz exhibited Rodin's watercolors at 291 in 1908, just after O'Keeffe had arrived in New York, and over the years he published numerous images of his sculpture in *Camera Work,* which O'Keeffe read.[4] Her sculpture, modeled in clay, then cast in plaster and later in bronze, was titled *Abstraction,* although she herself described it in figural terms as a nun bowing her head in mourning.[5] When Stieglitz photographed the piece again in 1919, titling his image *Interpretation* (fig. 12), he tacitly acknowledged his different

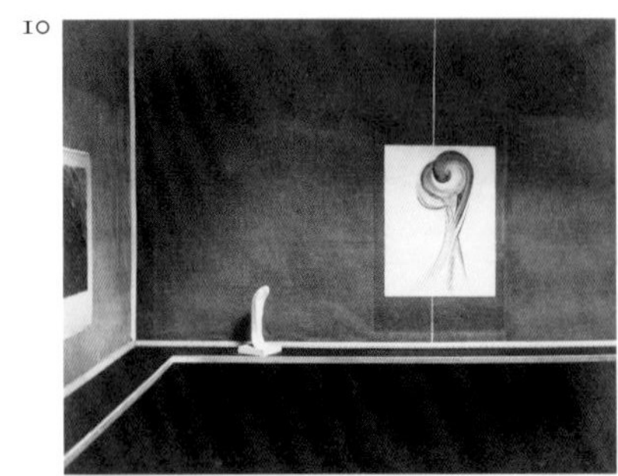

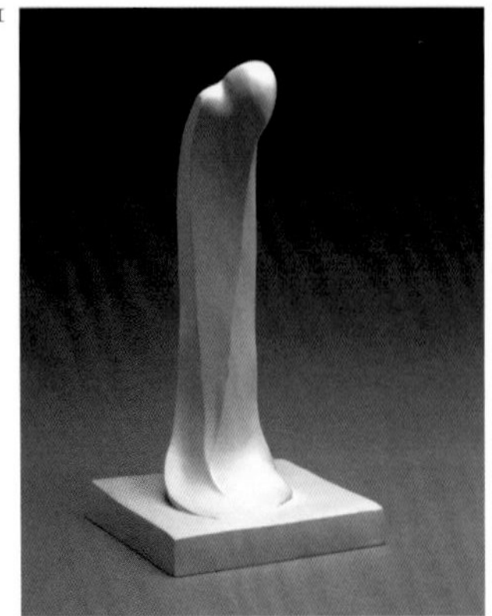

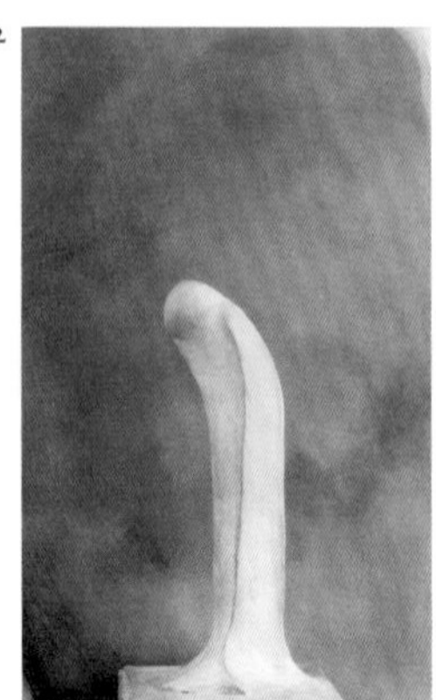

understanding of the work. The 1919 photograph emphasized the ambiguous nature of this piece, with its sexually charged form, and he included the sculpture in several early portraits of O'Keeffe.[6] In one, O'Keeffe holds the sculpture close to her chest; in another, the sculpture is placed in front of her painting *Music — Pink and Blue No. 1, 1918*, which, as scholars have noted, forms a vaginal-like backdrop for the sculpture. In another series of images, Stieglitz shows O'Keeffe fondling the sculpture with her bare feet (fig. 13). A Stieglitz photograph of the O'Keeffe sculpture was included in his 1921 exhibition, where he first unveiled his nude portraits of his protégé. In a review of the show, the art critic Paul Rosenfeld merged the two artists' interpretations in describing the work: "A tiny phallic statuette weeps, is bowed over itself in weeping, while behind, like watered silk, there waves the sunlight of creation."[7]

Stieglitz had begun his extended portrait series of O'Keeffe during her trip to New York in 1917,[8] and it both revived his photographic career and set the parameters for much of the Freudian criticism of her work over the next decade.[9] These photographs, as well as Stieglitz's discussions of O'Keeffe's work, promoted the sexual interpretations of her imagery to which she objected. But enrapt in the throes of her love affair with the much older and professionally influential art dealer, O'Keeffe was in no position or mind to discourage his making portraits of her in the nude, often posed before her art. One of the most frequent backdrops for Stieglitz's early O'Keeffe portraits was her 1916–1917 charcoal drawing *No. 15 — Special* (Philadelphia Museum of Art), before which she posed both fully clothed (fig. 14) and baring her breasts.[10] Although Stieglitz never exhibited his O'Keeffe nudes after 1921, art critics and writers knew of their existence, and they continued to color interpretations of her art.

The sexual content of Stieglitz's early portraits of O'Keeffe is often noted, but many images also refer to the essential dilemma of her art — the tension between abstraction and realism.[11] In 1919 Stieglitz posed O'Keeffe's hands reaching up as if to pluck a round object from one of her drawings, *No. 17 — Special* (fig. 15). The photograph can be seen as a

13 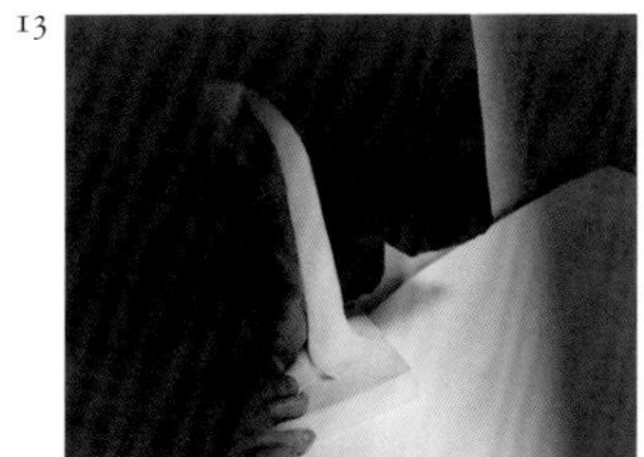 14 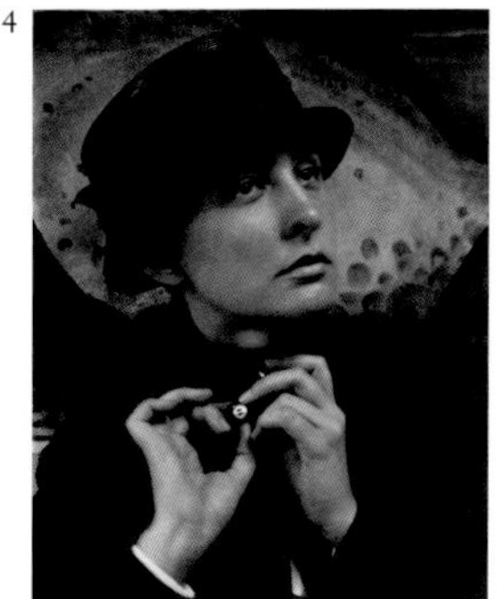 15 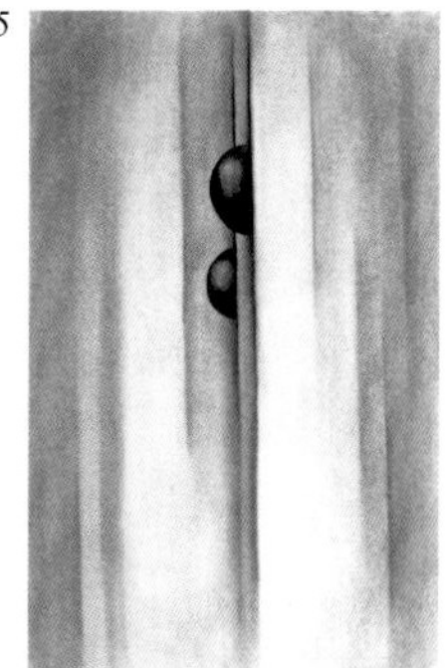

modern-day reference to the ancient Greek story about a contest between two famous artists, Zeuxis and Parrhasius, to produce the most realistic painting. Zeuxis depicted a still life of grapes so real that birds pecked at the fruit. But Parrhasius painted a curtain that was even more convincing, fooling his rival, who attempted to pull the drapery aside to see what lay behind. Stieglitz's photograph of O'Keeffe's hands attempting to grasp what appears to be a three-dimensional object from a two-dimensional drawing underscores the essential conceit of trompe l'oeil illusionism (fig. 16). O'Keeffe's painting of the same subject, *Green Lines and Pink*, with its more nuanced color and simpler definition of space, moves even farther toward abstraction (fig. 17).

In 1923 Stieglitz organized an important show of a hundred works by O'Keeffe at the Anderson Gallery in New York (fig. 18). The exhibition included both abstract works, such as *Green Lines and Pink* and *Blue Line* (see page 44), and a lively series of nude watercolors that were more explicitly sexual in nature (fig.19). The works in that exhibition and the critics' response to it cemented O'Keeffe's reputation as an artist.[12] Significantly, the critic Herbert Seligmann singled out the nudes as especially important advances in color and suggested parallels between the female form and abstraction: "Color is her language. Her body acknowledges its kindred shapes and renders the visible scene in those terms. A few bold delicate strokes lay upon paper a woman's figure in vibrant red, or green and slate shot with rose."[13]

From the outset, Stieglitz's photographs of O'Keeffe and her art encouraged the critics to conflate her art and her persona as a female artist. Henry Tyrrell observed that her work was "an extraordinary manifestation of modern art expression and feminine self-revelation through the medium of semi-abstract symbolistic painting."[14] Helen Appleton Read noted that "O'Keeffe's work is the expression of a powerful personality. It is entirely personal."[15] And in an attempt to combine O'Keeffe's art, her facial features, and aspects of her personal life, one critic went so far as to speculate about the connection between her genius and her poor health: "Miss O'Keeffe

16 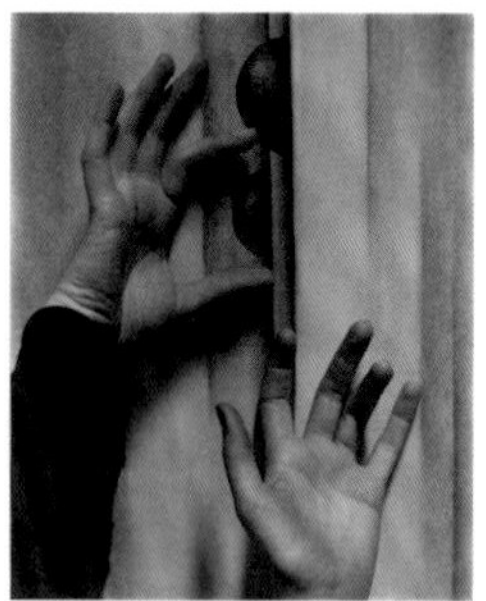

17 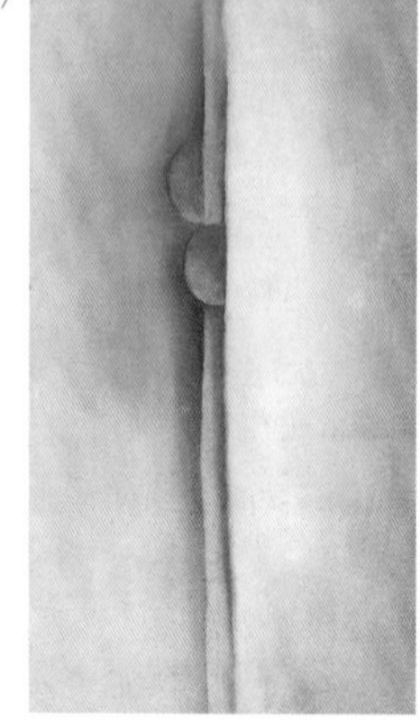

18 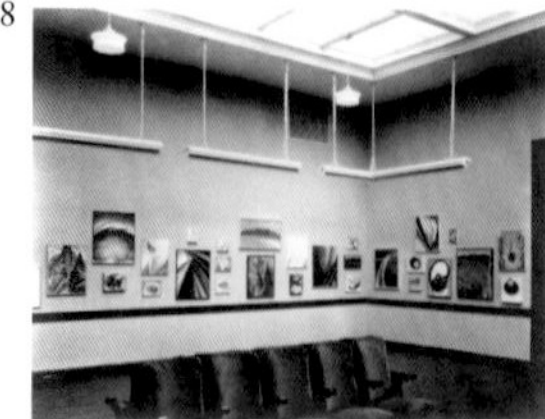

has known a great deal of illness in her life: she has, we imagine, been
thrown back on her own resources to a large extent. She is intellectual and
introspective — for an artist, a curiously austere type. Her face is an interest-
ing study — the features extremely sensitive and fine, the nose slender and
straight, the mouth wide and thin lipped."[16] It is here that we begin to see a
new understanding of her persona, as "intellectual and introspective," an
image that counters the sexual aura promoted by Stieglitz.

O'Keeffe's mental and physical health in these years has been
detailed by biographers.[17] Her bouts with influenza and perhaps tubercu-
losis, recurring periods of unhappiness, and a nervous breakdown in
1933 all indicated a frailty belied by her image as a strong, vibrant artist.
Much of her deep anxiety was brought about by the failure of her Radio
City Music Hall commission and by rifts in her relationship with Stieglitz:
his affairs with other women, notably Dorothy Norman, and his need
to control her career, promoting her art in ways she did not agree with.[18]
Her travels in these years were dictated largely by Stieglitz's need to be
near his family during summers at Lake George in upstate New York,
and O'Keeffe rarely left his side.[19] Then in 1929, seeking both a break
from the intensity of her marriage and a new source of inspiration for
her career, O'Keeffe left New York for New Mexico.

She traveled to Santa Fe with her friend Rebecca Strand, the wife
of photographer Paul Strand. The two women were then taken to Taos, at
the insistence of Mabel Dodge Luhan, who welcomed them to her home,
Los Gallos, and provided them with a studio. During their three-month
visit, they explored the neighboring Indian pueblos, went on sketching and
camping trips, and sunbathed in the nude. O'Keeffe purchased a Model A
Ford, and both women learned to drive. According to Rebecca Strand,
O'Keeffe was a timid driver but loved the car, nicknaming it Hello. In a
letter to her husband, Strand captures the sense of fun and relaxation of
the trip: "This afternoon, G. and I put on our bathing suits, connected
the hose, and washed the Ford. Much shrieking with laughter and it came
out shining like a new button. Then we disappeared into the pink patio

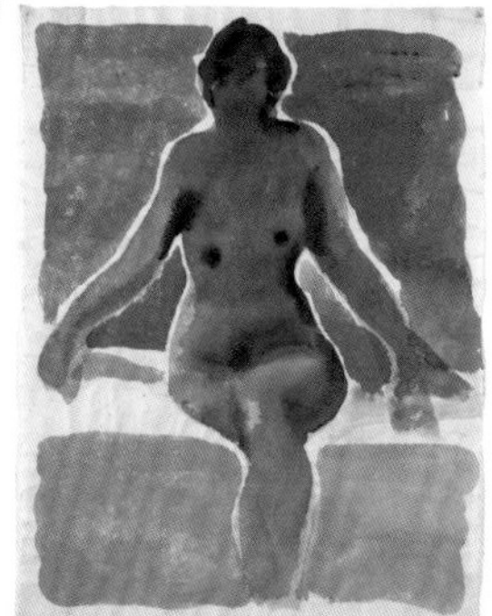

and took off our suits and hosed ourselves, then went to the house, made jasmine tea and [had] some of Mrs. Schauffler's marvelous orange bread."[20]

Just as O'Keeffe's personal life was undergoing significant changes, so was her art. Even Stieglitz seemed to recognize O'Keeffe's new spirit of independence. His 1929 portrait of her, significantly titled *Georgia O'Keeffe—After Return from New Mexico,* shows a coyly smiling woman, engaging the camera lens with a self-assured expression (see fig. 5). Her right arm is propped on the side of an automobile, the symbol of her new-found sense of freedom. While in New Mexico, O'Keeffe began sketching and painting landscapes of the rugged terrain, and she later exhibited the finished oils in New York at Stieglitz's new gallery, An American Place. His portrait of a confident O'Keeffe, dressed in nunlike black, with the suggestion of a cross formed by her lapel (fig. 20), poses the artist in front of her abstracted landscape *After a Walk Back of Mabel's,* 1930, painted near Luhan's house in Taos. The photograph was probably taken when the painting was shown at his gallery in 1930 and differs significantly from his earlier images of O'Keeffe posed with her work. Gone are the allusions to sensuality, either personal or aesthetic, and instead we see the artist as a saintly desert ascetic. The odd clothing she wears in the photograph was not a new affectation, however. O'Keeffe had always preferred to wear simple clothes: long dresses that she often fashioned herself and flat shoes. She rarely donned jewelry and usually tied her long hair in a bun at the nape of her neck and covered it with a headscarf, as in this picture. On her annual trips to New Mexico she acquired Navajo silver bracelets, and one figures prominently in another Stieglitz portrait of her taken in 1933 (fig. 21). In this image, O'Keeffe leans wistfully against the rim of an automobile wheel, the metallic shine of the bracelet echoing the graceful curve of the spare tire.[21]

In addition to buying Navajo silver and a new car, O'Keeffe collected bones in New Mexico, shipping them back to Lake George in 1931. Although Stieglitz complained about the shipping costs, O'Keeffe placed the bones around the farmhouse, and he began to include them in portraits

20 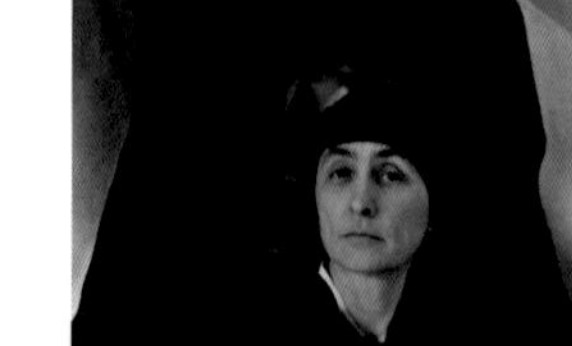

21 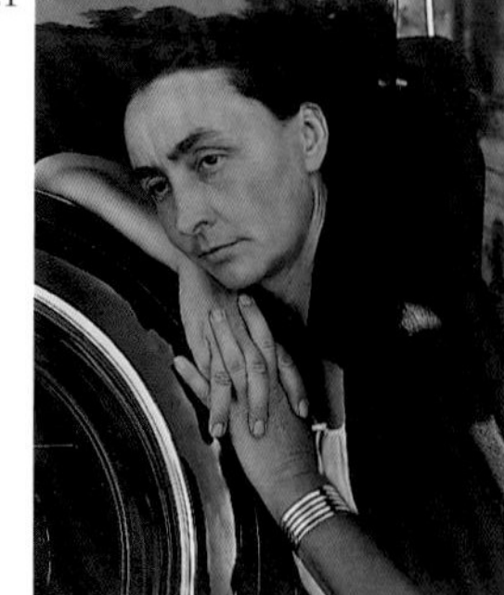

of her (fig. 22). Expanding on his previous portraits of her hands, Stieglitz
included these memento mori skulls juxtaposed with O'Keeffe's artfully
positioned fingers. That year he made several other portraits of her with
horse and cow skulls in addition to four images of her wrapped in an Indian
blanket — all symbols of the Southwest that she also incorporated into
her paintings (fig. 23).[22] When Stieglitz exhibited his portrait of O'Keeffe's
hands and a deer skull with the variant title *Life and Death — Hands and
Skull,* he underscored his ideas about the latent symbolism of her imagery.
By the time *Life* published this photograph in 1943 it could be read as a
meditation on their waning relationship and his failing health.[23]

     After 1929, when she began to spend more time in New Mexico,
O'Keeffe found new ways to promote her career, and her reliance on Stieglitz declined. He still held annual exhibitions of her work in his gallery,
but other critics began to play a greater role in publicizing her growing
reputation as an artist. After his photographic work ceased in 1937, other
photographers gradually began to fill the void, producing images of the
artist that increasingly placed her specifically in the Southwest rather than
in New York.[24] These new photographers first came from the ranks of
the Stieglitz circle or were at least beholden to him for an introduction to
O'Keeffe. The young Ansel Adams (1902–1984) was the first to take an
interest in O'Keeffe and her art. He and O'Keeffe had met in 1929 when
both were staying with Luhan in Taos. Adams was working on a book
documenting the architecture of the Taos Pueblo with a text by the noted
writer Mary Austin.[25] The pueblo was fast becoming an attraction for
artists, writers, and tourists alike, and O'Keeffe clearly shared Adams's
special interest in it. She made several sketches and paintings of the nearby
church of San Francisco de Asis on that first trip and in later years produced several more oils that parallel Adams's formal concerns for the broad
massing of shapes and natural light. Writing about one of her paintings,
O'Keeffe remarked: "The Ranchos de Taos Church is one of the most
beautiful buildings left in the United States by the Spaniards. Most artists
who spend any time in Taos have to paint it, I suppose, just as they have to

22 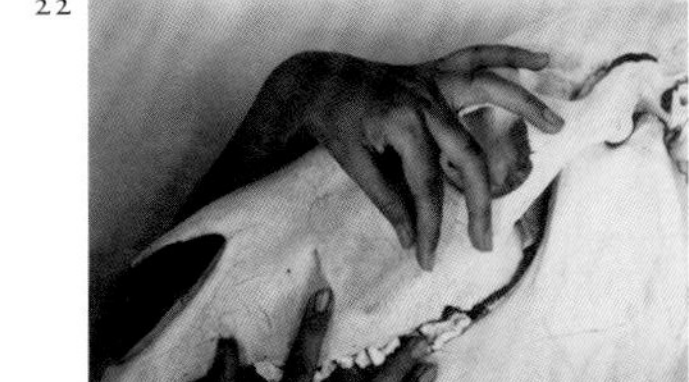

23 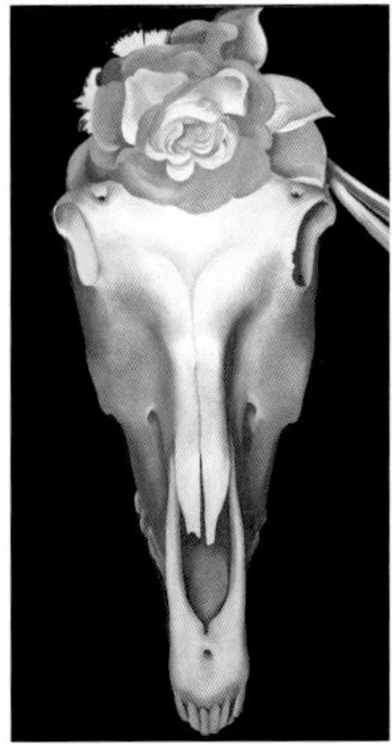

paint a self-portrait. I had to paint it—the back of it several times, the front once. I finally painted a part of the back…that said all I need to say about the church."[26]

In the 1920s O'Keeffe's architectural subjects had dealt with the more complicated urban skyline and dramatic lights of New York. In New Mexico, under the bright rays of the desert sun, the plain adobe walls provided simple areas for broad tonal modulation, and her colors seemed more subtly bleached. The parallels between Adams's photographs and O'Keeffe's paintings, especially in the 1930s, are dramatic.[27] Her introduction to his architectural photographs reinforced the formal concerns already present in her work but, more important, provided a new direction for her career. Although she had always been interested in vernacular architectural forms, they began to emerge as a major focus.[28] The artists' shared love of the Southwest's dramatic landscape and culture sealed their friendship, and Adams's portraits of her helped create the iconic image of O'Keeffe as a strong individualist and pioneering modern artist (see fig. 8).[29]

Adams's *Taos Pueblo* (1930), along with a portfolio of his work, caught Stieglitz's attention when the two photographers first met at An American Place in 1933.[30] Adams had hoped that Stieglitz, arguably the most influential advocate for modern photography in the country, would exhibit his photographs. Although Stieglitz did not immediately offer Adams an exhibition, the two began a friendly relationship and correspondence that lasted until Stieglitz's death. In 1936 Adams's hopes for success on the East Coast were realized when Stieglitz presented a solo exhibition of his photographs and sold one to David Hunter McAlpin, a wealthy collector and a founder of the Museum of Modern Art's photography department.[31] Adams had met McAlpin, a member of the Rockefeller family, through O'Keeffe earlier in the year, and the three of them, along with Godfrey Rockefeller and his wife, met again at O'Keeffe's house at Ghost Ranch in northern New Mexico the following year to make an extensive tour through the Southwest.

By the mid-1930s Ghost Ranch, owned and run by Arthur and Phoebe Pack, who were members of a wealthy East Coast lumber family, had become the center of O'Keeffe's artistic life.[32] Located sixty miles north-west of Santa Fe in the Chama River Valley, the guest ranch catered to well-to-do easterners, but it also provided a degree of privacy and remoteness that appealed to O'Keeffe. She first stayed there in 1934, and by the summer of 1937 she had rented one of the houses on the property, Rancho de los Burros. Situated at the base of a distinctive flat-topped mountain called the Pedernal, the traditional adobe home was surrounded by colorful cliffs and provided a vista of the distant Jemez Mountains and the deep blue desert sky.[33] O'Keeffe's 1937 painting of the Ghost Ranch house (fig. 24) was re-produced in an article in *Life* titled "Alfred Stieglitz Made Georgia O'Keeffe Famous." The piece concluded, perhaps to O'Keeffe's dismay: "A notable impresario of artists, [Stieglitz] has helped the onetime school teacher to become one of the country's most prosperous and talked-of painters."[34]

Despite its isolated location, Ghost Ranch provided O'Keeffe with a steady stream of visitors and potential patrons. During the day she retreated with her canvas or sketch pad into the hills, but in the evenings, before she moved to Ranchos de los Burros, she often ate with other guests in the communal dining room. Later, when she was settled in her house, O'Keeffe often invited friends to join her on the roof to watch the stars, a favorite pastime noted in the *Life* article and described in a letter to Stieglitz: "I've been up on the roof watching the moon come up—the sky very dark—the moon large and lopsided—and very soft—a strange white light creeping across the far away to the dark sky—the cliffs all black—it was weird and strangely beautiful."[35]

Shortly after O'Keeffe moved into the Burros house in September 1937, Ansel Adams and David McAlpin arrived at Ghost Ranch for the start of a two-week camping trip through the most scenic parts of the Southwest. The group traveled in style by car, guided by one of the ranch's most skilled hands, Orville Cox. The trip resulted in one of the best-known images of O'Keeffe, a rare Adams portrait that captured the smiling artist looking slyly out from under her wide-brimmed hat toward the cowboy, who assiduously avoids her gaze (fig. 25).[36] Among the more typical Adams landscapes taken

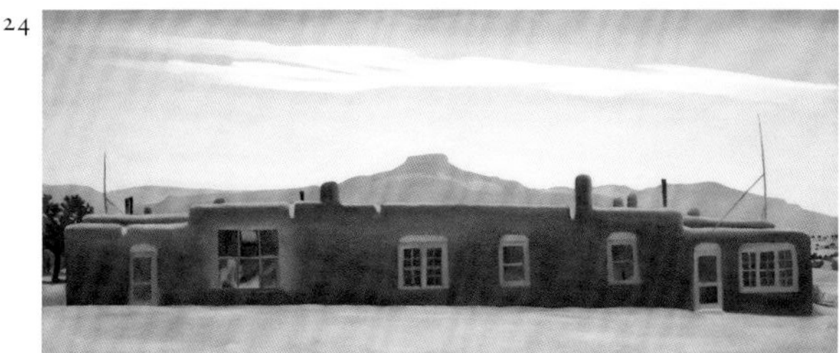

24

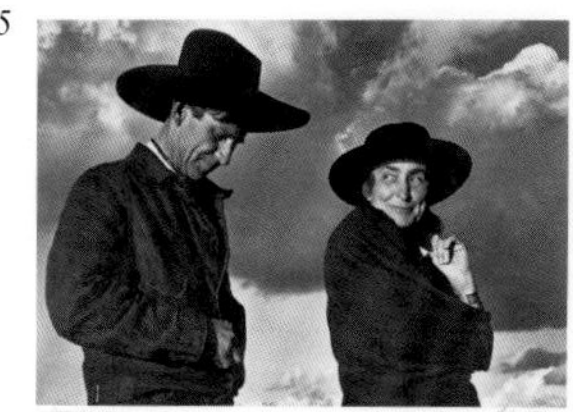

25

on this trip are those of the most famous sites in the West: Canyon de Chelly in Arizona, Monument Valley in Utah, and the Grand Canyon on the Colorado River. In addition to the numerous photographs en route, Adams photographed scenes at Ghost Ranch, providing an insider's view of O'Keeffe's new world—filled with friends, spectacular landscapes, moments of humor, and her work. In an unusual view of O'Keeffe painting, Adams captured her using the back seat of her car as a studio, its roof shielding her from the hot desert sun (fig. 26). The canvas propped up on the back seat, *Gerald's Tree II*, depicts a gnarled cedar stump named for her friend Gerald Heard, a poet and theosophist who also visited the artist at Ghost Ranch that year (fig. 27). As O'Keeffe noted, Heard had often hiked to the tree during his stay there, and "he must have been dancing around the tree before I started to paint it. So I always thought of it as Gerald's tree."[37]

Late in 1937 O'Keeffe sent nineteen paintings from her summer's work at Ghost Ranch to her annual exhibition at Stieglitz's gallery in New York. Among them were two versions of *Gerald's Tree, The House I Live In* (see fig. 24), and *Three Small Rocks Big* (fig. 28). The catalogue copy consisted of a long letter she sent Stieglitz describing the events of a typical day on the ranch—getting up late, eating lunch with the gardener, giving her car to Ansel Adams so that he could drive out into the landscape to take photographs, and going on an evening horseback ride with David McAlpin:

It was the best ride I've ever had here—up and down all sorts of places that we could only get the horse to go by getting off and pulling several times—places I would never dare to go alone and the cowboys wouldn't be much interested—perfectly mad looking country—hills and cliffs and washes too crazy to imagine all thrown up in the air by God and let tumble where they would.... The evening glow on a cliff much higher than these here in a vast sort of red and gold and purple amphitheatre while we sat on our horses on top of a hill of the whitish green earth.[38] [fig. 29]

Capping the evening was an impromptu piano concert from Adams on the Steinway owned by an absent Ghost Ranch resident, Robert Wood Johnson, the New Jersey pharmaceutical magnate. O'Keeffe's guests let themselves

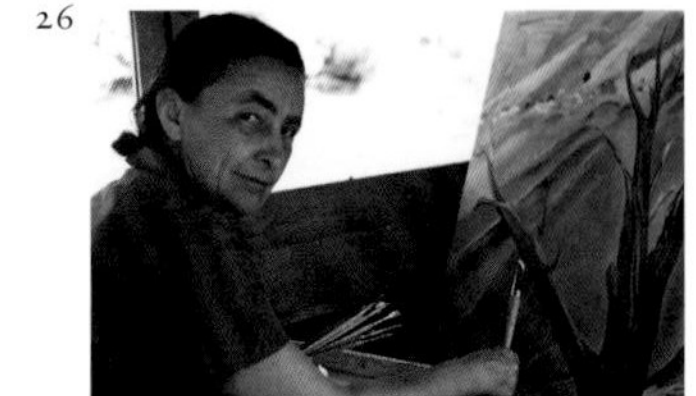

26

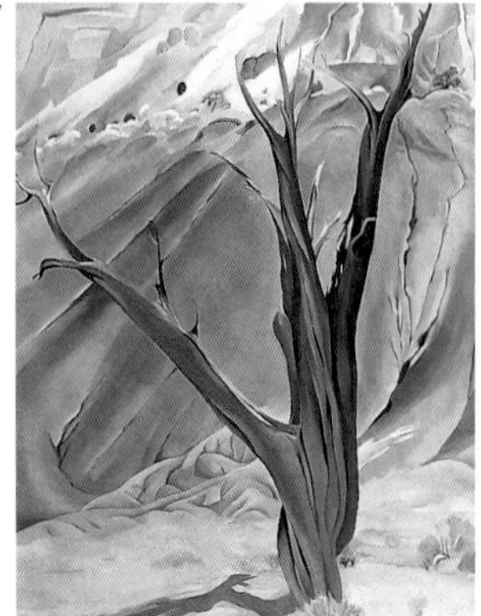

27

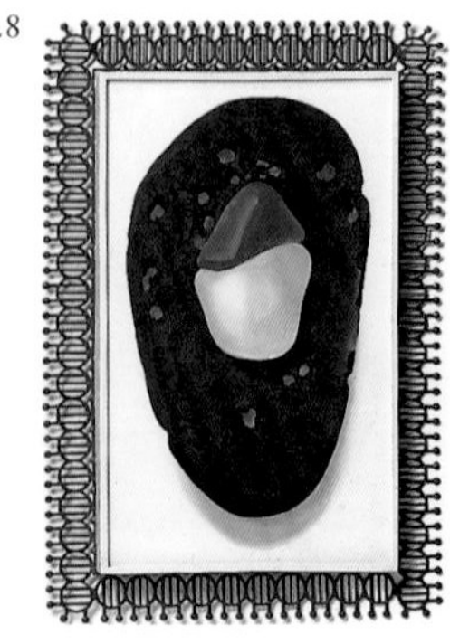

28

into his closed-up house, laid themselves down on newspapers covering
the carpet, and drank beer while Adams played. By including such details
in the exhibition catalogue, Stieglitz ensured that O'Keeffe's New York
audience had a full and romantic picture of her life out West.

Later that year Adams sent a set of proofs from the New Mexico
trip to McAlpin. O'Keeffe chided him for not charging his well-to-do pat-
ron, but Adams was grateful for McAlpin's financial support, conveying
his enthusiasm for the trip in a letter to Stieglitz: "By a miraculous sequence
of circumstances and the kindness of David McAlpin, I am in New Mexico
with three cameras, a case of film, a big appetite and a vigorous feeling
of accomplishment."[39] He continues: "O'Keeffe is supremely happy and
painting, as usual, supremely swell things. When she goes out riding with
a blue shirt, black vest, and black hat, and scampers around against the
thunderclouds—I tell you it's something."[40]

In addition to the Ghost Ranch photographs acquired from Adams
(fig. 30), McAlpin later purchased one of O'Keeffe's flower pictures for his
collection.[41] As the result of his 1937 trip and another with the same group
to Yosemite the following year, McAlpin became a staunch advocate of
modern photography, eventually donating funds for photography purchases
to both The Metropolitan Museum of Art and the Museum of Modern Art.
In May 1939, to celebrate MoMA's first exhibition devoted to photography, McAlpin entertained its new curator, Beaumont Newhall, and Adams,
Stieglitz, and O'Keeffe at dinner. Later that evening he took the group
(without the aging Stieglitz) on a boat ride to see the New York World's
Fair, which had named O'Keeffe as one of the twelve outstanding women
of the past fifty years.[42] During this visit to New York, Adams took photographs of O'Keeffe's paintings in the back room of Stieglitz's gallery. With
the paintings propped up on shelves and leaning against storage bins,
these photos were not installation shots of an exhibition but rather formal
geometric studies of frames, angles, and odd croppings. McAlpin bought
three prints from the series, one of which, *Detail of O'Keeffe Painting and
Reflections, An American Place, Gallery of Alfred Stieglitz*, features her

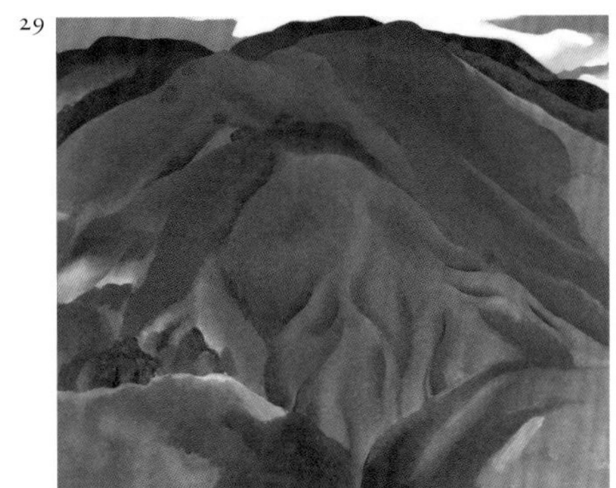

29

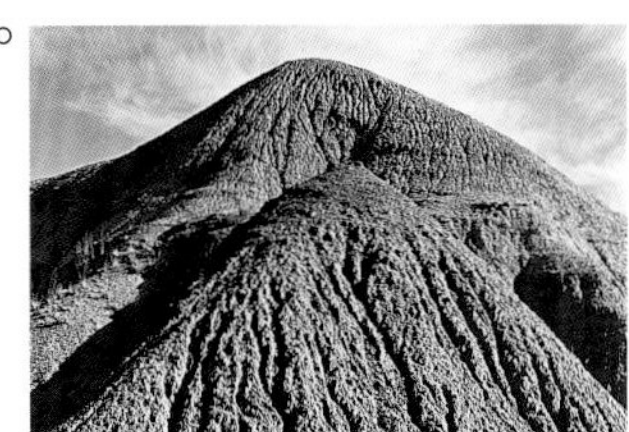

30

view of the industrial landscape of Manhattan (see page 118). The sheet
of glass covering the O'Keeffe painting reflects the window frames on the
opposite side of the room and the buildings beyond, further layering the
complexity of Adams's composition and turning O'Keeffe's realism into an
abstraction.[43]

Another of Stieglitz's stable of photographers who developed a long
relationship with O'Keeffe was Eliot Porter (1901–1990). Late in the winter
of 1938–1939, Stieglitz showed Porter's black-and-white prints in a solo
exhibition at An American Place. Trained as a research scientist in biochem-
istry, Porter was an amateur photographer with an interest in birds and
natural history. The year after his show with Stieglitz, Porter gave up
teaching and research to focus exclusively on photography. During a visit
to O'Keeffe at Ghost Ranch in 1940, Porter used black-and-white film to
photograph one of the characteristically twisted trunks of a dead cedar tree
(fig. 31)—just the type of stark vegetation that O'Keeffe featured in her
painting *Gerald's Tree II* (see fig. 27). By 1946, when he moved to Tesuque,
New Mexico, situated between Santa Fe and Ghost Ranch, Porter had
begun to earn a reputation as a noted color photographer. But in keeping
with his earlier practice of photographing O'Keeffe, Porter continued to
photograph the artist and her landscape in black and white. His image of
O'Keeffe posed with her portrait bust by the sculptor Mary Callery (fig. 32)
uses deep shadows to soften the artist's profile, the type of dramatic lighting
that nineteenth-century photographers described as "Rembrandt effects."[44]
Indeed, in composition and mood, Porter's image evokes the seventeenth-
century Dutch painter's famous portrait *Aristotle with a Bust of Homer,*
another meditation on artistic fame.

Porter's friendship with O'Keeffe developed during these years
because of their proximity to and shared love of the Southwest landscape.
In 1951 O'Keeffe and the Santa Fe writer Spud Johnson joined Porter
and his wife, Aline, on a trip to Mexico, where Porter photographed churches
and pyramids in both color and black and white. During the 1960s Porter
made several raft trips on the Colorado River through Glen Canyon,

31 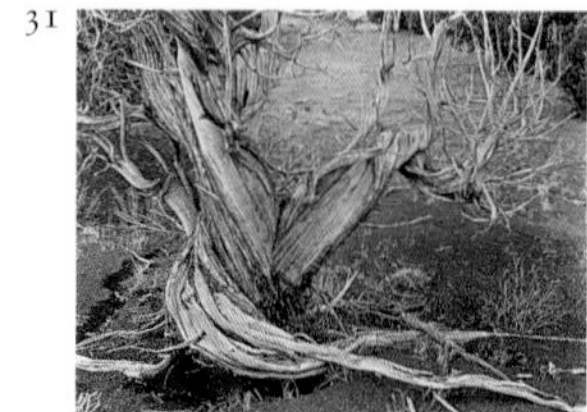

32 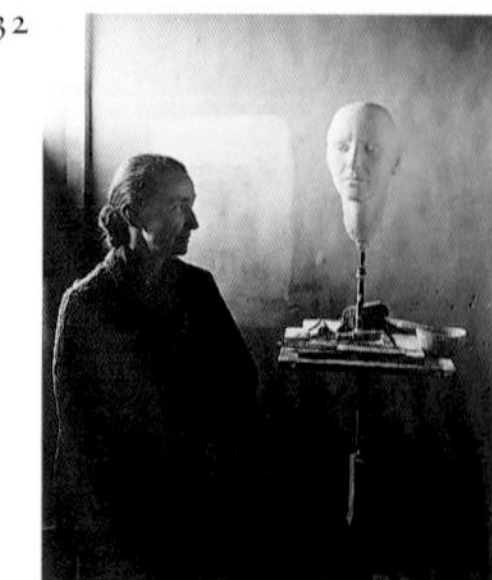

Utah, which was soon to be flooded to provide a source of water for the growing urban populations in the Southwest. O'Keeffe joined him on trips in 1961 and 1964 (fig. 33). On the first trip, while camping along the river's edge, Porter found a perfectly smooth, rounded black stone that he showed to O'Keeffe because he knew she collected such things. Although she was keenly interested in its shape and texture, Porter refused to give it to her. Sometime later at a party in Tesuque, the Porters decided to tempt her by placing the stone where she could see it. The rock vanished that evening, and Porter later found it at her house in Abiquiu. The story became part of family lore, and it was memorialized in a photograph by John Loengard, *The Rock from Eliot Porter, Abiquiu* (fig. 34) and retold in a somewhat different version in Calvin Tompkins's *New Yorker* profile of O'Keeffe.[45]

Abiquiu, where O'Keeffe bought a second home in 1945, was an old abobe village and home to descendents of the Spanish and native populations alike. Located some forty miles northwest of Porter's house, along the banks of the Chama River, Abiquiu offered a good supply of water and was closer to paved roads than Ghost Ranch. For almost a decade O'Keeffe had been trying to buy the ruins of the old hacienda and the adjoining three acres from the archdiocese of Santa Fe. She finally succeeded and began an extensive project to restore the house and grounds that was formulated and carried out by her friend Maria Chabot.[46] The Abiquiu village church had been recently rebuilt with assistance from New Mexico's most prominent preservation architect, John Gaw Meem, and the urge to rebuild the region's historic structures was in vogue.

O'Keeffe's interest in traditional building forms had begun at Ghost Ranch in a painting called simply *The Patio — No. 1,* with its emphasis on a close-up view of the traditional roof structure and adobe walls (fig. 35). But Abiquiu, with its older history and opportunity for a large walled garden, provided O'Keeffe with other architectural elements that did not exist at Ghost Ranch. In Abiquiu she was particularly drawn to the traditional entryway into the patio courtyard, a feature of the house frequently photographed by visitors, including Eliot Porter (fig. 36). O'Keeffe put

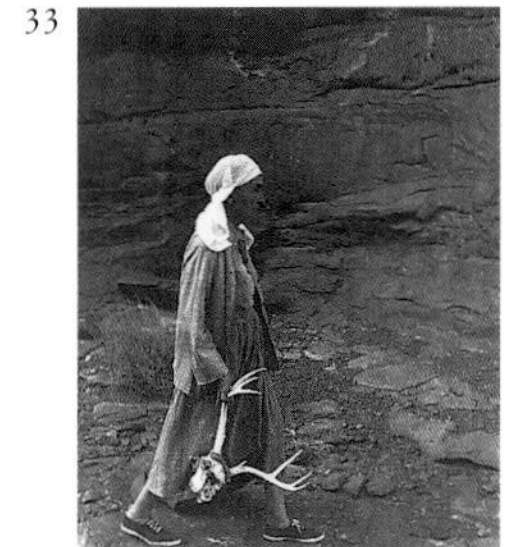

33

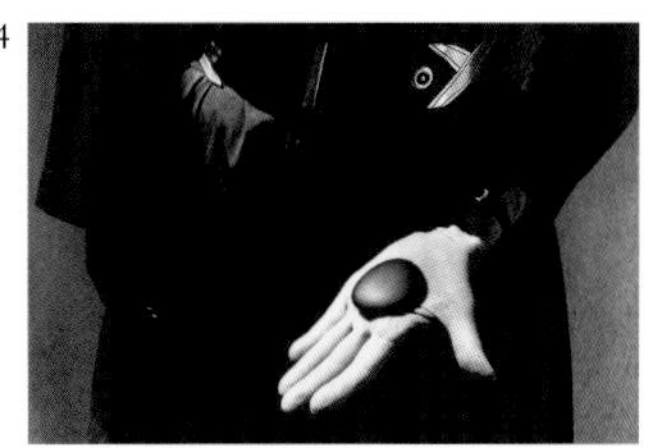

34

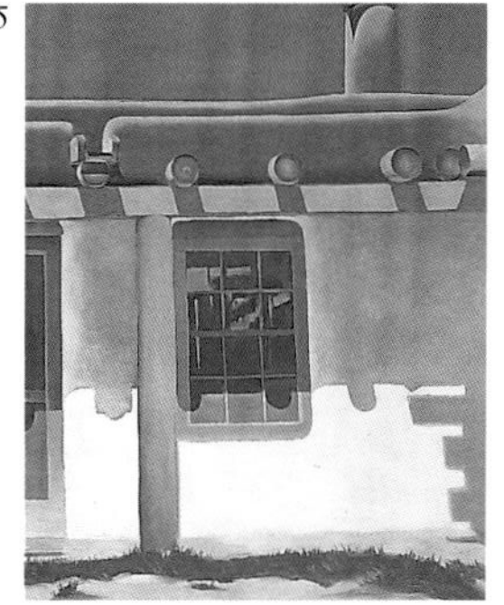

35

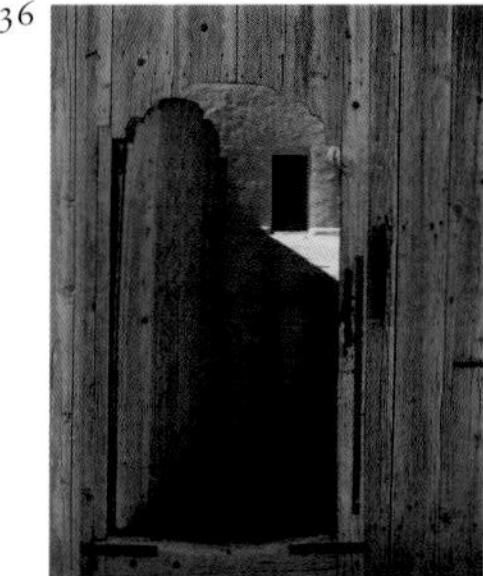

36

Chabot in charge of rebuilding and replastering the house's adobe walls and adding modern plate-glass windows, transforming the carriage house into a studio, and building a high adobe wall around the garden for privacy (fig. 37). In 1949, after almost three years of restoration, O'Keeffe was able to begin dividing her time between her two homes at Ghost Ranch and Abiquiu.

Both homes were simply outfitted with a few pieces of modern furniture, her paintings, and an increasingly well known collection of rocks and bones artfully arranged on window sills and ledges. Skulls, pelvic bones, and antlers hung on the porch railing at Ghost Ranch (fig. 38) and greeted visitors in the entryway into the Abiquiu house (fig. 39). As early as 1938, her Ghost Ranch bone collection was featured in an article in *Life* that identified O'Keeffe as the "best known woman painter in America today." The feature reproduced one of her horse skull pictures, noting that "experts, collectors, and connoisseurs will vehemently assure doubters that it is a thing of real beauty and rare worth."[47]

By the 1950s O'Keeffe's fame as an artist was well established, and her houses had become as important as her paintings and the photographs of her in the public imagination. One photographer who helped create the popular portrait of O'Keeffe as the consummate artist of the Southwest was Todd Webb (1905–2000). Like Adams and Porter, he came to know her because of his connection to Stieglitz.[48] Shortly before Stieglitz's death, Webb had shown Stieglitz a portfolio of his work. In 1946 he also photographed O'Keeffe's solo show at the Museum of Modern Art, the first devoted to a woman at that prestigious institution (fig. 40). As Stieglitz had done in his installation shots of her first exhibition, Webb emphasized the spare detail of the hanging, using the inherent geometry of the gallery spaces to frame the images. When Webb applied for a Guggenheim grant to photograph the Santa Fe Trail in 1954, he turned to O'Keeffe for a letter of recommendation. While working on that project in 1955, he stopped briefly to see her in Abiquiu and visited her again for two weeks the following year when his Guggenheim grant was extended. In exchange for her help and

37 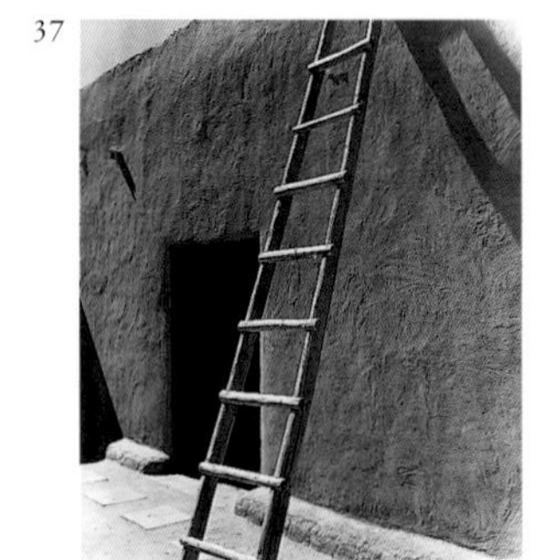

38 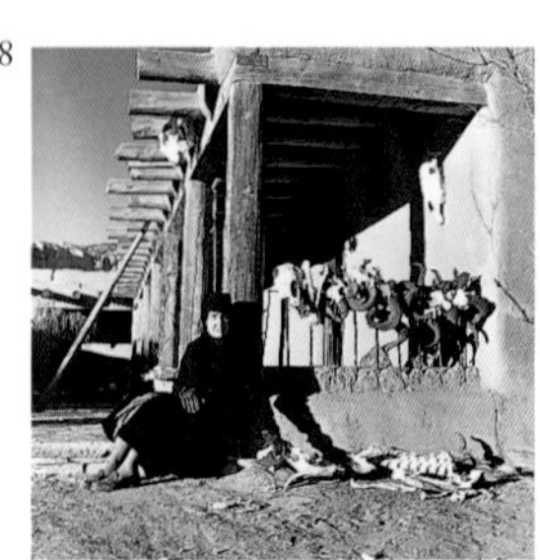

39 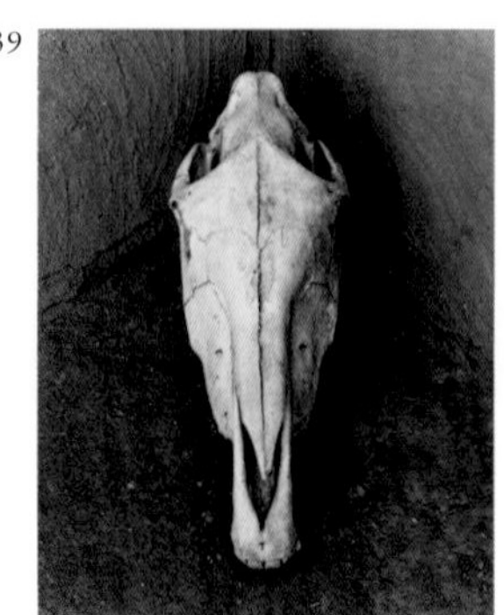

40 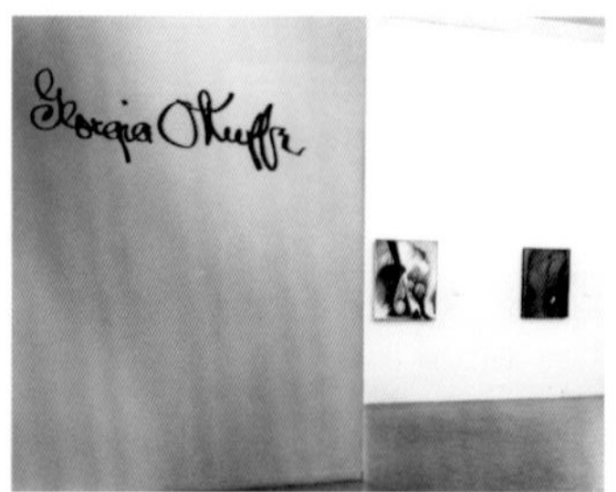

hospitality, Webb gave O'Keeffe her first Polaroid camera, showed her
how to use it, and even printed photographs for her when he returned to
New York (fig. 41).[49]

Prompted by O'Keeffe's life in the West and the dramatic southwestern landscape, Webb was determined to leave New York and move to
New Mexico. He settled in Santa Fe in 1961 and accompanied O'Keeffe and
Eliot Porter on their 1961 and 1964 trips down the Colorado River, taking
memorable pictures of O'Keeffe in Glen Canyon (fig. 42; see fig. 33). Her
bone collection became a staple of his O'Keeffe repertoire and was featured
among the many pictures that he published in his 1984 book *Georgia
O'Keeffe: The Artist's Landscape* (fig. 43). Several of Webb's architectural
images of O'Keeffe's patio, taken in the 1970s at Abiquiu, echo the simple
geometry and abstract patterns that appear in her paintings from the 1950s
(fig. 44). He also photographed the interior of her studios at Ghost Ranch
and Abiquiu, with paintings and props hanging on the wall. In one image
Webb positioned an O'Keeffe painting, *From the River—Pale,* next to the
barren branch that had served as its source of inspiration (figs. 45 and 46).
Without the photograph, the viewer might easily assume that the painting is
an aerial landscape view of the nearby Chama River. In another photograph
of the Ghost Ranch studio, the clutter of detail in the foreground contrasts
markedly with the high degree of abstraction in the O'Keeffe painting on
the easel (figs. 47 and 48).

Celebrity Portraits

In addition to allowing her photographer friends to take numerous pictures
of her home, her landscape, and her face, beginning in the late 1940s the
nominally reclusive O'Keeffe made herself available to celebrity portrait
photographers. The widespread popularity of news and fashion magazines
such as *Life, Time,* and *Vogue* increased Americans' appetite for images of
famous people. O'Keeffe, already acclaimed as one of the most important

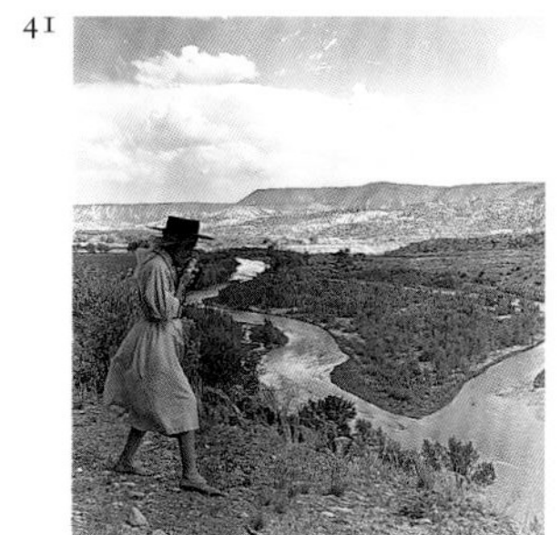

41

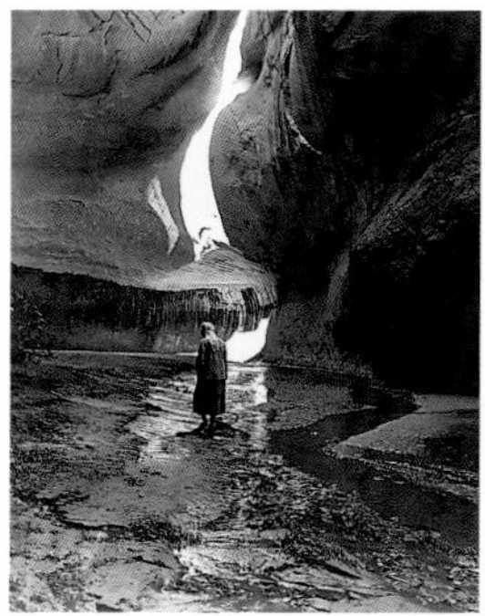

42

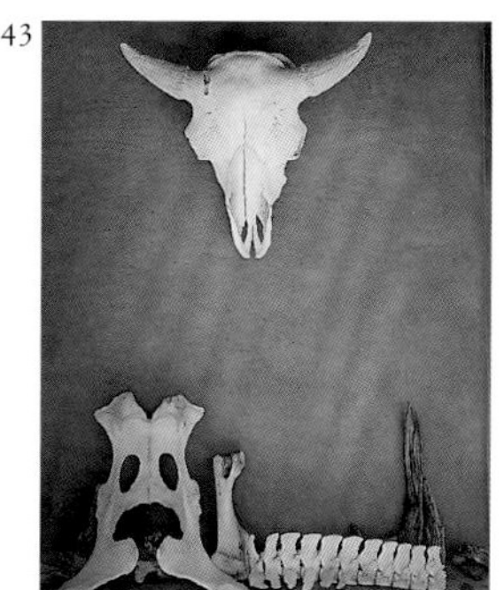

43

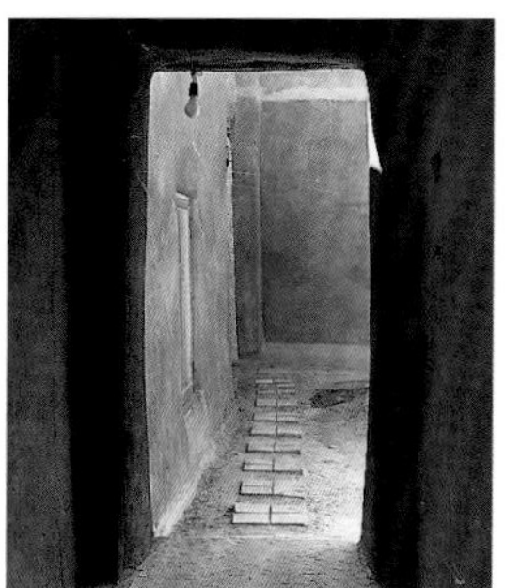

44

modern women painters of the era, played both sides of the celebrity
coin—she was aloof and private, but she made sure her face was known
to the public. *Vogue* was among the first popular magazines to cover
O'Keeffe's career, beginning with an article in 1923 by Herbert Seligmann.
His piece, titled "Why 'Modern' Art," included a Stieglitz portrait of
O'Keeffe and a reproduction of her work, compared her early abstract
art to music, and discussed her oeuvre within an eclectic framework of
El Greco's mannerist paintings, Congolese sculpture, the jungle scenes
of French modernist Henri Rousseau, and the work of the Stieglitz circle,
including Arthur Dove and John Marin.[50] But by the late 1940s, *Vogue*
and other popular magazines were more interested in O'Keeffe's celebrity
status than in criticism of her art.

As part of his extensive study of famous people in the arts, Irving
Penn (b. 1917) photographed O'Keeffe for *Vogue* in 1948. Penn posed
O'Keeffe in a tight corner between two temporary walls in his New York
studio. In one version of the image, we see the edges of those false walls,
emphasizing the contrived nature of the studio environment. Dressed
characteristically in black, O'Keeffe looked to the photographic historian
Colin Westerbrook "as if she [were] still in mourning for Alfred Stieglitz,
who died two years earlier. With Stieglitz now gone, O'Keeffe has lost
her mythic proportions. Penn's singular portrait repudiates the many
Stieglitz had done in which this tiny woman seems Amazonian, an incar-
nation of a Lawrentian sexual energy."[51] In the variant reproduced here,
Penn has made O'Keeffe appear even more vulnerable and frail, wedged
farther into the corner with her hands tucked behind her back and
feet turned slightly off center (fig. 49). Penn used the idiosyncratic corner
format for a number of other celebrity portraits that year, but none of
his other subjects seem so overwhelmed by the surrounding props. George
Grosz sits uncomfortably on a chair ready to rise, Spencer Tracy smiles
nonchalantly with his elbow resting on the wall next to his head, and
Charles Sheeler leans back resolutely on a mound of old carpeting. A master portraitist, Penn was adept at drawing out a variety of psychological

45 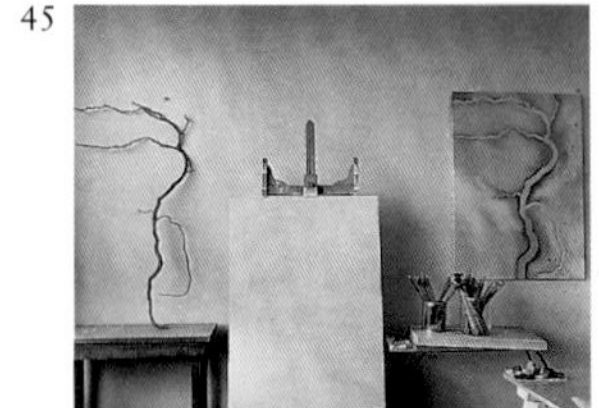

46 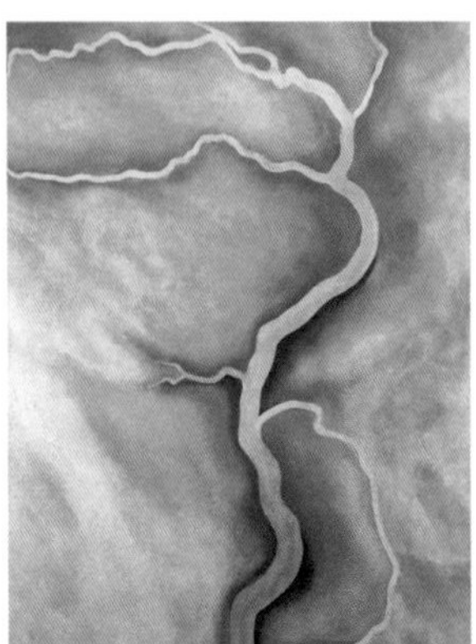

47 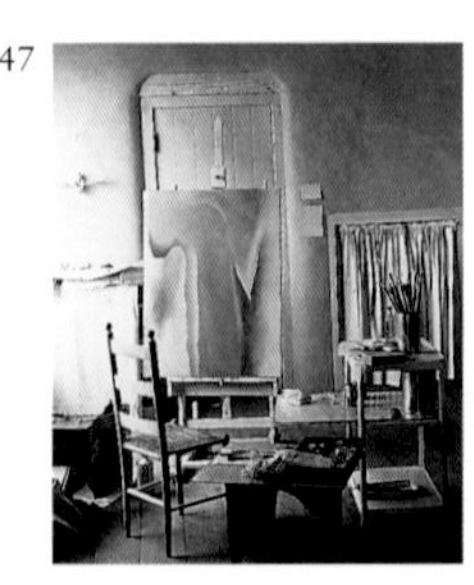

48 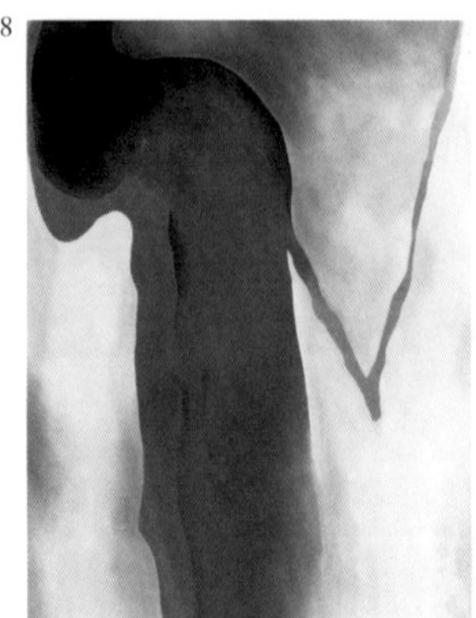

nuances from O'Keeffe's pose and facial expression. With the hint of a
smile and one raised eyebrow, her face conveys a sense of skepticism and
authority, despite the frailty.

Philippe Halsman's portraits of the artist, taken on two assign-
ments for *Life* in 1948 and 1967, are all about O'Keeffe's famous sense of
style.[52] In a portrait from the early series, Halsman (1906–1979) set
O'Keeffe's kerchief-covered head in profile against a black background,
creating an image that is classical in its simplicity and elegance (fig. 50).
With its allusions to aristocratic Roman and Italian Renaissance portraiture,
this iconic image set the stage for other celebrity portraitists of the day,
such as Yousuf Karsh and Arnold Newman. Other photographs from
this session show the artist seated outdoors in front of her home at Ghost
Ranch contemplating her famous collection of bleached animal bones
and stones.[53] In one outdoor scene she wears a broad-brimmed black hat
with a favorite pin bearing her initials and made by the sculptor Alexander
Calder prominently displayed on her lapel. The same pin peeks out from
under her suit collar in a later close-up image from 1967 that emphasizes
the streaks in her graying hair and the wrinkles on her face. These are
images of an older woman—self-assured and confident in her position and
comfortable in her surroundings. In 1986 *Newsweek* featured another
Halsman portrait of O'Keeffe holding a set of vertebrae taken at the same
session. Clearly identifying her persona with the landscape, this homage
to the recently deceased artist concluded with a plea for a more restrained
development in the West: "With the Southwest sprawling into the future,
with the American sublime closeted in parks, people sorrow for O'Keeffe
as they would for the last pioneer."[54]

When Yousuf Karsh (1908–2002) traveled to Abiquiu to photograph O'Keeffe in 1956, he, too, produced an image that suggested her self-
assurance and reflected her artistic concerns. Seated in profile in the entryway of her house, O'Keeffe posed under a large set of antlers that appeared
in many of her paintings (fig. 51).[55] Karsh wrote that he "expected to find
some of the poetic intensity of her paintings reflected in her personality.

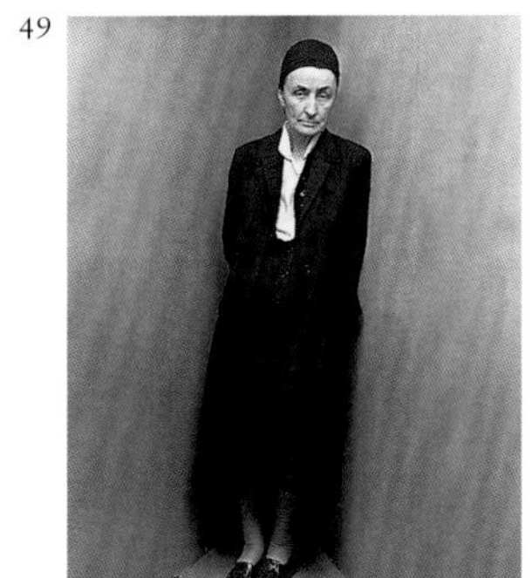

49

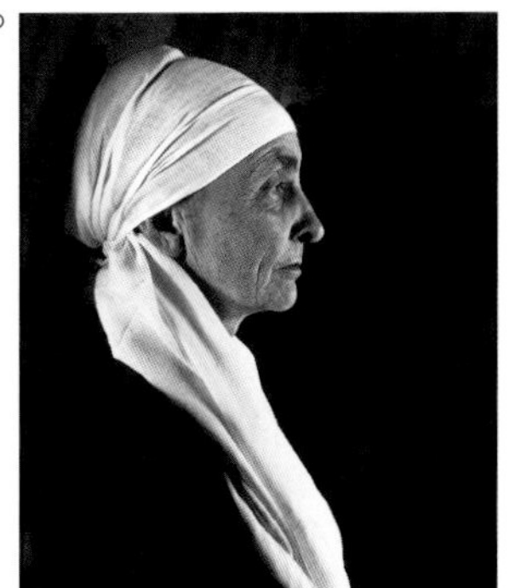

50

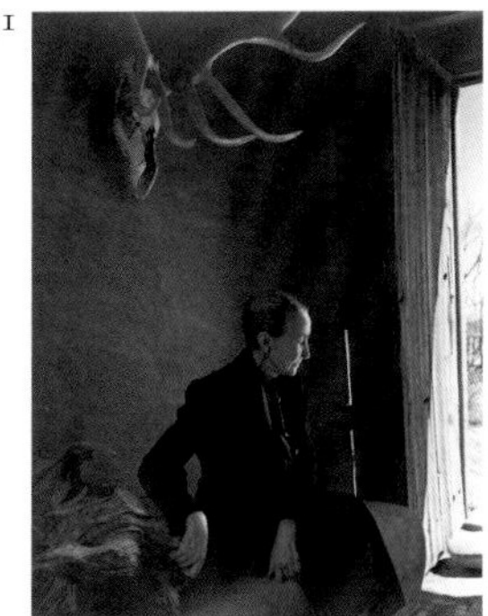

51

Intensity I found, but it was the austere intensity of dedication to her work, which has led Miss O'Keeffe to cut out of her life anything that interferes with her ability to express herself in paint."[56] As Stieglitz had done in his portraits of the young O'Keeffe, Karsh drew attention to the artist's hands. But for his image of the sixty-nine-year-old artist, he posed her bent fingers next to a gnarled tree stump and placed her under a deer's skull, alluding to the passage of time and to death. As if to balance those dark elements, a streak of light coming in from the open doorway falls on O'Keeffe's forehead, wrist, and still-life objects in the composition, reminding the viewer of the inspiration and vitality of the still-practicing artist. According to Karsh, his photograph once hung in her house at Abiquiu.[57]

Like Halsman, the European-born Karsh had come to North America at the outbreak of World War II. He, too, established his photographic reputation taking portraits of famous people — politicians, scientists, writers, actors and actresses, musicians, and artists. In the late 1940s and 1950s, he produced a series of images of hands, clearly in homage to Stieglitz, and among the first artists he photographed in 1958 was Georgia O'Keeffe. In the 1960s and 1970s, Karsh would capture likenesses of other well-known painters, sculptors, and photographers, including Pablo Picasso, Alexander Calder, Joan Miró, Man Ray, Edward Steichen, and Ansel Adams. Perhaps more than any other late-twentieth-century photographer, Karsh has become synonymous with the concept of celebrity.

Arnold Newman (1918–2006) is another O'Keeffe photographer whose artistic reputation derives from his portraits of the famous.[58] After studying art at the University of Miami, Newman worked at a series of commercial portrait studios. On a trip to New York in 1939 he met Stieglitz, and two years later, encouraged by Stieglitz and Beaumont Newhall at MoMA, Newman set out on his own as a photographer. In his 1946 double portrait of O'Keeffe and Stieglitz, the photographer, not the painter, dominates the composition (see fig. 7). Although the critic Estelle Jussim observes that this picture may be more about Newman's psychology than that of his sitters, Newman has clearly managed to capture the sense of estrangement between his subjects.[59] Both present almost expressionless faces, and neither engages either the camera or the other subject.

Newman's later portrait of O'Keeffe alone, taken at Ghost Ranch, is from a group of artists' portraits featuring background elements that convey distinctive aspects of each subject's style. For example, Newman's portrait of Piet Mondrian features a gridwork of shapes formed by Mondrian's easel and two squares tacked to the wall behind his head. Willem de Kooning stands immediately in front of a wall with scraps of canvas covered with his expressionist brushwork, creating an artistic halo behind his head. And for his portrait of Isamu Noguchi, Newman placed the artist's head in the void at the center of one of his sculptures. The photographer took the unusual step of setting up the O'Keeffe portrait outdoors (fig. 52). The artist, wearing a denim shirt, is shown in profile seated in front of a blank canvas propped on an easel to which is attached a ram's skull and horns. The distinctive landscape surrounding her home at Ghost Ranch forms the backdrop. Like other celebrity photographers, Newman often worked for the popular press, and a variant of this image appeared in an article on Santa Fe in *Holiday* the following year.[60]

Promoting O'Keeffe and Santa Fe Modern Style

The growth of Santa Fe as a cultural center, attracting artists and writers from the East Coast as well as the Southwest, was in full swing when O'Keeffe arrived there from New York in 1929.[61] With the renaissance of Hispanic architecture, prompted by the work of John Gaw Meem and others in the following decades, Santa Fe came to represent a unique melding of modernism and the traditional adobe style.[62] The photographer Laura Gilpin (1891–1979), who lived in Santa Fe and was a long-time friend of the artist,[63] noted the affinity between O'Keeffe's work and the local architectural idiom in an article for *House Beautiful* in 1963: "Beauty of spacing and simplicity of design are the two major qualities that dominate the

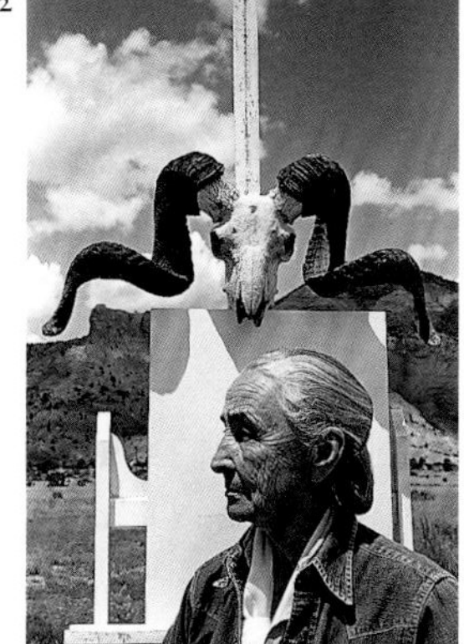
52

painting of Georgia O'Keeffe. They are also the dominant characteristics of her house in Abiquiu, New Mexico. Indeed, her house and her painting are all of a piece, and most of her 'decorations' are nature objects picked up off the desert."[64] Gilpin's photographs accompanying the article included interior shots of the Abiquiu house, details of the now-famous collection of stones and bones, and a view of the Chama River Valley from the panoramic window of O'Keeffe's studio, where a decade earlier Gilpin had photographed O'Keeffe sitting beside this same window, with a still life of paintbrushes on the sill (fig. 53).

The most comprehensive picture of O'Keeffe's homes and their furnishings appeared in a 1968 photo essay in *Life* and later in a book by the photographer John Loengard (b. 1934).[65] His profile portrait of the artist seated on the rooftop and framed by a chimney pot atop her home at Ghost Ranch was featured on the cover of *Life* (see fig. 6). The magazine piece also included examples of her paintings alongside Loengard's portraits, views of the interiors of her houses (fig. 54), and scenes of the surrounding landscape (fig. 55). The accompanying text combined quotations by O'Keeffe with the observations of an unnamed writer that, together with the images, strove to demonstrate the "interlocking of her life and art." Among the Loengard photos are the inevitable still-life arrangements of bones (fig. 56), about which she reminisced: "When I came to New Mexico in the summer of 1929, I was so crazy about the country that I thought, how can I take part of it with me to work on? There was nothing to see in the land in the way of a flower. There were just dry white bones. So I picked them up. People were pretty annoyed having their cars filled with those bones. But I took back a barrel of bones to New York. They were my symbols of the desert, but nothing more."[66]

The *Life* article also featured a Loengard photograph captioned, "A favorite stone and a favorite belt." It showed O'Keeffe holding a smooth, rounded dark stone that was identified later in his book as *The Rock from Eliot Porter, Abiquiu* (see fig. 34). Loengard's introduction mentions the story of the rock stolen long ago from Porter and provides details about the

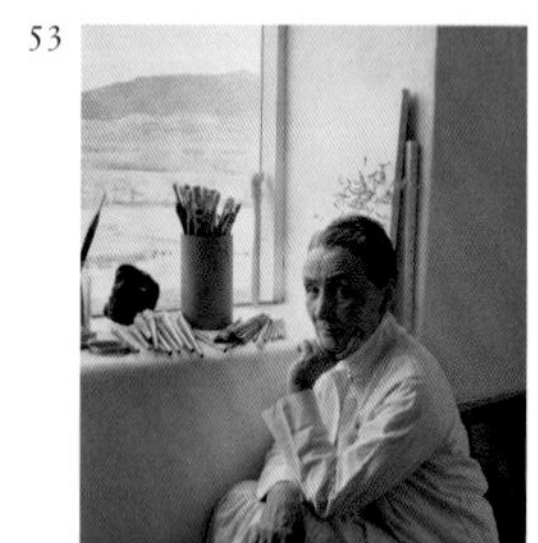

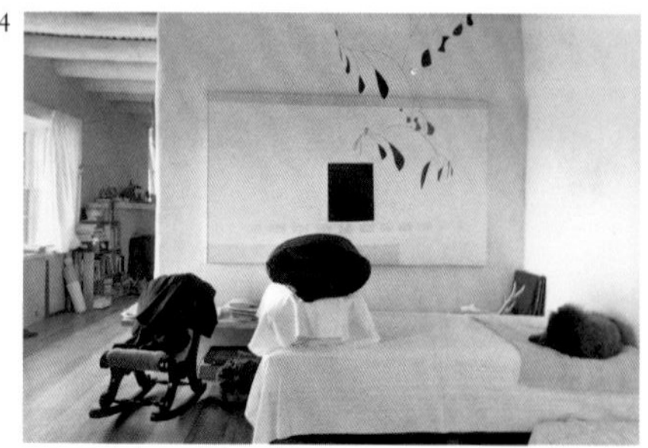

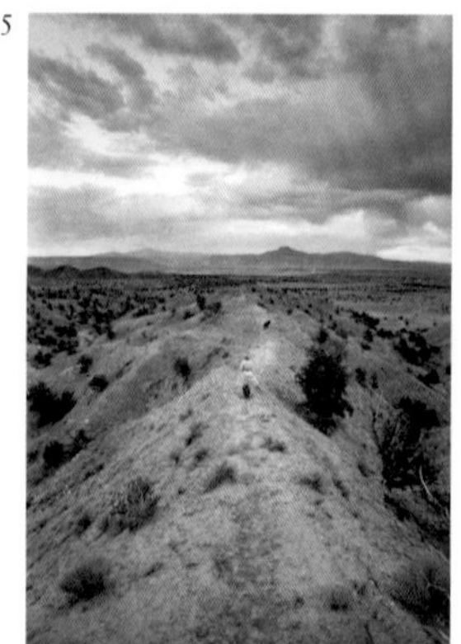

three-day photo shoot in 1966. During the time Loengard spent with the artist, "she talked a great deal, often with amusement. O'Keeffe played the role not so much of a painter, but of a wealthy woman, interested in the arts. She paid considerable attention to the smooth management of her household." After following his subject through the routine of a typical day, he concluded, "Clearly, O'Keeffe was no hermit"—morning and evening walks with her favorite chow-chows, visits from friends and family, and work in the garden filled her days with much activity even at the age of seventy-nine.

Although O'Keeffe did not pose at her easel for Loengard, her art is evident in his images. Hanging on the wall in her uncharacteristically cluttered bedroom or standing alone on an easel, her paintings are formal elements that the photographer skillfully weaves into his compositions. The dark rectangle of the door in *My Last Door* (1952–1954, Georgia O'Keeffe Museum) serves as foil to the Calder mobile that hung over her bed (see fig. 54), and the shape of the stretched canvas in *Studio, Ghost Ranch* emphasizes the corners of doors, windows, and cupboards in her studio (fig. 57). But Loengard's photographic approach to O'Keeffe was largely personal and related to her art only indirectly. His reverential close-up portraits capture her lined face; his scenes of her house show O'Keeffe alone fingering her rock collection or stooping as she works in the garden. In the last image in the book, *Evening Walk, Ghost Ranch* (see fig. 55), O'Keeffe, long skirt billowing in the wind, seems almost to disappear in the expanse of the New Mexican desert.

Whereas Gilpin's and Loengard's photographs stress the traditional New Mexican aspects of O'Keeffe's home, others, such as those by George Daniell, Don Worth, Balthazar Korab, and Myron Wood, capture the modernist side of her art and life.[67] George Daniell (1911–2002), a celebrity photographer best known for his portraits of Hollywood stars, was perhaps the first photographer to emphasize the affinity between her persona and Santa Fe modernism. He and O'Keeffe had met in New York in the 1940s at Stieglitz's gallery, and he photographed her once on a visit to Fire Island. But it was on a trip to New Mexico around 1952, when he juxtaposed the

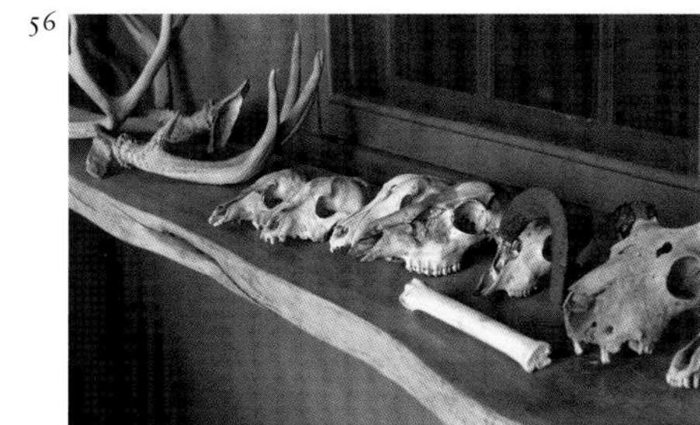

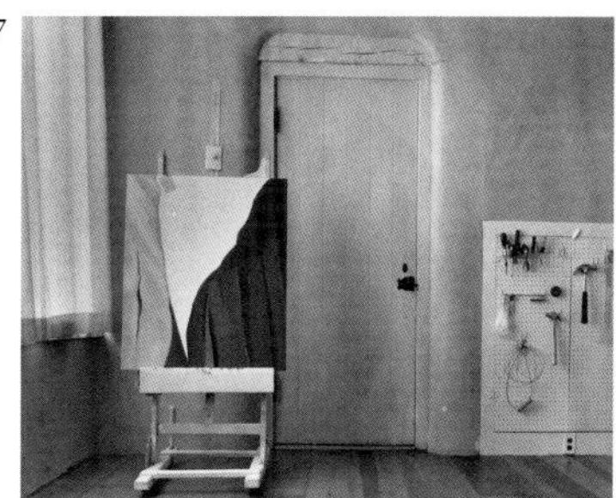

austerity of shadows on an adobe wall with O'Keeffe's black hat and
coat (fig. 58), that Daniell captured her affinity for abstraction, the quality
that he admired most in her work. His lasting memory of the artist
was of her relaxing in a modern chrome reclining chair in her house at
Abiquiu.[68]

Don Worth (b. 1924), who worked as an assistant to Ansel Adams,
photographed O'Keeffe around 1958 standing next to a doorway on the
Abiquiu patio (fig. 59) that appears in some of her most minimalist paintings, such as *Wall with Green Door* (fig. 60). In addition to emphasizing
the repetitive pattern of the square stepping stones, Worth places the metal
frame of a butterfly chair in the foreground as if it were abstract sculpture.
The stylish butterfly chair, designed by the Argentine architect Jorge Ferrari-
Hardoy in 1938, would normally be covered in a fabric sling. The fabric's
absence makes the empty angular frame seem especially enigmatic, as
does O'Keeffe's downcast gaze. Devoid of the usual array of animal skulls,
antlers, and stones, the unadorned adobe wall lacks reference to the usual
O'Keeffe icons. Even the artist's attire, a simple checked skirt and jacket,
seems subdued compared to the more self-consciously contrived black-and-
white outfits she wears in photographs by celebrity photographers like
Irving Penn and Philippe Halsman.

At O'Keeffe's behest, in April 1965 *House Beautiful* sent the noted
architectural photographer Balthazar Korab (b. 1926) to photograph her
house at Abiquiu as part of a series of articles on artists' homes. Author
Mary Roche explained the magazine's motivation: "An artist is a person
with a constellation of special gifts, and for those of us who are constantly
nourished by those gifts, the life of the artist at home has tremendous
fascination."[69] Telling Korab he reminded her of the young Ansel Adams,
O'Keeffe greeted him at the door and gave him a tour of the house. In
recollecting that day, Korab noted that he worked "without as much as
moving a chair. Everything was in the right place." Probably at O'Keeffe's
request, Korab took the by-now requisite shots of traditional southwestern
elements in her home—the adobe wall and ladder, the wooden viga roof

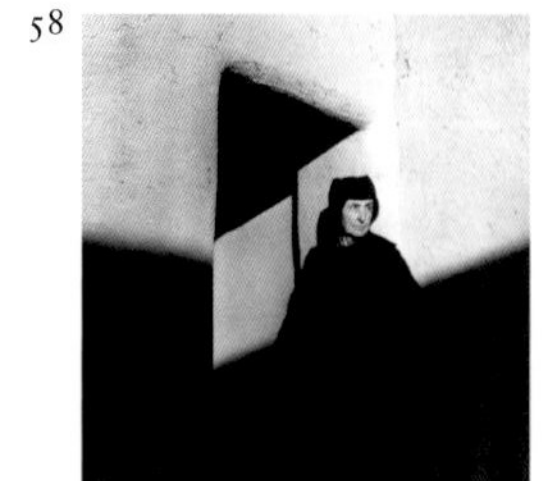
58

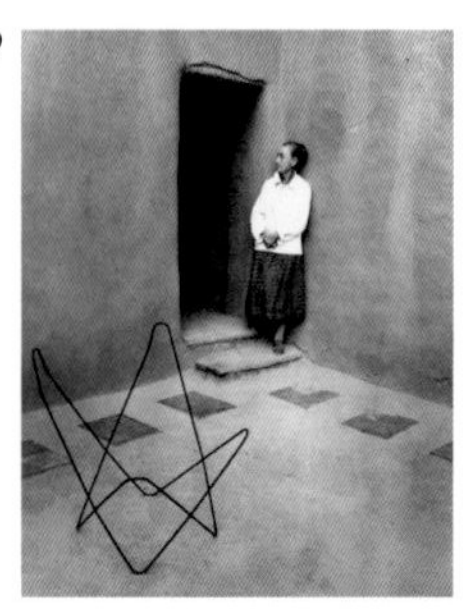
59

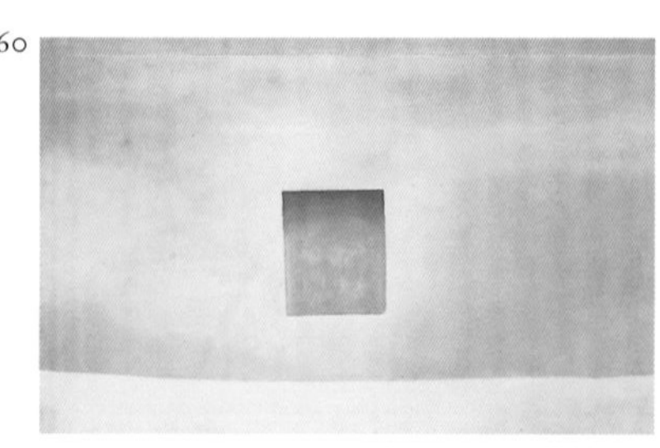
60

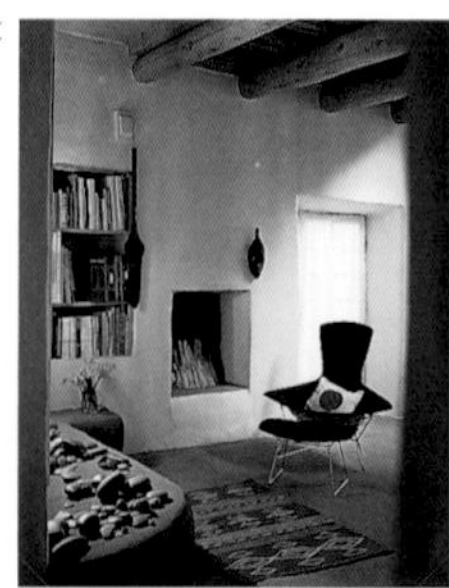
61

supports, and her famous collection of bones and stones. But he was drawn
to her "hard edge modern, chairs by Eames, Saarinen, Bertoia," as is evident in his photograph of the living room, which features designer-sculptor
Harry Bertoia's famous bird chair and ottoman (fig. 61).[70] The captions
for his pictures stress how well the modern design elements and O'Keeffe's
art, especially her cloud paintings, complement the traditional architecture
(figs. 62 and 63).

Popular fascination with O'Keeffe's homes continues today. Korab's
photographs of Abiquiu were republished in *Western Interiors and Design,*
and this time, the thrust of the article was even more overtly about O'Keeffe
and modernism: "While many people think of Georgia O'Keeffe as the high
priestess of Southwestern style, her soul belonged to one true faith: modernism." The author, one of O'Keeffe's biographers, reiterates the importance
of her early training with the Japanese-inspired artist Arthur Wesley Dow
and the influence of Stieglitz and the modern art, including photography,
that he championed at 291. But more than Stieglitz, the author believes,
O'Keeffe understood modernism as a "way of life." "She demonstrated it in
the geometry of her usually black clothing, her neat hair, her lean body type,
her bold, precise penmanship."[71] At Abiquiu in the end, O'Keeffe "rejected
the rustic" and instead interspersed a Bertoia wire-frame chair and a molded
Eames chair with her own muslin-covered seating cubes and simple ply-
wood and sawhorse dining table. The artist's penchant for a modernist
aesthetic at Abiquiu is perhaps best expressed in Korab's views of her studio,
with its large window dominating the room and reflecting the sky and hills
beyond (figs. 64 and 65). O'Keeffe's admiration for Frank Lloyd Wright's
organic modernism, which melded landscape and architecture, found ample
expression in her new studio.[72]

In 1979 the public library in Pueblo, Colorado, commissioned
Myron Wood (b. 1921) to photograph O'Keeffe's home at Abiquiu as part
of a large documentary project recording important sites and landscapes of
southern Colorado and northern New Mexico. Although O'Keeffe initially
rejected the library's request, she eventually invited Wood to Abiquiu and

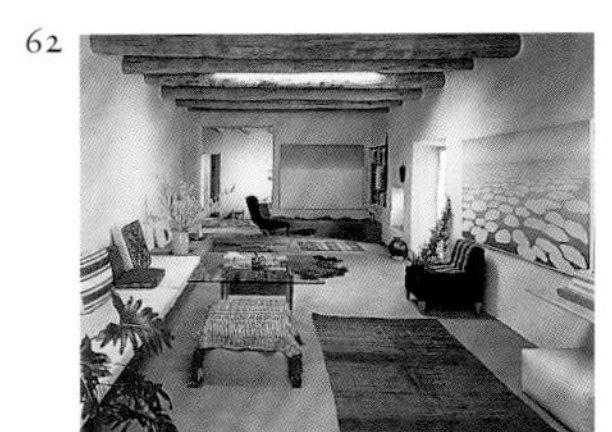

62

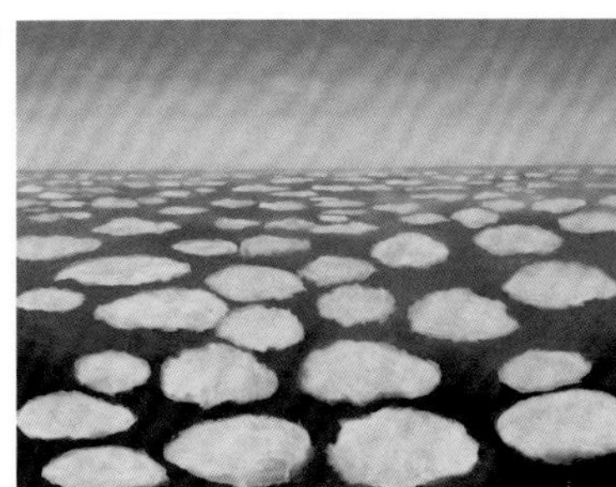

63

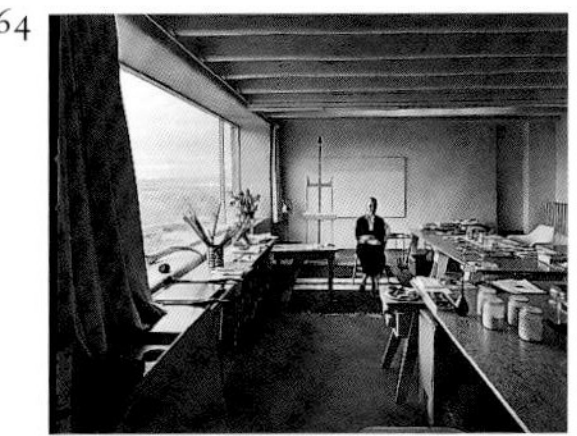

64

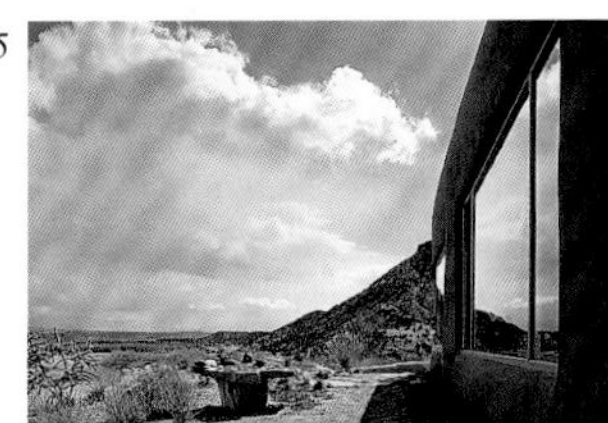

65

gave him permission to photograph there and at Ghost Ranch. The project spanned more than two years and resulted in a book that reflects Wood's notion that O'Keeffe's "effect upon these dwellings was natural and it was so sustained that it is perhaps clearer and more innocent than anything she expressed in any other medium. In her homes as in her life there was no pretense — bare light bulbs, lean furniture, and adobe walls served their purposes" (fig. 66). Like many other photographers and writers who met O'Keeffe late in life, Wood revered the aging artist: "Miss O'Keeffe had a walk of queenly splendor. Upon entering a room, she changed that room by her presence; never mind that she could barely see. It was the magnetism of her will that caught everyone up."[73] His portraits show a smiling woman, seated next to her young companion, the artist Juan Hamilton, or deep in thought as she fondles her collection of smooth stones. Wood's interior views focus on simple details — doorways and windows embedded in thick adobe walls, the modern banquette and chairs in the living room, the kiva-style fireplace with its artfully arranged sticks of wood. And his landscapes taken at Ghost Ranch show the low adobe building dwarfed by the surrounding cliffs and softened by the surrounding sage and stunted pines.

For Wood and other photographers who specialized in scenes of the Southwest in the 1960s and 1970s, O'Keeffe had become a venerated symbol of modernism in the West.[74] Her homes were seen as the embodiment of the new and increasingly popular pueblo revival, a regional idiom that combined traditional architectural forms with modern design. A love of natural materials, rooted in the minimal vegetation and dramatic rock formations that surrounded her houses, was the basis of her art. And although her imagery vacillated between the real and the abstract, it often derived from her observations of the natural world, especially after she moved to New Mexico. The numerous photographs that show her late, more abstract paintings sparingly displayed in her homes among her favorite bits of modern design and beloved collection of natural objects demonstrate how conscious she was of their combined effect. O'Keeffe's willingness and what even might be considered compulsion to have her homes

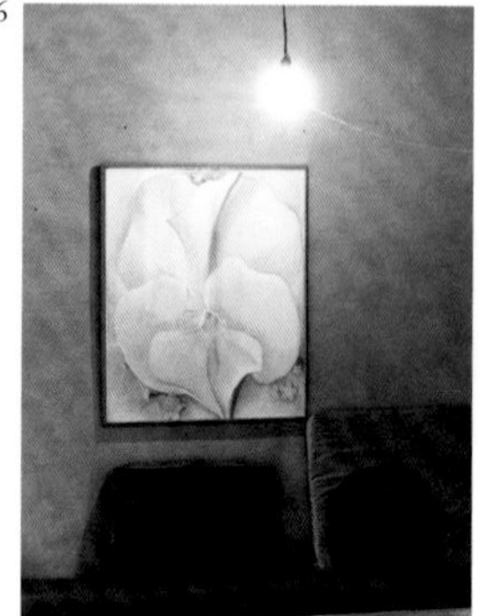
66

and private spaces photographed and published so frequently in popular magazines speak to her need to create a new image of herself. This image of an older, self-reliant woman, alone but fulfilled by her dedication to her art and her landscape, would eventually replace the Stieglitz-generated view of O'Keeffe as a young avant-garde painter of sexually charged images of flowers and shells.[75]

O'Keeffe and the Popular Press

O'Keeffe's image in the news and fashion magazines of her day emerged alongside critical writings about her art shaped by Stieglitz.[76] From the beginning, women's magazines in particular linked her persona with changing notions about the role of women artists in the modern era. As early as 1922, *Vanity Fair* identified O'Keeffe as one of five "women painters of America whose work exhibits distinctiveness of style and marked individuality."[77] The article included an early Stieglitz portrait of O'Keeffe with a lengthy caption that easily could have come from his pen: "Her history epitomizes the modern artist's struggle out of the mediocrity imposed by conventional art schools, to the new freedom of expression inspired by such men as Stieglitz. Her work was undistinguished until she abandoned academic realism and discovered her own feminine self. Her more recent paintings seem to be a revelation of the very essence of the woman as Life Giver."[78]

A decade later, Frank Crowninshield, an editor at *Vanity Fair* and an O'Keeffe collector, pointedly featured a Stieglitz portrait of O'Keeffe (see fig. 5) along with reproductions of her paintings, including *Coxcomb* (fig. 67), when the magazine ran a series on the Museum of Modern Art's most popular American painters. The museum had polled its visitors on their favorite artists, and O'Keeffe led a group made up of male artists that included Eugene Speicher, Maurice Sterne, Edward Hopper, Charles Burchfield, and Preston Dickinson. Making certain that his readers were aware

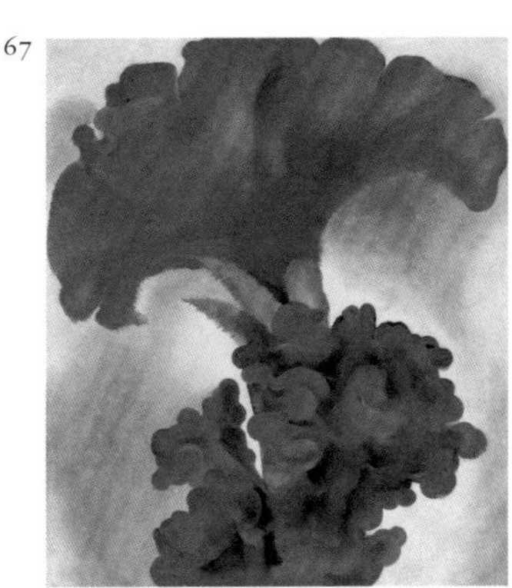
67

that "Miss O'Keeffe is, in private life, the wife of Alfred Stieglitz, the photographer," Crowninshield praised her work with its "extraordinary interest in form, a natural gift for design and a sensitized, almost uncanny feeling for color. These qualities, imposed upon a rich emotional nature, have produced a painter for whom it is impossible to find a counterpart among modern artists."[79]

The link between O'Keeffe's paintings and contemporary style, the primary thrust of these women's magazines, is perhaps most obvious in a brief article that appeared in *Town and Country* in 1937. The article, titled "Beauty Is Fun," featured an O'Keeffe flower painting, *Jimson Weed*, that once hung in the mirrored exercise studio of Elizabeth Arden's upscale Fifth Avenue beauty salon in New York. As the unnamed author described it, the large painting (almost six feet by eight feet) "dominates the yellow and white splendor reflected in the many mirrors of this latest in exercise floors."[80] In an interview with Andy Warhol late in life, O'Keeffe told of Elizabeth Arden's attempt to transform her face with make-up. She went home, looked in her mirror, and immediately washed it all off.[81]

O'Keeffe's public persona also became fodder for popular magazines such as *Life, Look, Time, Newsweek*, and the *New Yorker*. These publications tended to run articles on her life and art when major retrospective exhibitions of her work were being held. In its review of her 1946 show at the Museum of Modern Art, *Time* praised the "brilliant hardness of her most ambitious paintings" and retold the story of the early Stieglitz-O'Keeffe exhibitions.[82] In 1960 *Newsweek*, referring to the seventy-two-year-old artist as "the grand old lady of painting," discussed her solo exhibition at the Worcester Art Museum and its emphasis on her more recent "brilliant semi-abstract work, paintings of clouds, earth, rivers and airscapes."[83] Robert Hughes, writing for *Time* about the Whitney's 1970 show, attempts to "scotch the myth of her provinciality forever," approves of the "aloofness and precision" of her painting style, and concludes that her "life and work are one."[84] O'Keeffe's own popular picture book about her art and life, published by Viking Press, was the subject of a lengthy essay by Sanford Schwartz in the *New Yorker* in 1978.[85] In the review he takes umbrage at the "very stagy photograph" of O'Keeffe on the back cover, which like many images in the popular press shows O'Keeffe walking off into the desert landscape as if it were a "parody of the last scene in a Western." But Schwartz goes on to remark on the unusual longevity of her successful career, the book's seamless melding of text and pictures, and the importance of Stieglitz's portraits in the public's understanding of the artist's persona. And he addresses the nature of her fame: "O'Keeffe was a figure with a national renown that cut through art circles and reached the widest public—a public that often had little or no interest in the art world. O'Keeffe's fame was special in that it was based equally on what people knew of her work and of her life."[86]

Vogue, perhaps more than any other popular magazine, was fascinated by O'Keeffe's celebrity status late in her life. In 1967 the magazine featured an article illustrated with photographs of her homes at Abiquiu and Ghost Ranch by Cecil Beaton. Although the article begins, "Georgia O'Keeffe's name is engraved on the cornerstone of modern American art," it goes on to claim that "her extraordinary contribution to twentieth-century art [has been] obscured by her fame." The piece provided readers with details of her relationship with Stieglitz and her move to the Southwest, discussed her role as a woman artist and place among contemporary abstract artists, and even described the modern decor of her adobe houses. Like any good celebrity piece, it gave *Vogue*'s readers an insider's look at her life: "O'Keeffe *can* kill a rattlesnake, even in her eightieth year.... [S]he rides from the new house in Abiquiu to her first Western home, the Ghost Ranch, in an air-conditioned automobile like any other sensible Westerner. She rises early, eats lightly, has a figure any woman more than half her age would envy, dresses classically, simply....No provincial in any sense, but thoroughly sophisticated, she has always been more modern than her contemporaries."[87]

That same interest in O'Keeffe's personal life permeates art historian Barbara Rose's two feature articles on the artist that appeared in *Vogue* in

1986 and 1987. The first is a memorial piece following the artist's death at age ninety-nine, the second a reminiscence about Rose's visit with O'Keeffe in the 1960s. Titled "The Self, the Style, the Art of Georgia O'Keeffe," the later article is full of anecdotal incident and speculation about the nature of her fame. The artist "remains as much a mystery and a myth as she was when she was alive, controlling everything that was published about her work, and, wherever possible, what was written about herself. The making of that myth was one of O'Keeffe's greatest creations." Illustrated by one of her famous flower paintings and a Stieglitz photograph of her bare breasts and hand, Rose's essay concludes: "Her painting and her persona together provide a lasting drama of artistic and human interest. She wanted to leave an indelible mark of her identity and vision of the world. She did it by understanding the concept of style and creating her own unforgettable personal version of it."[88]

"Ruler of the Art World": O'Keeffe and Popular Culture

The famed artist and publicity addict Andy Warhol invited the aging O'Keeffe to take part in an interview and photography session for his magazine, *Interview,* in January 1983. A "crystal ball of pop culture," his trendy publication featured articles and images of celebrities from the varied worlds of fashion, politics, society, and the arts. In addition to O'Keeffe, the rather idiosyncratic group of artists Warhol interviewed over the years included Salvador Dalí, Bruce Nauman, Jamie Wyeth, William Wegman, Robert Rauschenberg, and David Hockney. O'Keeffe lacked the edginess and hip quality of Warhol's usual subjects and, at the age of ninety-three, required assistance from Juan Hamilton to answer Warhol's queries.[89] According to Hamilton, later she was annoyed that her portraits were reproduced without her permission and scoffed at the notion that she and Warhol should exchange paintings, saying that her work didn't belong in Andy Warhol's house.[90]

68

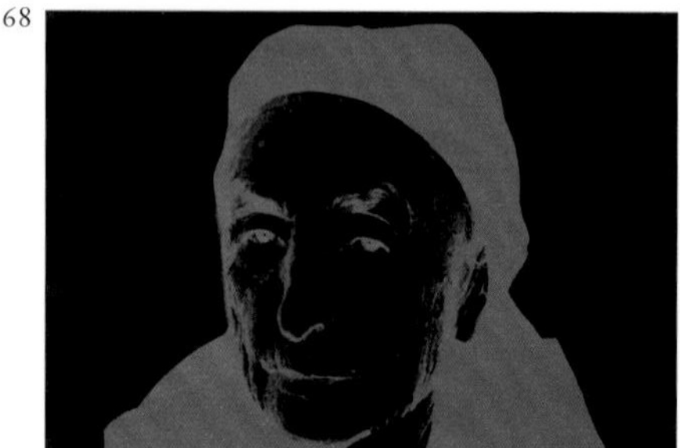

In addition to the photographs of O'Keeffe and Hamilton by
Christopher Makos that appeared in the magazine, Warhol took informal
Polaroids of O'Keeffe, one showing the artist, grim-faced with her arms
folded, seated next to a pile of cardboard boxes.[91] Warhol used another,
more frontal photograph of O'Keeffe as the basis for a series of silk-screen
prints, reversing the tonal relationship in the image so that the print appears
to be a colored negative, exploiting the photographic properties of his
source. He also experimented with the colors, making three versions with
diamond dust sprinkled on the surface: one in black on peach paper (fig. 68),
another in orange on cream paper, and the third in blue on black paper.[92]
Warhol used diamond dust in several other celebrity portraits, such as
those of the artist Joseph Beuys and Senator Edward Kennedy, and it figures
prominently in his *Myth* series, prints that included pop culture icons
such as Uncle Sam, Mickey Mouse, and a Warhol self-portrait in the guise
of the radio-play character known as the Shadow.

If the company that O'Keeffe keeps in Warhol's "glitterati" world
seems odd, the interview itself, conducted over lunch in Warhol's studio,
is even stranger. It began with O'Keeffe saying that she felt lost without
her cane, to which Warhol responded solicitously: "You have me. You can
use me as a cane." Throughout the interview, Juan Hamilton prompted
O'Keeffe's answers to the questions that Warhol posed, most of which
had little to do with her art and more to do with famous people she knew,
such as the architect Philip Johnson, cosmetics maven Elizabeth Arden,
and fashion designer Calvin Klein. In talking about her failing eyesight, the
artist seemed frail and dependent on Hamilton for direction. And in the
resulting print series, her identity is almost lost, her facial features described
in an eerie black and her clothes in uncharacteristically bright colors. She
would be unrecognizable except for the myriad photographic portraits that
preceded Warhol's image.

Like Chairman Mao and Marilyn Monroe, O'Keeffe entered Warhol's
galaxy of stars because of her celebrity status, made possible through
photography. As Barbara Rose astutely noted, O'Keeffe created her own

public persona "the same way Andy Warhol became larger than life, by imitating the image-making that creates stars."[93] These two artists are linked in pop culture fame: many museum stores carry an inexpensive tchotchke, a wooden ruler, that lists chronologically the "Rulers of the Art World" from Apelles to Warhol. Among the thirty-six listed, Warhol and O'Keeffe are the only twentieth-century Americans.[94] And at a food counter at the San Francisco airport, John Loengard's portrait of O'Keeffe (see fig. 6) serves as the menu marker for the "O'Keeffe Sandwich"—an overstuffed concoction of turkey, ham, cheese, lettuce, and tomato of which the abstemious artist would no doubt have disapproved. As the title of a *Ms.* review of O'Keeffe biographies suggests—"Georgia on Our Mind: Portrait of the Artist as a Pop Star"—her image also resonates in the world of contemporary music.[95]

For the most part, however, O'Keeffe's lasting fame rests on the strength of her work and the romantic story of her life. Photographs made by her art dealer husband, her friends, celebrity portraitists, and photojournalists all tell various versions of that tale. By consciously cultivating press coverage of her career and her life, O'Keeffe achieved and maintained a celebrity status for decades, not only in the art world, but also in the population at large. O'Keeffe's astute understanding of the power of the photographic image became a critical tool in fashioning her popular identity and a key to her abiding fame.

Notes

Epigraph: Dorothy Seiberling, "A Flowering in the Stieglitz Years," *Life,* March 1, 1968, 50–53.

1. Recent books about the artist include Hunter Drohojowska-Philp, *Full Bloom: The Art and Life of Georgia O'Keeffe* (New York: W. W. Norton, 2004); Sarah Whitaker Peters, *Becoming O'Keeffe: The Early Years,* rev. ed. (New York: Abbeville, 2001); and Roxana Robinson, *Georgia O'Keeffe: A Life* (New York: Harper and Row, 1989).

2. Sarah Greenough discusses the history of Stieglitz's galleries in the exhibition catalogue *Modern Art and America: Alfred Stieglitz and His New York Galleries* (Washington, D.C.: National Gallery of Art and Boston: Bulfinch, 2000).

3. For a discussion of O'Keeffe's early years in New York, her friendship with Anita Pollitzer, and her relationship with Alfred Stieglitz, see Drohojowska-Philp, *Full Bloom.*

4. In the April–July 1911 issue of *Camera Work,* Stieglitz published collotype reproductions of Rodin's drawings and a series of photogravures of his sculptures taken by Edward Steichen. One of the Steichen images of Rodin's sculpture, *Balzac—The Silhouette, 4 a.m.,* may be a source for the O'Keeffe piece.

5. Drohojowska-Philp, *Full Bloom,* 563, n. 11.

6. Sarah Greenough, *Alfred Stieglitz: The Key Set* (Washington, D.C.: National Gallery of Art and New York: Harry N. Abrams, 2002), nos. 584–591.

7. Paul Rosenfeld, "Stieglitz," *The Dial,* April 1921, 408–409. The image to which Rosenfeld referred is also titled *Interpretation;* see Greenough, *Stieglitz,* no. 586.

8. Georgia O'Keeffe, *Georgia O'Keeffe: A Portrait by Alfred Stieglitz* (New York: The Metropolitan Museum of Art, 1978). In the introduction, O'Keeffe discusses her early relationship with Stieglitz and the circumstances under which she posed for the portrait series. Between 1917 and 1933, Stieglitz took 331 photographs of O'Keeffe.

9. For a full discussion of critical interpretations of O'Keeffe's early work, see Barbara Buhler Lynes, *O'Keeffe, Stieglitz, and the Critics, 1916–1929* (Ann Arbor: UMI Research Press, 1989; 2nd ed., Chicago: University of Chicago Press, 1991).

10. In several images O'Keeffe wears a coat and hat (Greenough, *Stieglitz,* nos. 471–477), a deep V-necked sweater (nos. 478–482), and an open kimono (nos. 494–498).

11. One of the most cogent discussions of the portrait series appears in Anne Middleton Wagner, *Three Artists (Three Women): Modernism and the Art of Hesse, Krasner, and O'Keeffe* (Berkeley: University of California Press, 1996), 29–103.

12. The exhibition, *Alfred Stieglitz Presents One Hundred Pictures, Oils, Water-colors, Pastels, Drawings by Georgia O'Keeffe, American,* was on view at the Anderson Gallery, January 29–February 10, 1923. For reprints of the critical response, see Lynes, *O'Keeffe, Stieglitz, and the Critics,* 184–197. Other studies of O'Keeffe's critical reception and the role of gender also emphasize the importance of this exhibition; see Anne Middleton Wagner, "O'Keeffe's Femininity," in Wagner, *Three Artists,* 29–103; Barbara Lynes, "The Language of Criticism," in Christopher Merrill and Ellen Bradbury, eds., *From the Faraway Nearby: Georgia O'Keeffe as Icon* (Albuquerque: University of New Mexico Press, 1998): 43–54; and Marcia Brennan, *Painting Gender, Constructing Theory* (Cambridge, Mass.: MIT Press, 2001), 2–8.

13. Herbert J. Seligmann, "Georgia O'Keeffe, American," MSS., March 1923, 10, reprinted in Lynes, *O'Keeffe, Stieglitz, and the Critics,* 195–196.

14. Henry Tyrrell, "Art Observatory: High Tide in Exhibitions Piles up Shining Things of Art: Two Women Painters Lure with Suave Abstractions," *The* [New York] *World,* February 1923, 9M, reprinted in Lynes, *O'Keeffe, Stieglitz, and the Critics,* 193.

15. Helen Appleton Read, "Georgia O'Keeffe's Show an Emotional Escape," *Brooklyn Daily Eagle,* February 11, 1923, 2B, reprinted in Lynes, *O'Keeffe, Stieglitz, and the Critics,* 191–192.

16. "'I Can't Sing, So I Paint!' Says Ultra Realistic Artist; Art Is Not Photography— It Is Expression of Inner Life! Miss Georgia O'Keeffe Explains Subjective Aspect of Her Work," *New York Sun,* December 5, 1922, 22, reprinted in Lynes, *O'Keeffe, Stieglitz, and the Critics,* 180–182.

17. For a discussion of O'Keeffe's health and its impact on her relationship with Stieglitz, see Drohojowska-Philp, *Full Bloom*, 248.

18. Speculations about the impact of Stieglitz's love affairs on O'Keeffe are discussed extensively in Benita Eisler, *O'Keeffe and Stieglitz: An American Romance* (New York: Doubleday, 1988), and in Drohojowska-Philp, *Full Bloom*, 5–6.

19. The main exceptions were short trips O'Keeffe made to visit her friends Marjorie and Bennet Schauffler in York Beach, Maine, in the 1920s and visits to her family in Wisconsin in 1928.

20. Rebecca Strand to Paul Strand, June 16, 1929, Paul Strand Archives, Center for Creative Photography, Tucson (AG17:41:5–7).

21. This portrait is from a series of nine images that Stieglitz took of O'Keeffe in 1933 posing with her new Ford v-8 convertible coupe; see Greenough, *Stieglitz*, nos. 1515–1522. In two, she wears a Navajo blanket across her shoulders, further associating the car with her western sojourns.

22. For a listing of these photographs and paintings, see Greenough, *Stieglitz*, nos. 1427–1437.

23. "Speaking of Pictures… These Are by One of Photography's Pioneers," *Life*, April 5, 1943, 9; see Greenough, *Stieglitz*, no. 1427.

24. For a discussion of O'Keeffe's shift from New York to New Mexico, see Barbara Buhler Lynes, "Georgia O'Keeffe: Identity and Place," in *Georgia O'Keeffe: Circling around Abstraction* (West Palm Beach, Fla.: Norton Gallery and School of Art, 2007), 39–51.

25. Ansel Adams and Mary Austin, *Taos Pueblo* (San Francisco: Ansel Adams, 1930).

26. From an unidentified article on Georgia O'Keeffe in the Ansel Adams papers, Center for Creative Photography. O'Keeffe exhibited nineteen paintings of New Mexico in her annual exhibition at Stieglitz's gallery in 1930. Only two were landscapes; the others were views of the Ranchos de Taos church and crosses.

27. Anne Hammond curated a traveling exhibition on this topic for the Georgia O'Keeffe Museum; see her catalogue *Georgia O'Keeffe and Ansel Adams: Natural Affinities* (Boston: Little, Brown, 2008).

28. Her interest in vernacular architecture dates back to the early 1920s, with images of barns in the countryside near Lake George, but intensified in the series on the Taos church in the 1930s and culminates in the 1950s with her series of views of her patio at Abiquiu.

29. For an overview of the relationship between Adams and O'Keeffe and its cultural context, see Rebecca A. Senf, "Ansel Adams in the American Southwest," in the exhibition catalogue *Ansel Adams in the Lane Collection* (Boston: Museum of Fine Arts, 2005), 53–75.

30. Mary Alinder, *Ansel Adams: A Biography* (New York: Henry Holt, 1996), 109. This book provides a detailed account of Adams's relationship with O'Keeffe and Stieglitz.

31. Clearly a key figure in his life, McAlpin receives a chapter in Adams's book *Ansel Adams: An Autobiography* (Boston: Bulfinch, 1985), 221–235.

32. Leslie Poling-Kempes's extensive history of Ghost Ranch includes a chapter on O'Keeffe and her activities; see *Ghost Ranch* (Tucson: University of Arizona Press, 2005).

33. O'Keeffe eventually bought the house in 1940. For a detailed survey of that landscape and its many manifestations in O'Keeffe's art, see Barbara Buhler Lynes, Lesley Poling-Kempes, and Frederick W. Turner, *Georgia O'Keeffe and New Mexico: A Sense of Place* (Princeton, N.J.: Princeton University Press and Santa Fe, N.Mex.: Georgia O'Keeffe Museum, 2004); Charles C. Eldredge, *Georgia O'Keeffe* (New York: Harry N. Abrams and Washington, D.C.: National Museum of American Art, Smithsonian Institution, 1991), 103–116.

34. *Life*, February 14, 1938, 31.

35. Quoted in Poling-Kempes, *Ghost Ranch*, 134. Among the diverse array of guests that O'Keeffe entertained that year at Ghost Ranch were Margaret Bok, her husband, the filmmaker Henwar Rodakiewicz, and their three young children; the Santa Fe writer Spud Johnson and painter Cady Welles; and college professors Haniel Long of Carnegie-Mellon University and Gerald Heard of Duke University. Although many scholars stress O'Keeffe's isolation at Ghost Ranch, she clearly enjoyed having visitors.

36. Among the seventy-five images in James Alinder and John Szarkowski, *Ansel Adams: Classic Images* (Boston: Bulfinch, 1985), there are only six portraits, among them the double portrait of Cox and O'Keeffe. The book also features three landscapes from the 1937 trip and a portrait of Stieglitz posed in front of one of O'Keeffe's paintings at An American Place in 1944.

37. See Poling-Kempes, *Ghost Ranch,* 135–136, and Georgia O'Keeffe, *Georgia O'Keeffe* (New York: Viking, 1976), 90. There are two versions of this painting: see Lynes, *O'Keeffe,* nos. 936 and 937. Lynes identifies the first, now in the collection of the Georgia O'Keeffe Museum, as the version in the Adams photograph.

38. O'Keeffe to Stieglitz, August 26, 1937, published in the exhibition catalogue *Georgia O'Keeffe: Catalogue of the Fourteenth Annual Exhibition* (New York: An American Place, 1938), 10.

39. Alinder, *Ansel Adams,* 146. A selection of the four-by-five-inch proof prints that Adams gave to McAlpin, now in a private collection, were shown in 2002 at the Fitchburg Art Museum in an exhibition organized by Stephen Jareckie: *Adams and O'Keeffe on the Road.* In a letter to McAlpin, Adams said he was sending McAlpin three albums as Christmas presents: one for McAlpin, one for his cousin Godfrey Rockefeller, and one for O'Keeffe (December 7, 1938, McAlpin Family archive). In another letter Adams told McAlpin: "I have no illusions over the prints; they are just records of the trip. So all the recipients must consider them as such, not as collections of fine photography. Some fine prints will follow, but they would be out of place in such an album" (December 18, 1939, McAlpin Family archive). The "fine prints" owned by McAlpin are now at the Princeton University Art Museum, and other large prints from the 1937 trip are in the Ansel Adams archives at the Center for Creative Photography.

40. Adams to Stieglitz, September 21, 1937, on Ghost Ranch stationery, Beinecke Rare Book and Manuscript Library, Yale University.

41. McAlpin bought a pastel, *Narcissa's Last Orchid,* 1941, now at the Princeton University Art Museum. For further details about McAlpin's photographic interests, see Peter C. Bunnell, *Photography at Princeton* (Princeton, N.J.: Princeton University Art Museum, 1998), 1–3.

42. Alinder, *Ansel Adams,* 154–155; Eldredge, *Georgia O'Keeffe,* 155.

43. The painting, *East River No. 1,* 1927–1928, is now in the collection of the New Jersey State Museum; see Lynes, *O'Keeffe,* no. 614.

44. For a discussion of O'Keeffe's friendship with Callery, see Drohojowska-Philp, *Full Bloom,* 401, 418, 452. They met at Ghost Ranch in 1945, and O'Keeffe made her first trip to Europe with Callery and the photographer Todd Webb in 1953.

45. "Profiles: The Rose in the Eye Looked Pretty Fine," *New Yorker,* March 4, 1974, 40–66.

46. For an account of O'Keeffe's activities at Ghost Ranch and a history of the village of Abiquiu, see Leslie Poling-Kempes, *The Valley of the Shining Stone: The Story of Abiquiu* (Tucson: University of Arizona Press, 1997), and Barbara Lynes and Ann Paden, *Maria Chabot and Georgia O'Keeffe: Correspondence, 1941–49* (Albuquerque: University of New Mexico Press, 2003).

47. "Georgia O'Keeffe Turns Dead Bones to Live Art," *Life,* February 14, 1938, 28–30. Charles Eldredge reproduced the article in his chapter on O'Keeffe's bone paintings and reiterates the story of her shipping bones back east; see *O'Keeffe,* 119.

48. For a discussion of Webb's career, see his autobiography, *Looking Back: Memoirs and Photographs* (Albuquerque: University of New Mexico Press, 1991).

49. For details of their relationship, see Georgia O'Keeffe–Todd Webb correspondence (1952–1986) at the Beinecke Rare Book and Manuscript Library, Yale University; Lynes, *Georgia O'Keeffe and New Mexico,* 51–56; and Todd Webb, *Georgia O'Keeffe: The Artist's Landscape* (Pasadena, Calif.: Twelvetrees Press, 1984).

50. *Vogue,* October 15, 1923, 76–77, 110, 112.

51. Colin Westerbeck, "A Man of Many Parts," in *Irving Penn: A Career in Photography* (Chicago: The Art Institute of Chicago and Boston: Bulfinch, 1997), 11.

52. For an overview of his career, see Mary Panzer's essay in *Philippe Halsman: A Retrospective* (Boston: Little, Brown, 1998), 7–11.

53. For a selection of a dozen images from both the 1948 and 1967 sessions, see http://www.magnumphotos.com/Archive.

54. Mark Stevens, "The Gift of Spiritual Intensity," *Newsweek,* March 17, 1986, 77.

55. O'Keeffe pictured similar deer skulls with antlers in 1936; see Lynes, *O'Keeffe,* nos. 879 and 880. At this same session, Karsh photographed O'Keeffe in front of a painting from her 1955 "Black Door" series; see Lynes, *O'Keeffe,* no. 1283.

56. Yousuf Karsh, *Faces of Our Time* (Toronto: University of Toronto Press, 1971), 142.

57. See the caption for this picture in Yousuf Karsh, *Karsh: A Sixty-Year Retrospective,* rev. ed. (Boston: Bulfinch, 1996), 107. Her home at Abiquiu is now maintained by the Georgia O'Keeffe Museum.

58. See Alan Fern and Arnold Newman, *Arnold Newman's Americans* (Washington, D.C.: National Portrait Gallery and Boston: Little, Brown, 1992).

59. Estelle Jussim, "The Psychological Portrait," in *Karsh: The Art of the Portrait* (Ottawa: National Gallery of Canada, 1989), 102.

60. Charles Brossard, "Santa Fe, Our Last Unspoiled City?" *Holiday,* May 1969, 64–65.

61. For discussions of the development of Santa Fe as an artistic center, see Sharon Rohlfsen Udall, *Modernist Painting in New Mexico, 1913–1935* (Albuquerque: University of New Mexico Press, 1984), and Patricia Trenton, ed., *Independent Spirits: Women Painters of the American West, 1890–1945* (Los Angeles: Autry Museum of the American West, 1995).

62. Meem provided plans for a new church in Abiquiu, built in a traditional pueblo style and completed in 1937. For a discussion of his influence, see Chris Wilson, *Facing Southwest: The Life and Houses of John Gaw Meem* (New York: W. W. Norton, 2002), and Bainbridge Bunting, *John Gaw Meem: Southwestern Architect* (Albuquerque: University of New Mexico Press, 1983).

63. For a discussion of Gilpin's career and her contacts with O'Keeffe, see Martha A. Sandweiss, *Laura Gilpin: An Enduring Grace* (Fort Worth, Tex.: Amon Carter Museum, 1986), 95, 109–110.

64. Laura Gilpin, "The Austerity of the Desert Pervades Her Home and Her Work," *House Beautiful,* April 1963, 144–145, 198–199.

65. John Loengard, "Horizons of a Pioneer: Georgia O'Keeffe in New Mexico," *Life,* March 1, 1968, 40–49. An expanded version of this photographic essay appears in his book *Georgia O'Keeffe at Ghost Ranch* (New York: Neues, 1998). The continuing popularity of Loengard's books on O'Keeffe is attested to by a new edition of the work, *Image and Imagination, Georgia O'Keeffe* (San Francisco: Chronicle Books, 2007), first published in paperback editions in German, English, French, and Italian by Schirmer/Mosel Verlag in 2006.

66. The text was probably provided by *Life* editor Grace Seiberling, who returned to New Mexico with Loengard after the layout was finished in October 1967 to meet O'Keeffe and obtain the quotations for the article.

67. Architectural historians in the 1920s and 1930s were among the first to link the colonial and modern styles in New Mexico; see, e.g., Sheldon Cheney, *The New World Architecture* (London: Longmans, Green, 1930).

68. Unpublished transcript of an interview with the artist conducted by Sarah Burt, The Georgia O'Keeffe Foundation, June 23, 2002, Georgia O'Keeffe Museum Research Center.

69. [Mary Roche], "Five Famous Artists in Their Personal Backgrounds," *House and Garden,* December 1965, 176–177.

70. Balthazar Korab, "A Fine Day in Abiquiu," unpublished notes (August 1997), courtesy of the author. Korab also notes that he photographed Ghost Ranch on this assignment.

71. Hunter Drohojowska-Philp, "O'Keeffe in Abiquiu," *Western Interiors and Design* July–August 2004, 130–137. In addition to the article on O'Keeffe, this issue included photo essays on the homes of artists Fritz Scholder, John Baldessari, and Donald Judd.

72. She wrote a letter of appreciation to Wright in 1942 after visiting Taliesin East in Springreen, Wisconsin, quoted in Jack Cowart, Juan Hamilton, and Sarah Greenough, *Georgia O'Keeffe: Arts and Letters* (Washington, D.C.: National Gallery of Art, 1988), 233. Later in 1950, O'Keeffe, Eliot Porter, and the writer Frances O'Brien traveled to Scottsdale, Arizona, to visit Wright's architectural studio and home.

73. Myron Wood and Christine Taylor Patten, *O'Keeffe at Abiquiu* (New York: Harry N. Abrams, 1995), 13–15. Wood's daughter, who was O'Keeffe's nurse, provided additional text about the artist's life.

74. Other contemporary photographers who took pictures of O'Keeffe late in life are Dan Budnik, Bruce Weber, William Clift, and the designer Charles Eames. Examples of their work are located in the Georgia O'Keeffe Museum Research Center.

75. In her recent introduction to an issue of *American Art* devoted to O'Keeffe, Barbara Buhler Lynes persuasively argues that the artist herself orchestrated these later images; see "Visiting O'Keeffe," *American Art,* Fall 2006, 2–7.

76. For example, see Anna Chaves, "O'Keeffe and the Masculine Gaze," in Christopher Merrill and Ellen Bradbury, eds., *From the Faraway Nearby: Georgia O'Keeffe as Icon* (reprint ed., Albuquerque: University of New Mexico Press, 1998), 29–42.

77. "The Female of the Species Achieves a New Deadliness," *Vanity Fair,* July 1922, 50, reprinted in Lynes, *O'Keeffe, Stieglitz, and the Critics,* 175. Of the remaining four artists mentioned, only Marguerite Zorach is much discussed today.

78. The Stieglitz portrait is one of his 1918 images of O'Keeffe posed in front of her charcoal drawing *No. 15—Special,* 1916–1917, Philadelphia Museum of Art (Lynes, *Georgia O'Keeffe,* 154); see Greenough, *Alfred Stieglitz,* no. 472.

79. [Frank Crowninshield], "An Editor's Uneasy Chair: Woman Painter," and "A Series of American Artists— in Color," *Vanity Fair,* April 1932, 21, 40–41.

80. "Beauty Is Fun," *Town and Country,* April 1937, 52. The painting is titled *Miracle Flower* in the article.

81. Andy Warhol, "Georgia O'Keeffe and Juan Hamilton," *Interview,* September 1983, 54–56. For details of the relationship between Arden and O'Keeffe, see Drohojowska-Philp, *Full Bloom,* 366–367.

82. "Austere Stripper," *Time,* May 27, 1946, 74–75.

83. "My World Is Different…," *Newsweek,* October 10, 1960, 101.

84. Robert Hughes, "Loner in the Desert," *Time,* October 12, 1970, 64–67.

85. O'Keeffe, *Georgia O'Keeffe.* This popular book was reissued in a smaller format in 1977 in hardback (Viking) and paperback (Penguin) editions.

86. Sanford Schwartz, "Books: Georgia O'Keeffe Writes a Book," *New Yorker,* August 28, 1978, 87–93.

87. E.C. Goossen, "O'Keeffe," *Vogue,* March 1, 1967, 174–179, 221–224.

88. Barbara Rose, "O'Keeffe, 1897–1986: A Revolutionary Personality, a Creative Genius," *Vogue,* May 1986, 290–293; Rose, "The Self, the Style, the Art of Georgia O'Keeffe," *Vogue,* October 1987, 432–433, 482.

89. In the Warhol interview, O'Keeffe claimed to be ninety-six and, despite her failing eyesight, resisted his suggestion that she get contact lenses, saying proudly, "I haven't any glasses, I don't use them." Warhol, "O'Keeffe and Hamilton," *Interview,* 54.

90. See Hamilton to Warhol, November 13, 1980, Beinecke Rare Book and Manuscript Library, Yale University.

91. See the exhibition catalogue *Andy Warhol Photography* (Pittsburgh: The Andy Warhol Museum, 1999), 166, 273.

92. Frayda Feldman and Jorg Schellmann, *Andy Warhol Prints: A Catalogue Raisonné, 1962–1987* (New York: Ronald Feldman Fine Arts, Edition Schellmann, and The Andy Warhol Foundation for the Visual Arts, 1997), 218.

93. Rose, "The Self, the Style, the Art of Georgia O'Keeffe," 433. For a further discussion of parallels between the art of O'Keeffe and Warhol, see Barbara Lynes, *Georgia O'Keeffe and Andy Warhol: Flowers of Distinction* (Santa Fe, N.Mex.: Georgia O'Keeffe Museum, 2005).

94. Of the thirty-six artists listed, O'Keeffe and Mary Cassatt are the only two women. Among the others are Giotto, Dürer, Rembrandt, and Picasso and the earlier American artists John Singleton Copley and Winslow Homer.

95. Amei Wallach, "Georgia on Our Mind: Portrait of the Artist as a Pop Star," *Ms.,* November 1989, 38–41.

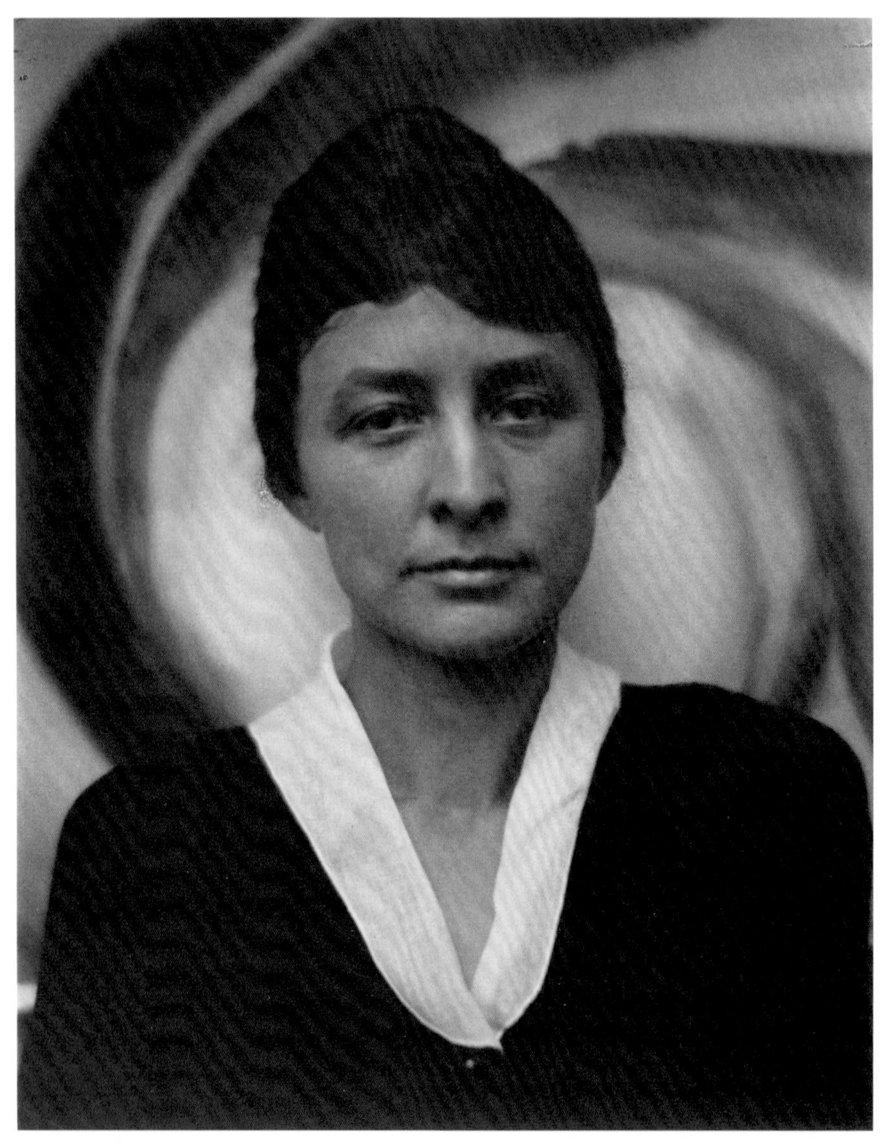

1.
Alfred Stieglitz,
Georgia O'Keeffe,
1917

2.
Alfred Stieglitz,
Georgia O'Keeffe
in Chemise,
1918

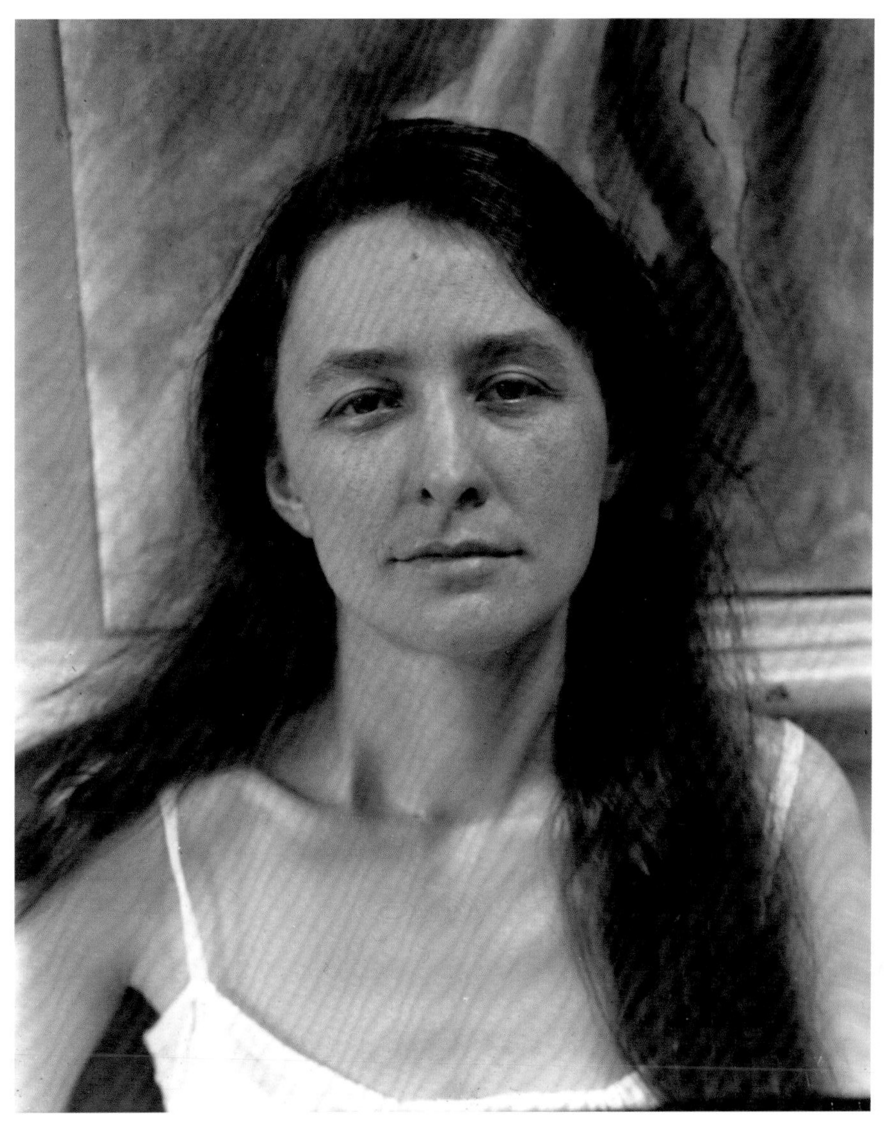

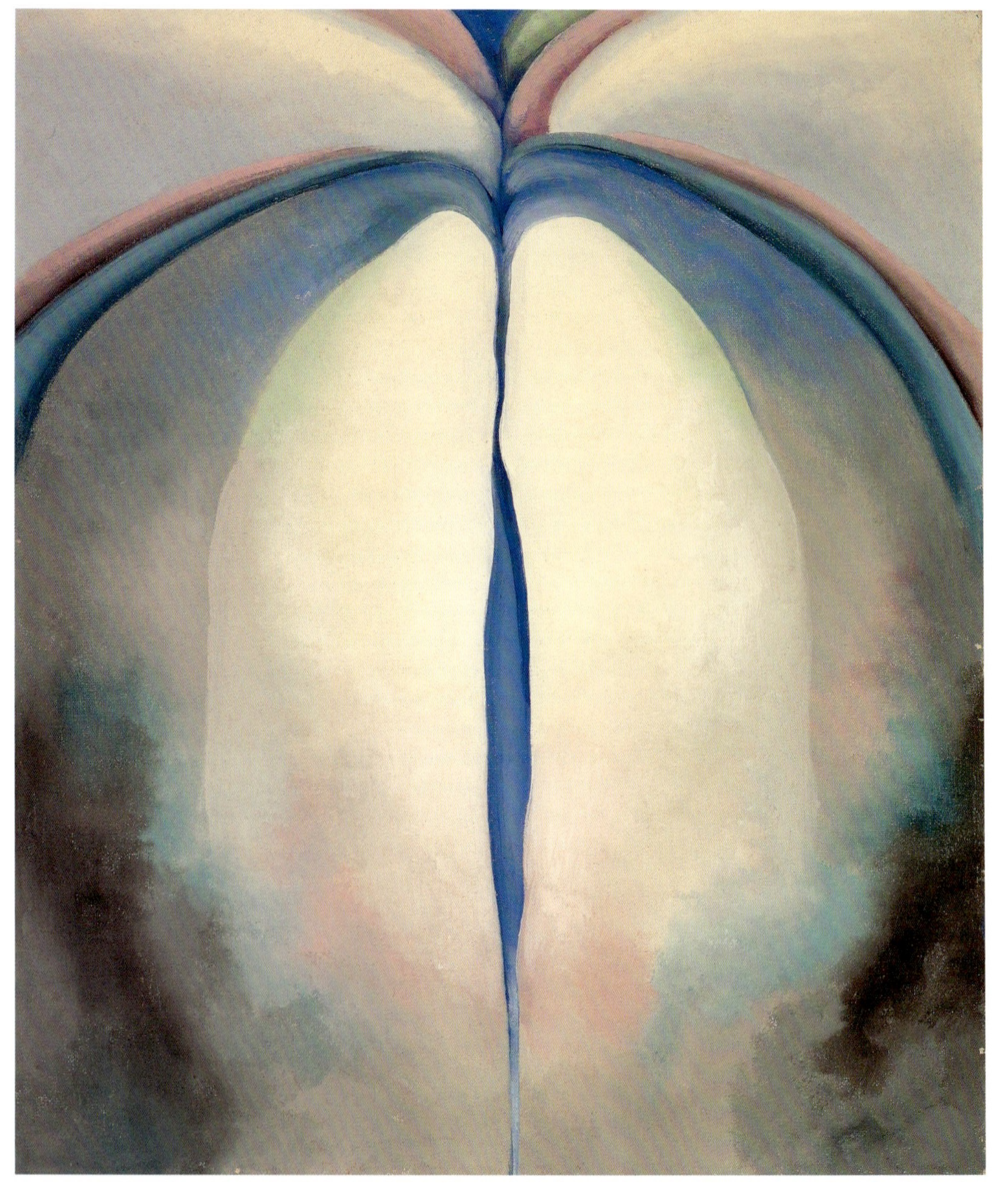

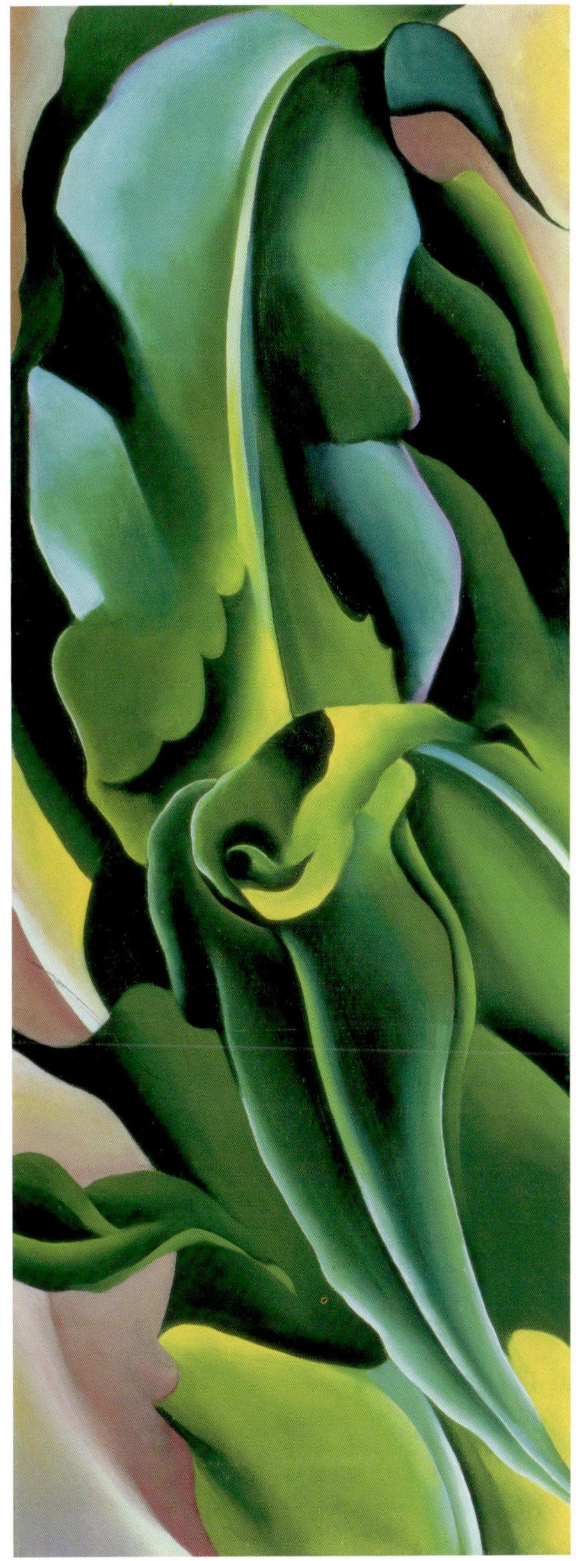

3.
Georgia O'Keeffe,
Blue Line, 1919

4.
Georgia O'Keeffe,
Corn, No. 2,
1924

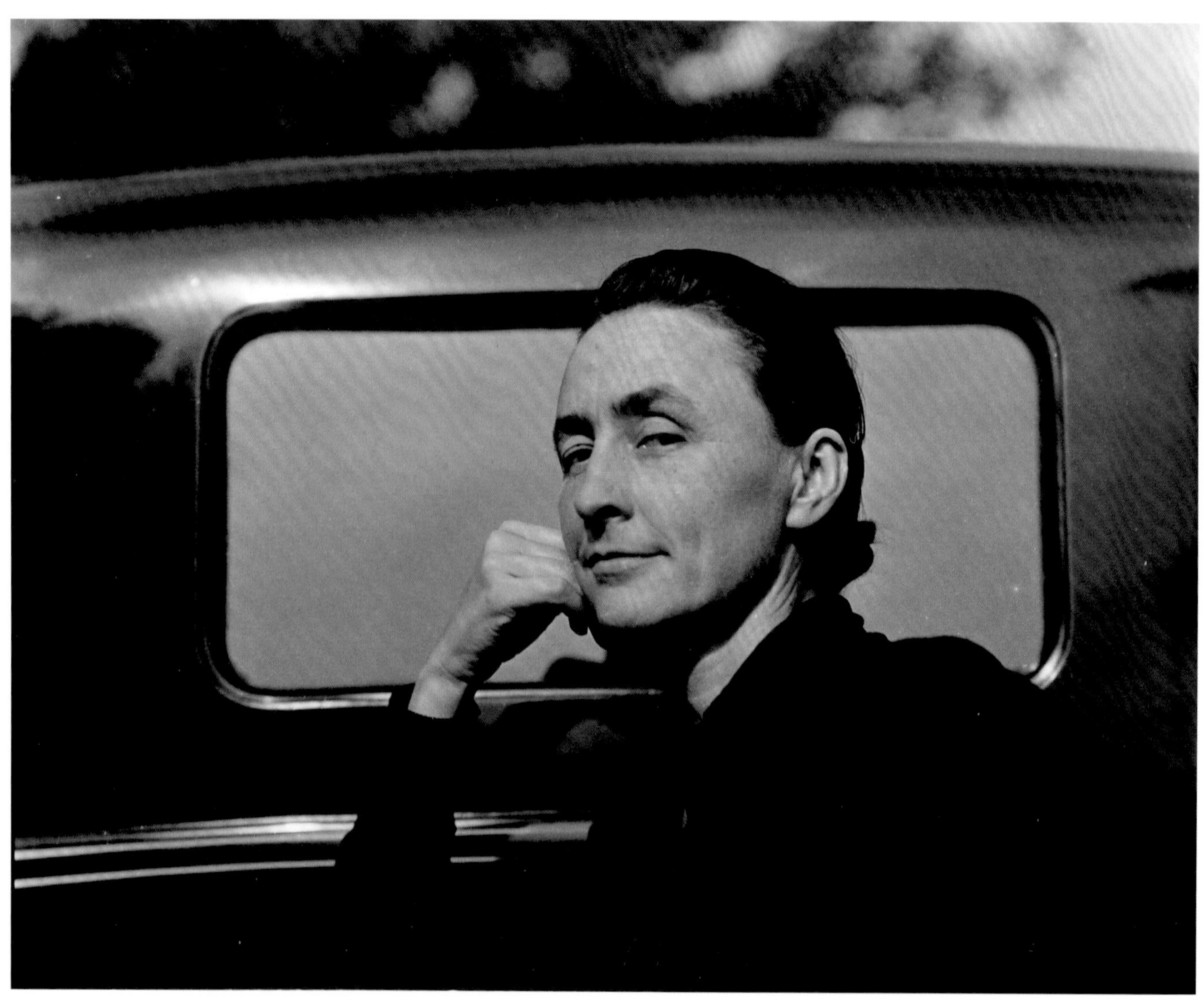

5.
Alfred Stieglitz,
Georgia O'Keeffe—
After Return
from New Mexico,
1929

6.
John Loengard,
On the Roof,
Ghost Ranch,
1967

7.
Arnold Newman,
Alfred Stieglitz and
Georgia O'Keeffe,
An American Place,
1944

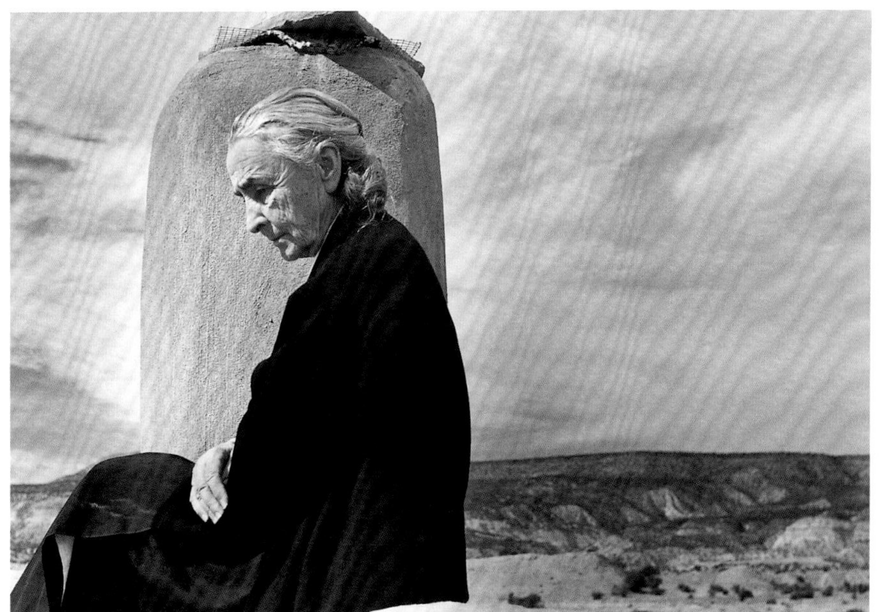

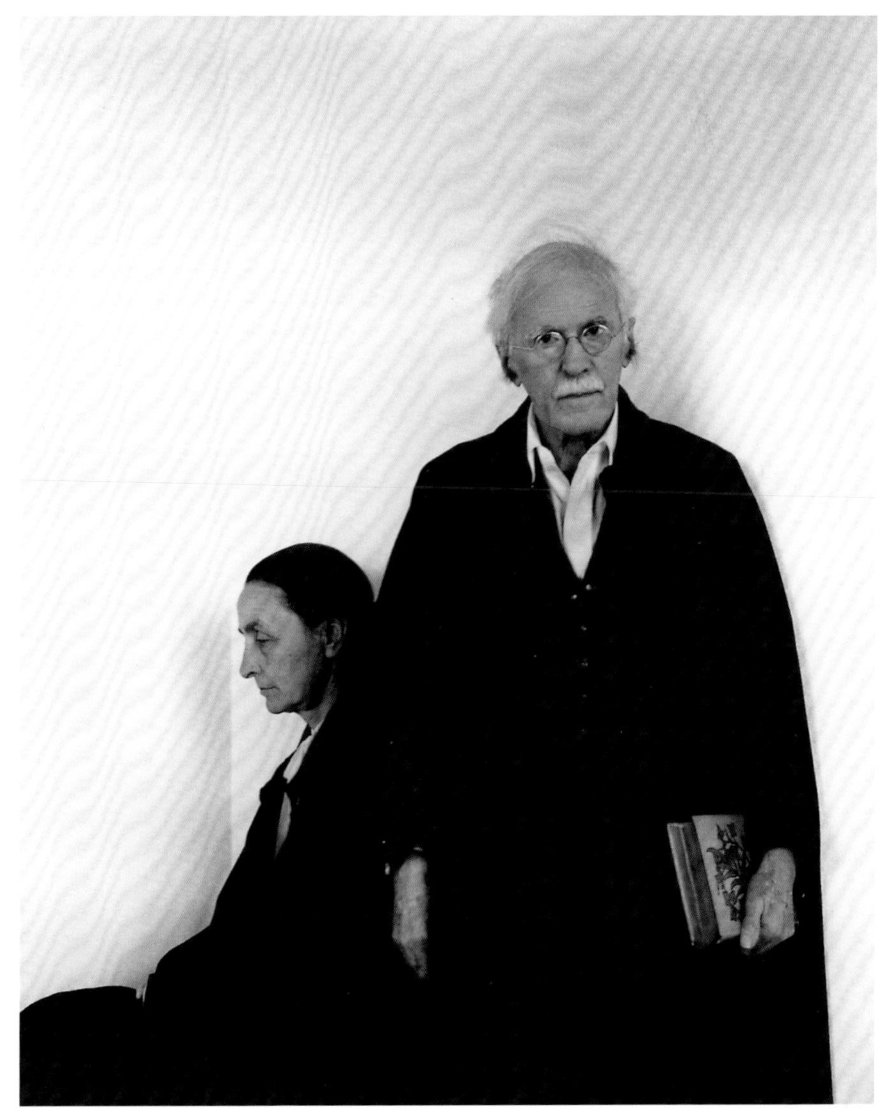

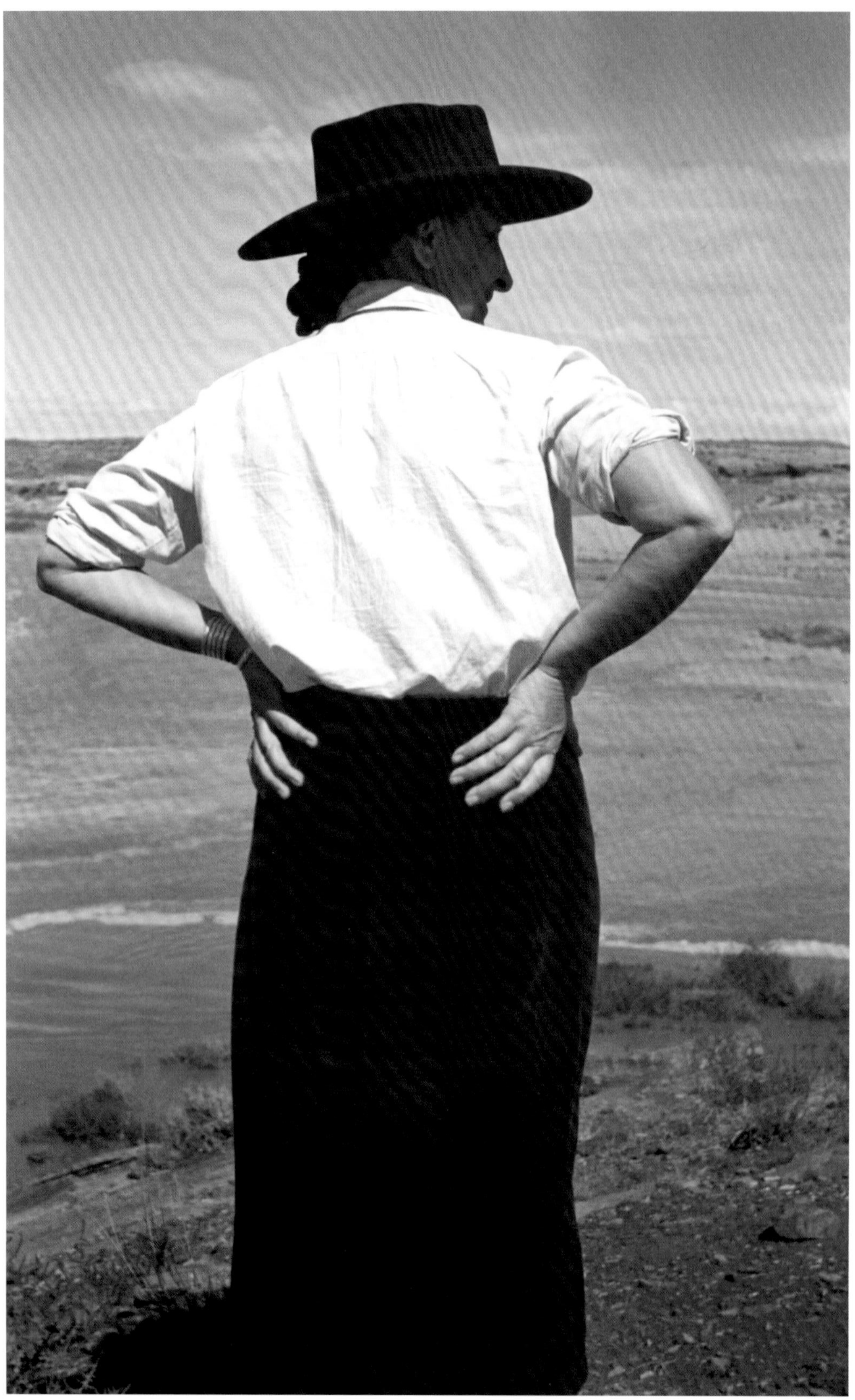

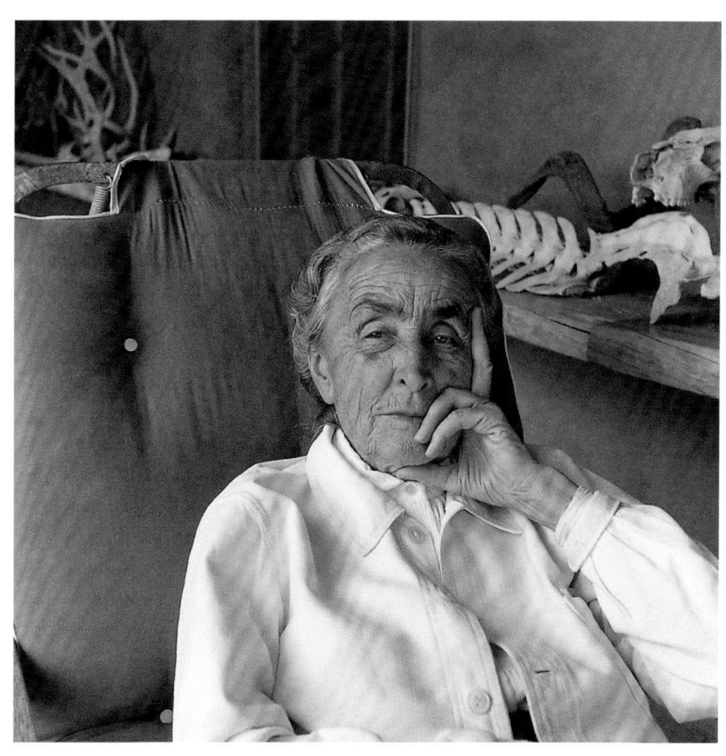

8.
Ansel Adams,
*Georgia O'Keeffe
in the Southwest,*
1937

9.
Todd Webb,
*Georgia O'Keeffe
at Ghost Ranch,*
1963

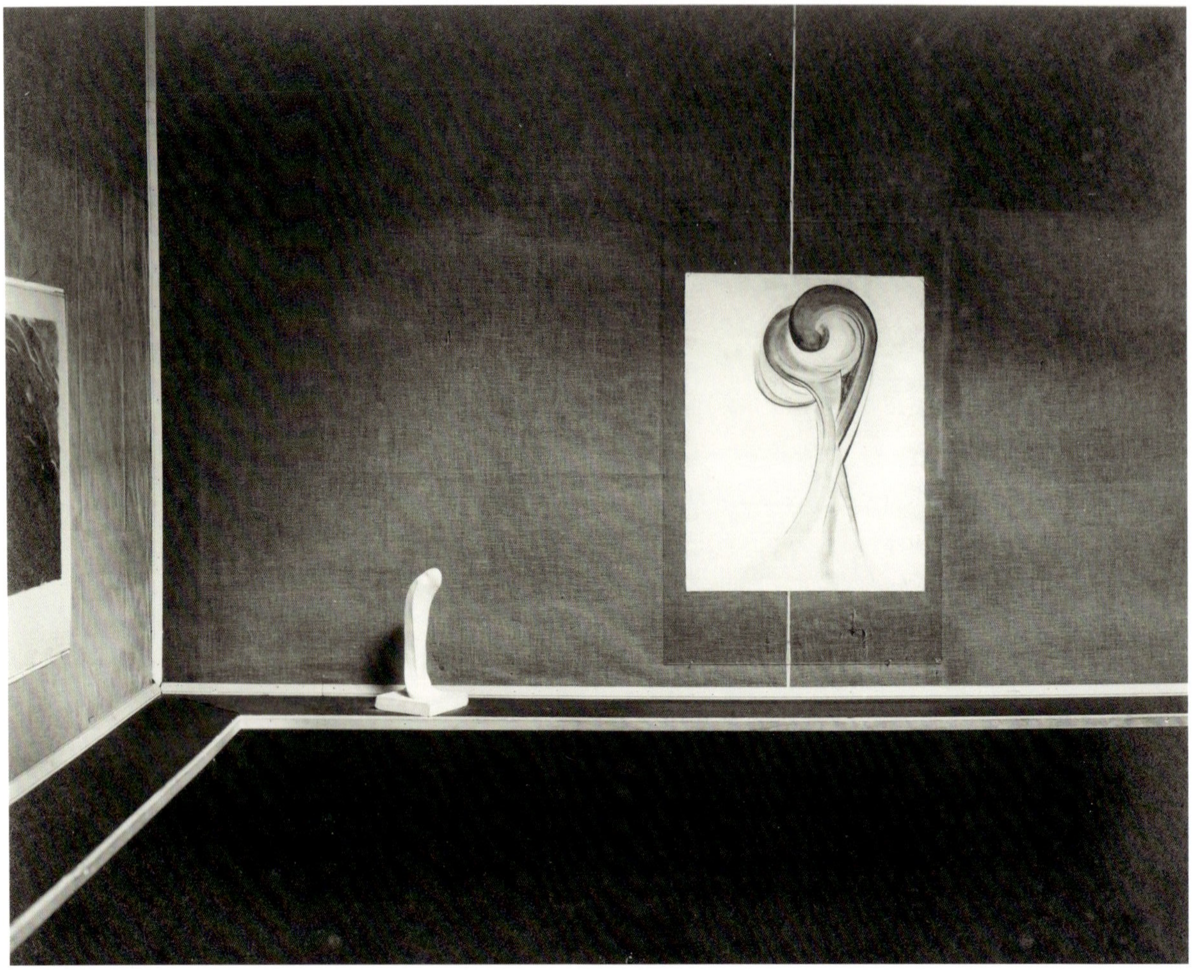

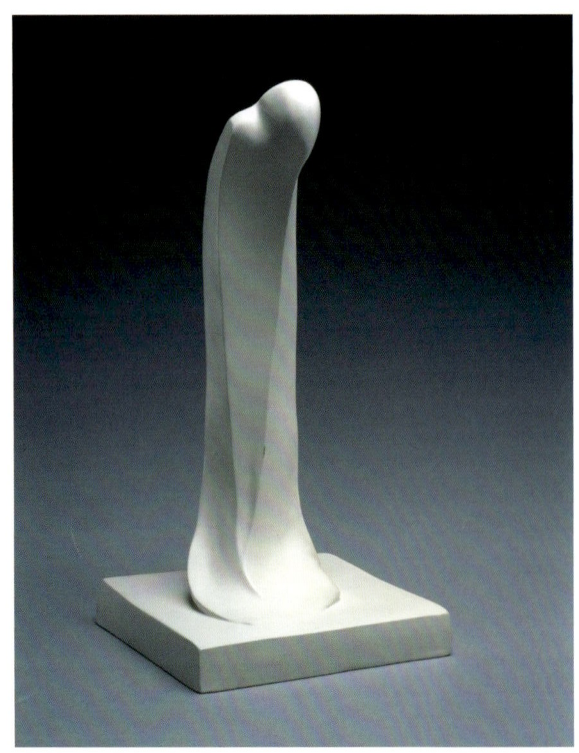

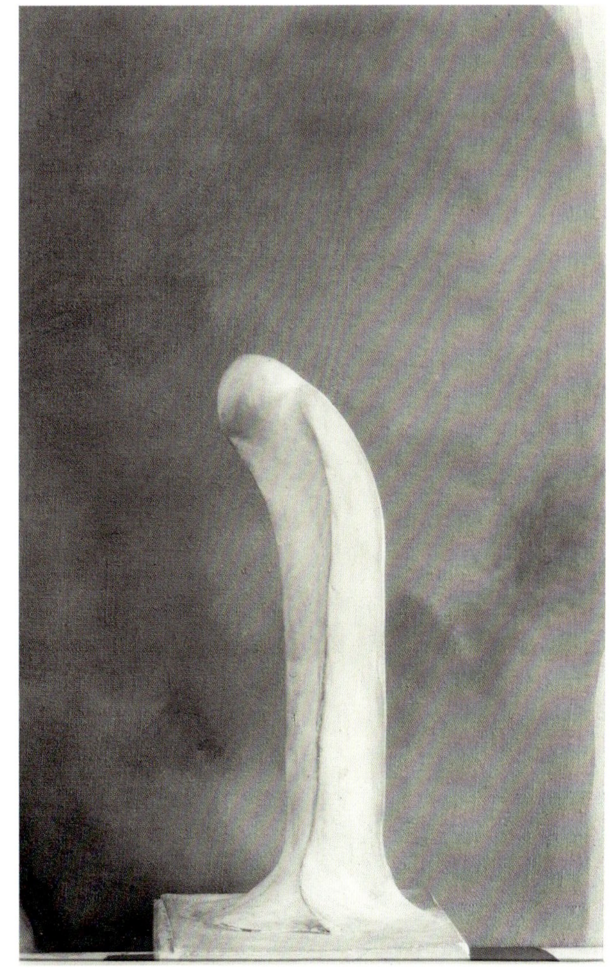

10.
Alfred Stieglitz,
*O'Keeffe Exhibition,
April 17, 1917,*
1917

11.
Georgia O'Keeffe,
Abstraction, 1916
(cast 1979–1980)

12.
Alfred Stieglitz,
Interpretation,
1919

13.
Alfred Stieglitz,
Georgia O'Keeffe,
1919

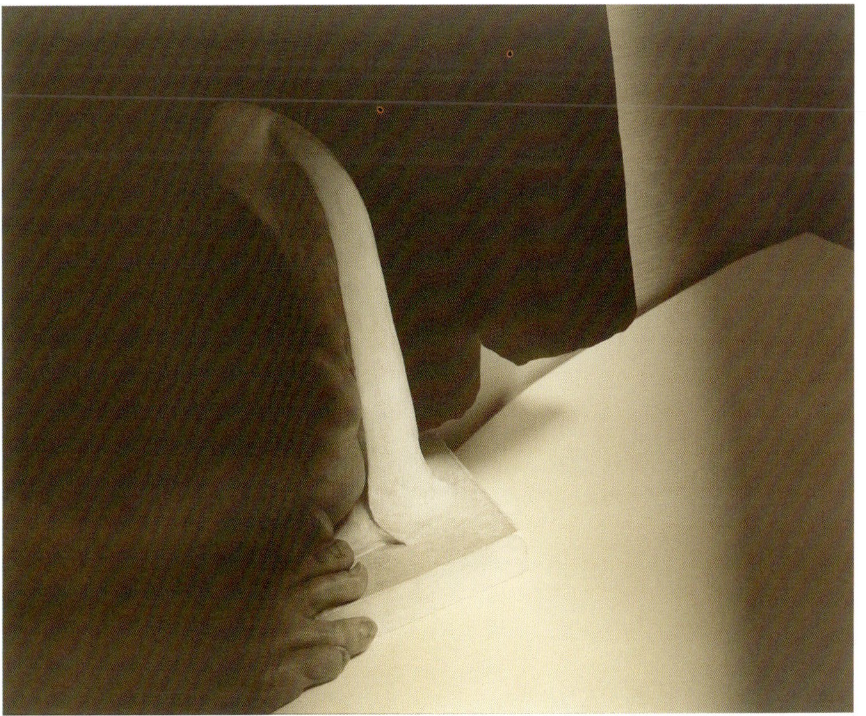

14.
Alfred Stieglitz,
Georgia O'Keeffe,
1918

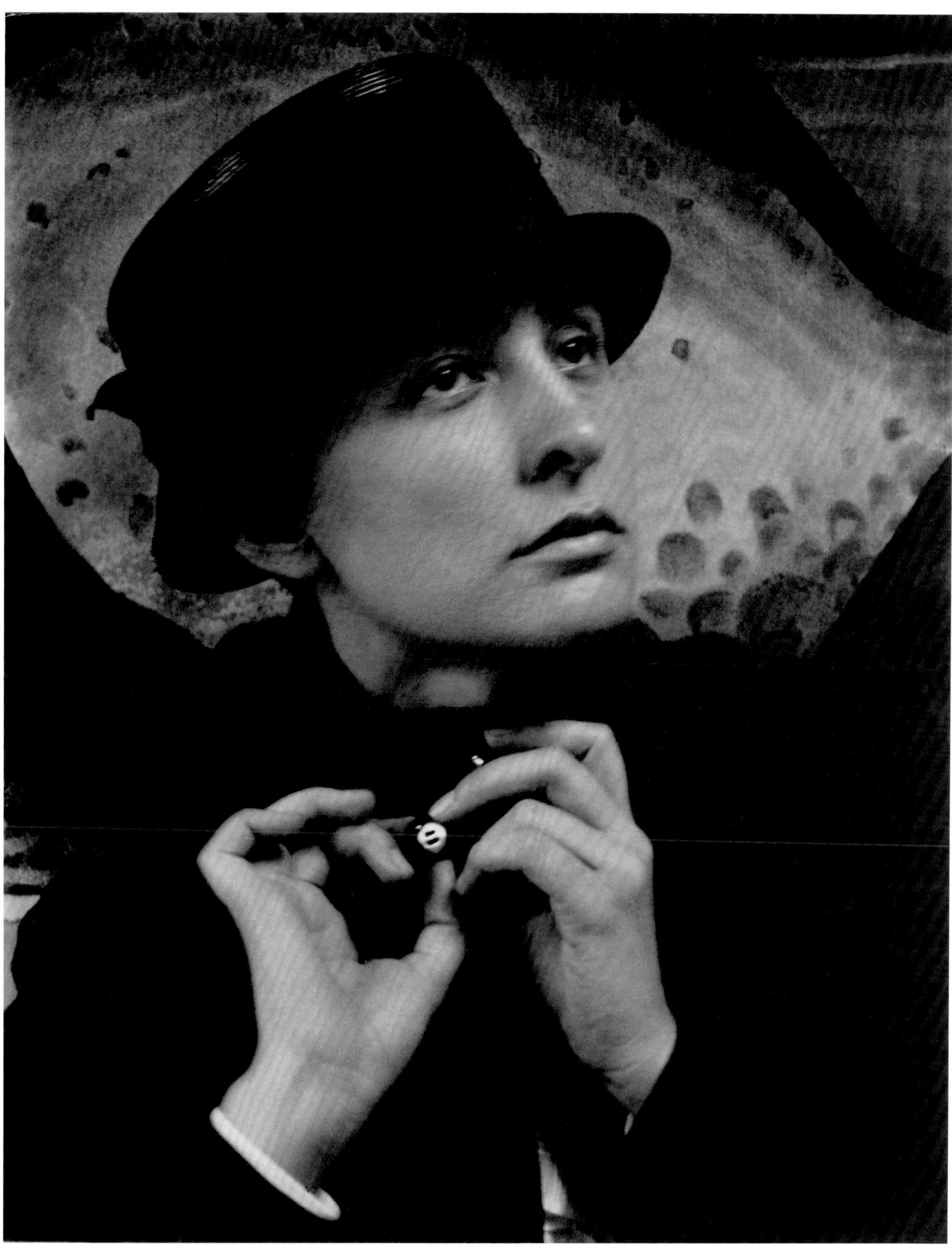

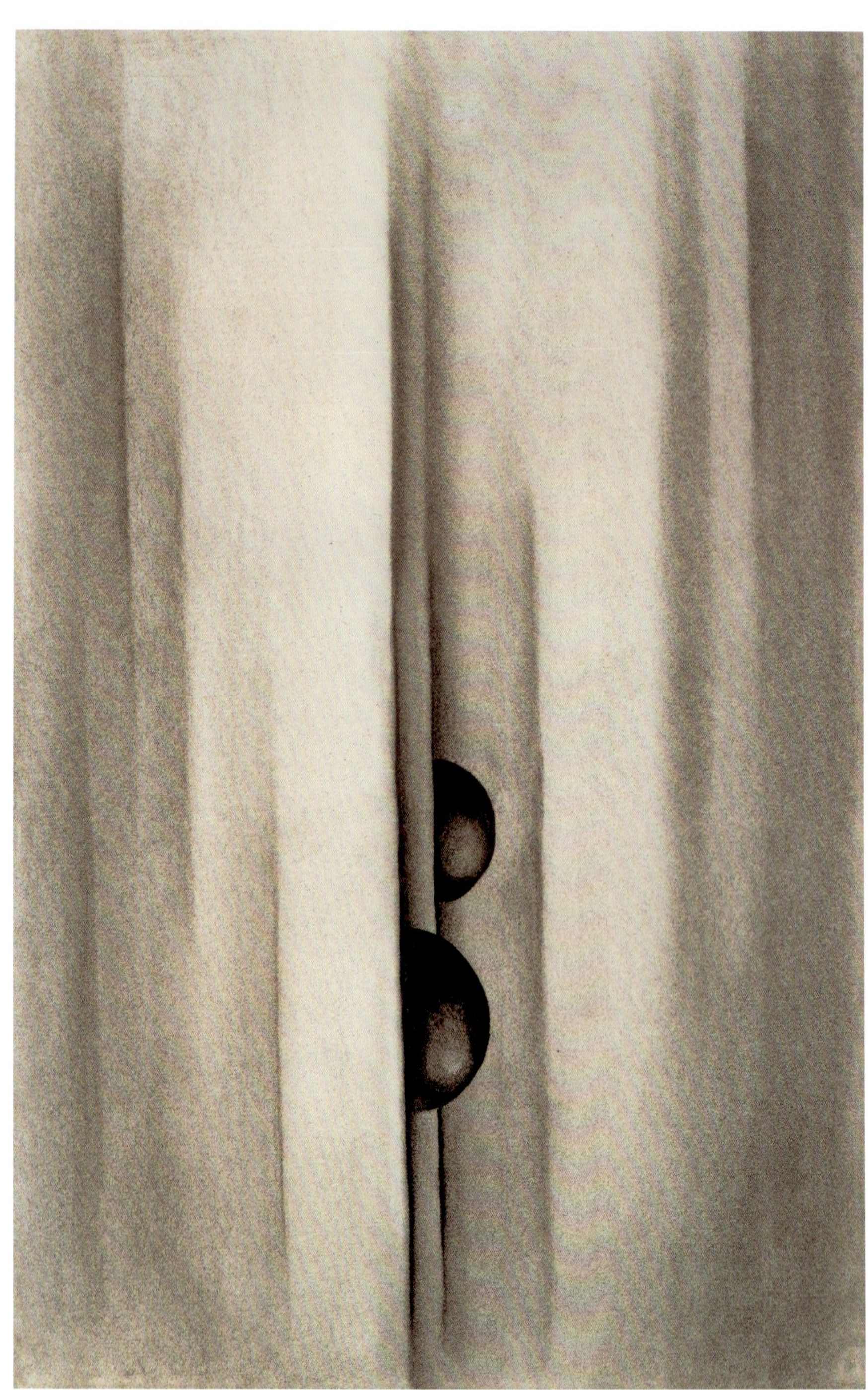

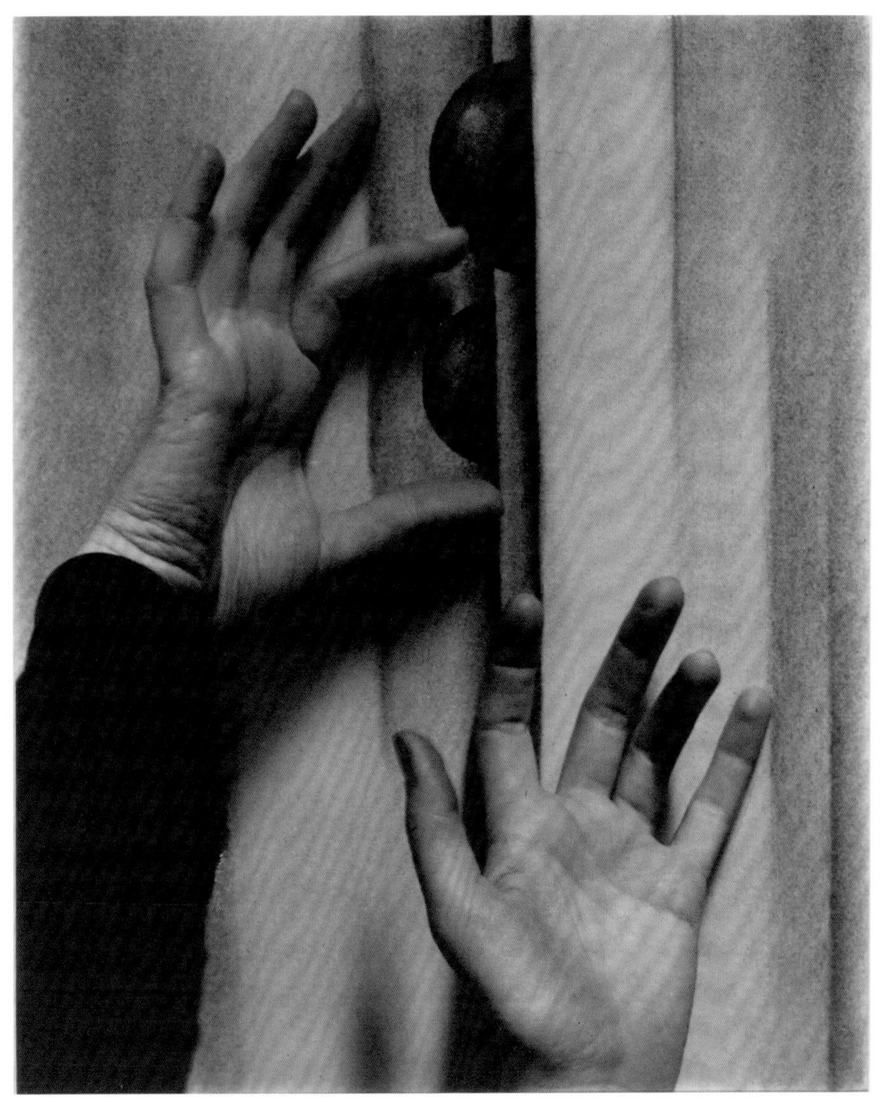

15.
Georgia O'Keeffe,
No. 17—Special,
1919

16.
Alfred Stieglitz,
Georgia O'Keeffe—
Hands, ca. 1919

17.
Georgia O'Keeffe,
Green Lines and Pink,
1919

18.
Alfred Stieglitz,
*O'Keeffe Exhibition at
Anderson Gallery*,
1923

19.
Georgia O'Keeffe,
Nude Series VII,
1917

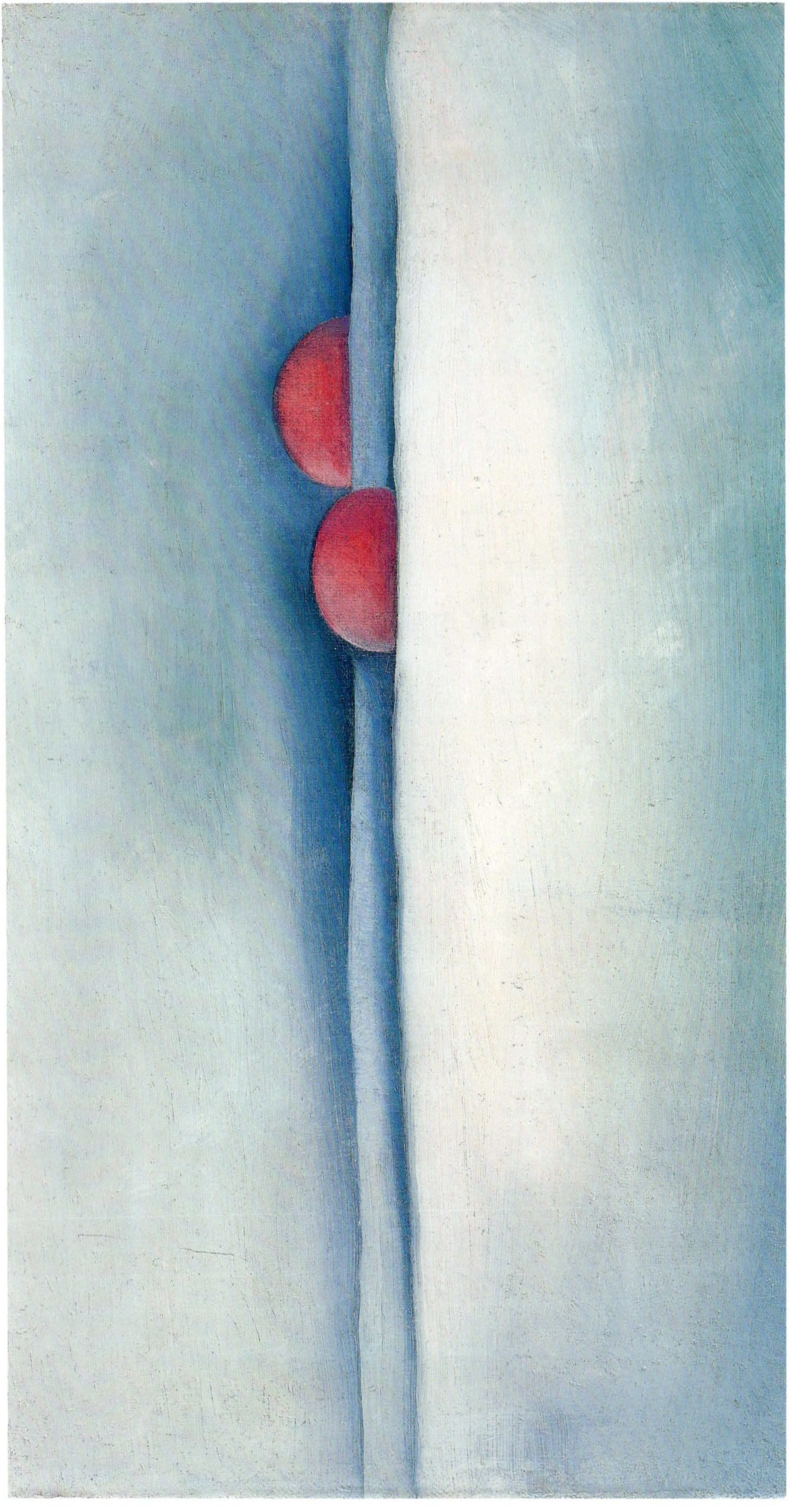

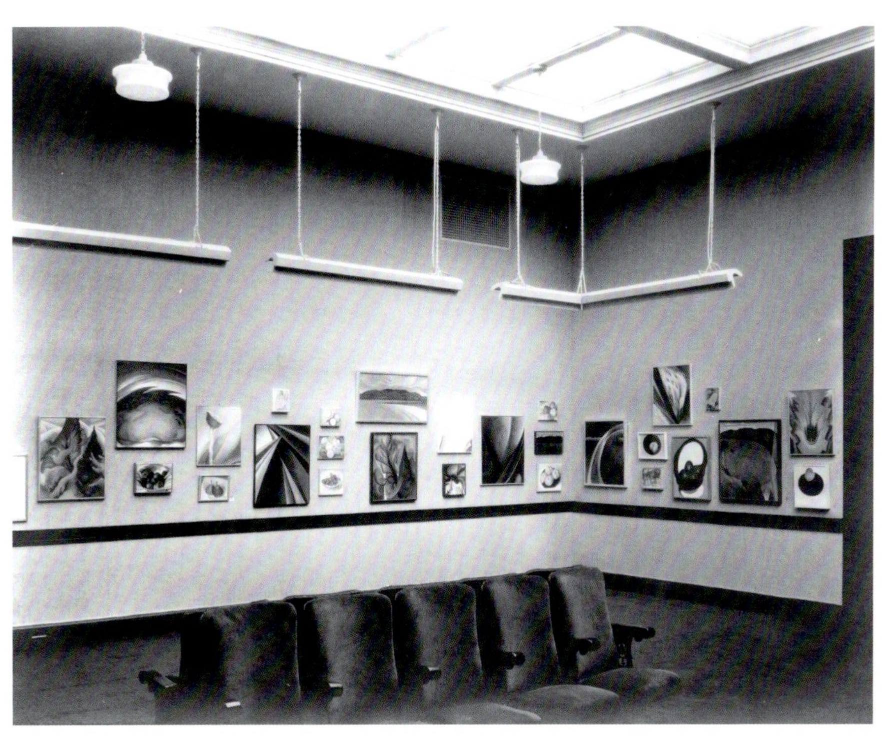

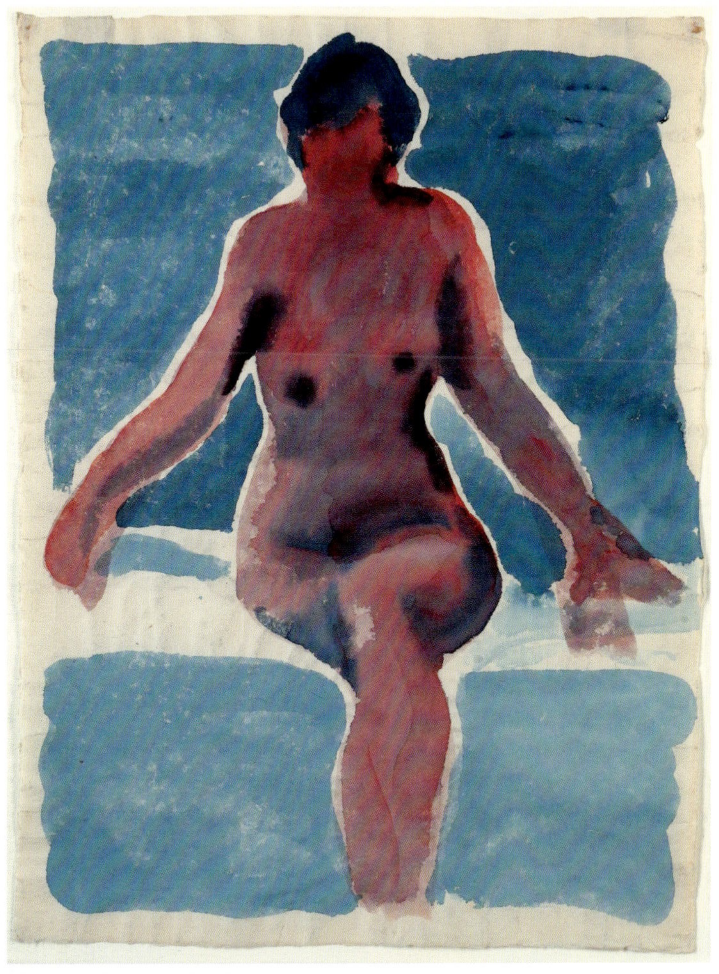

20.
Alfred Stieglitz,
Georgia O'Keeffe,
1930

21.
Alfred Stieglitz,
Georgia O'Keeffe,
1933

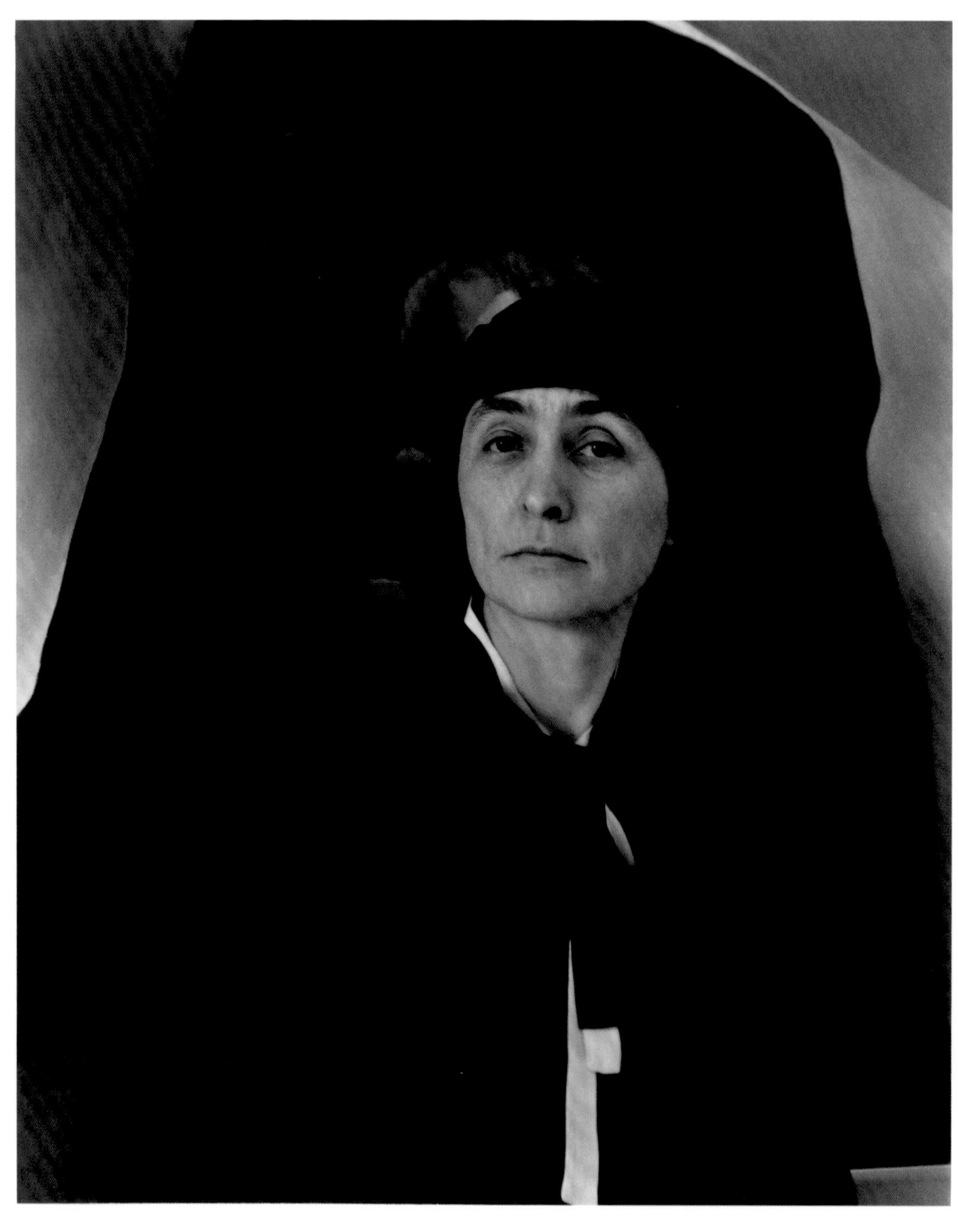

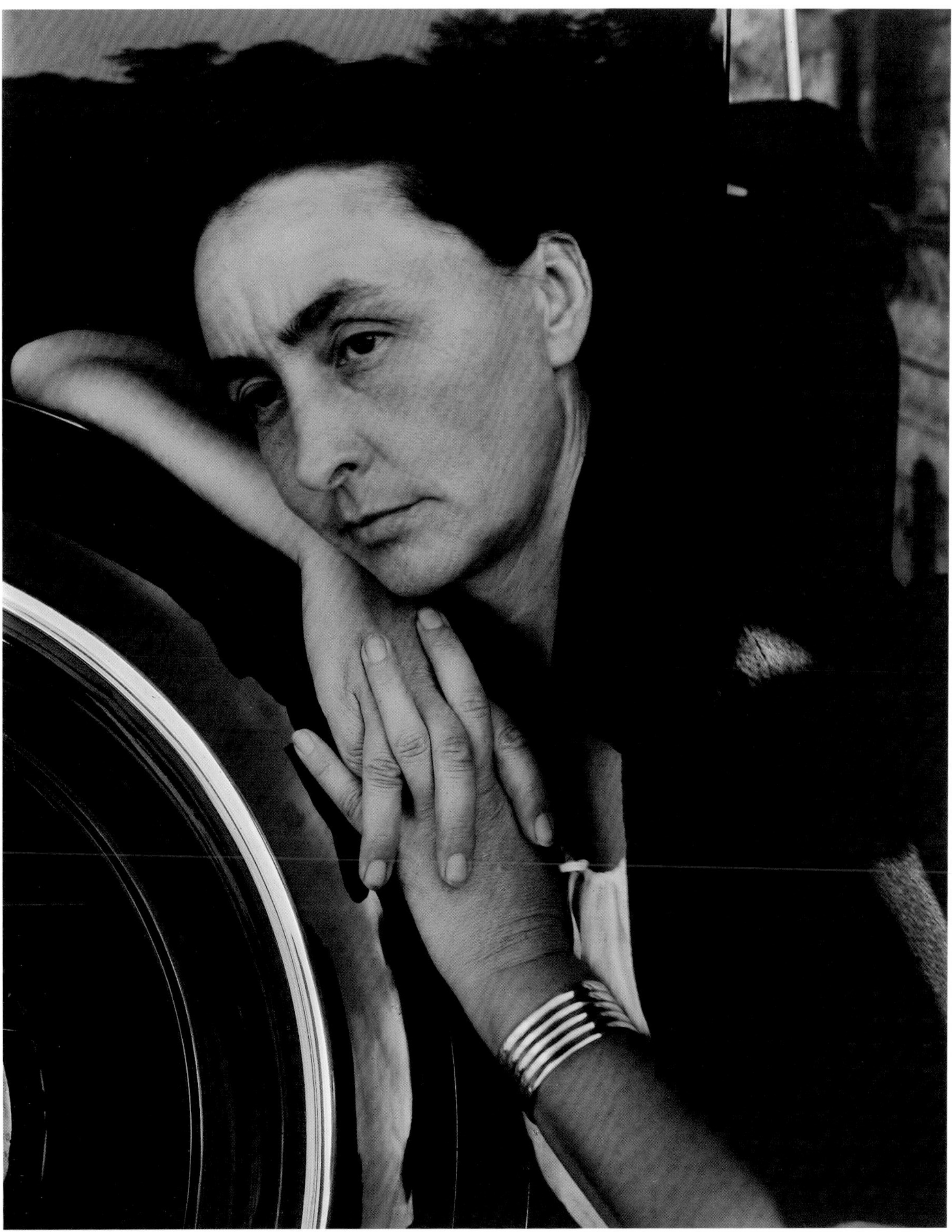

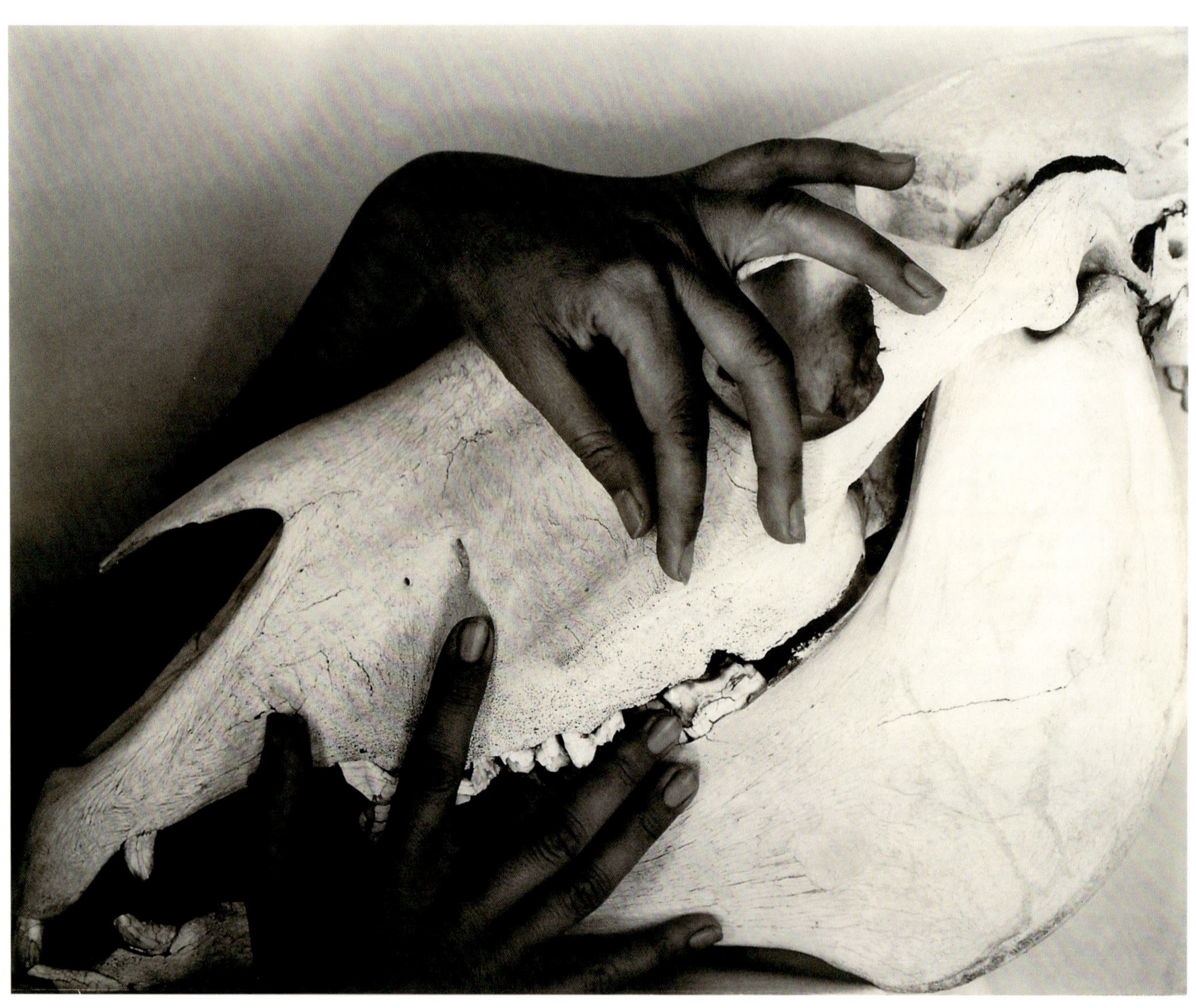

22.
Alfred Stieglitz,
Georgia O'Keeffe,
1931

23.
Georgia O'Keeffe,
Horse's Skull
with White Rose,
1931

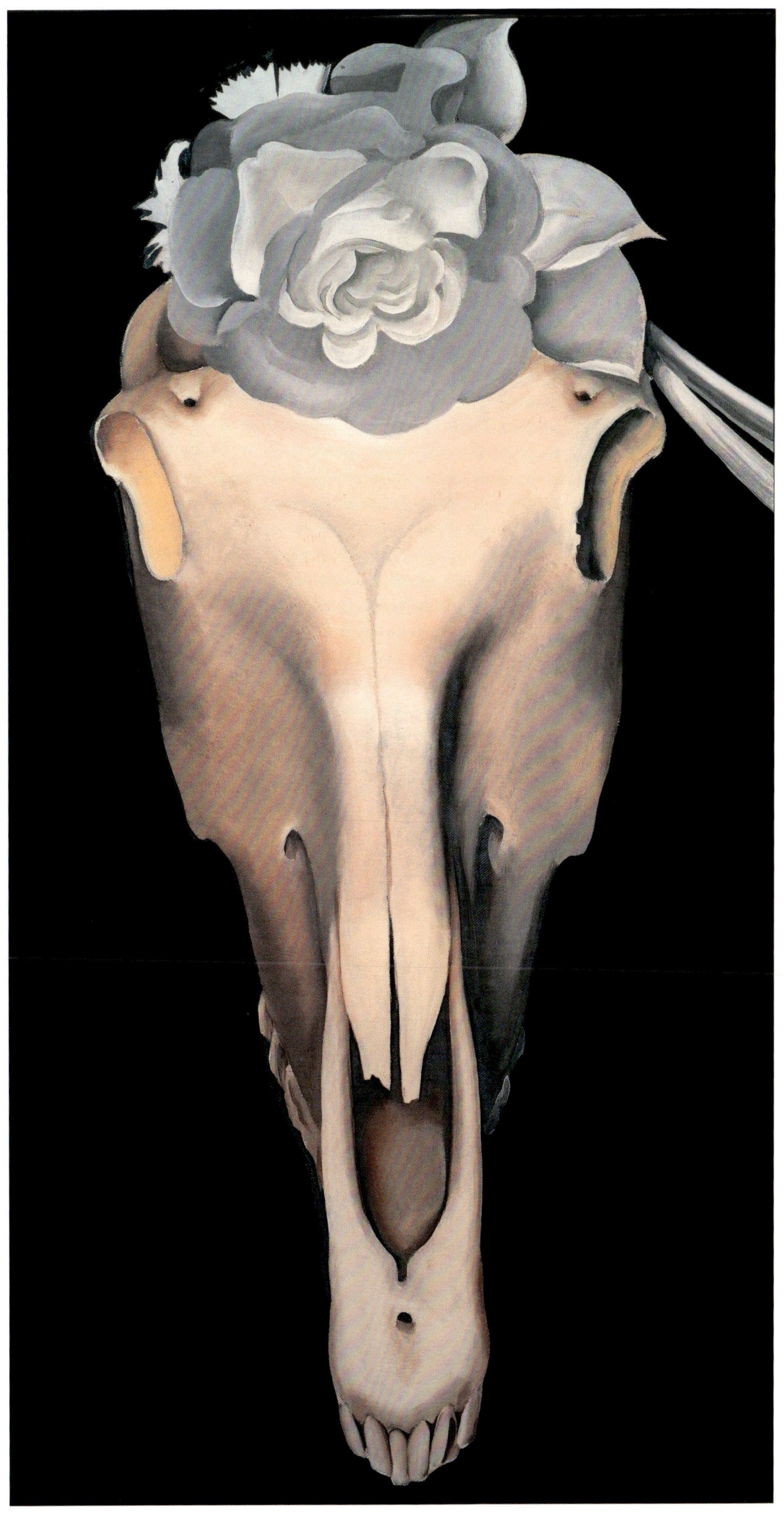

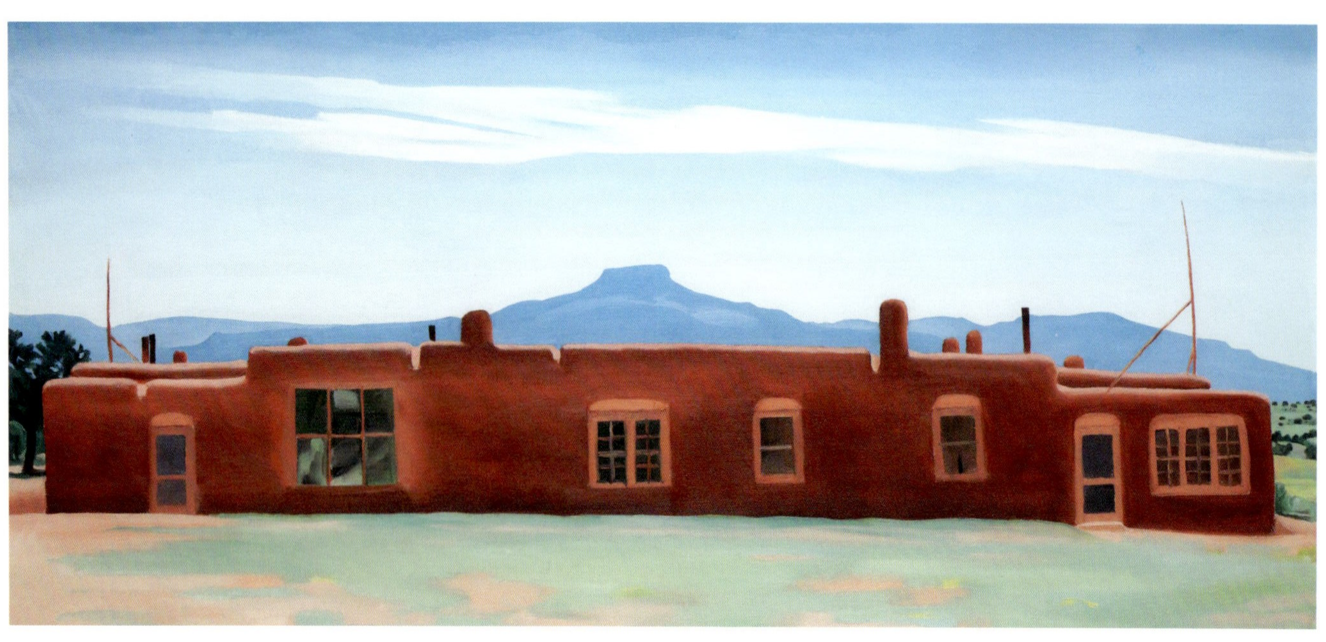

24.
Georgia O'Keeffe,
*The House
I Live In*, 1937

25.
Ansel Adams,
*Georgia O'Keeffe
and Orville
Cox, Canyon
de Chelly
National Park*,
1937

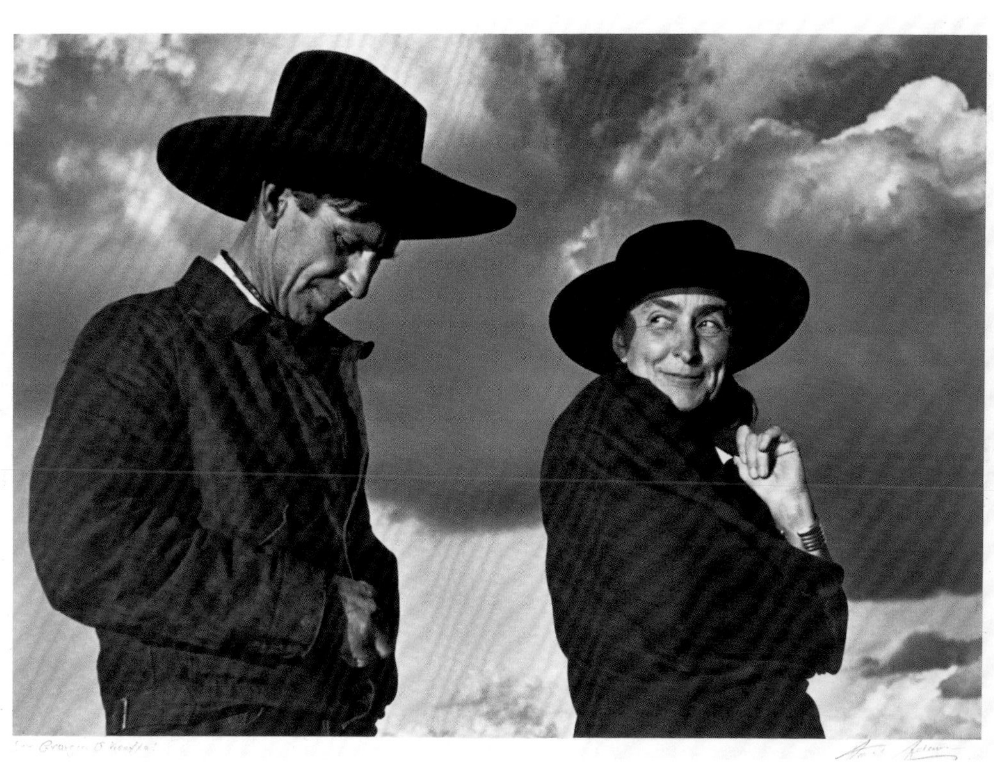

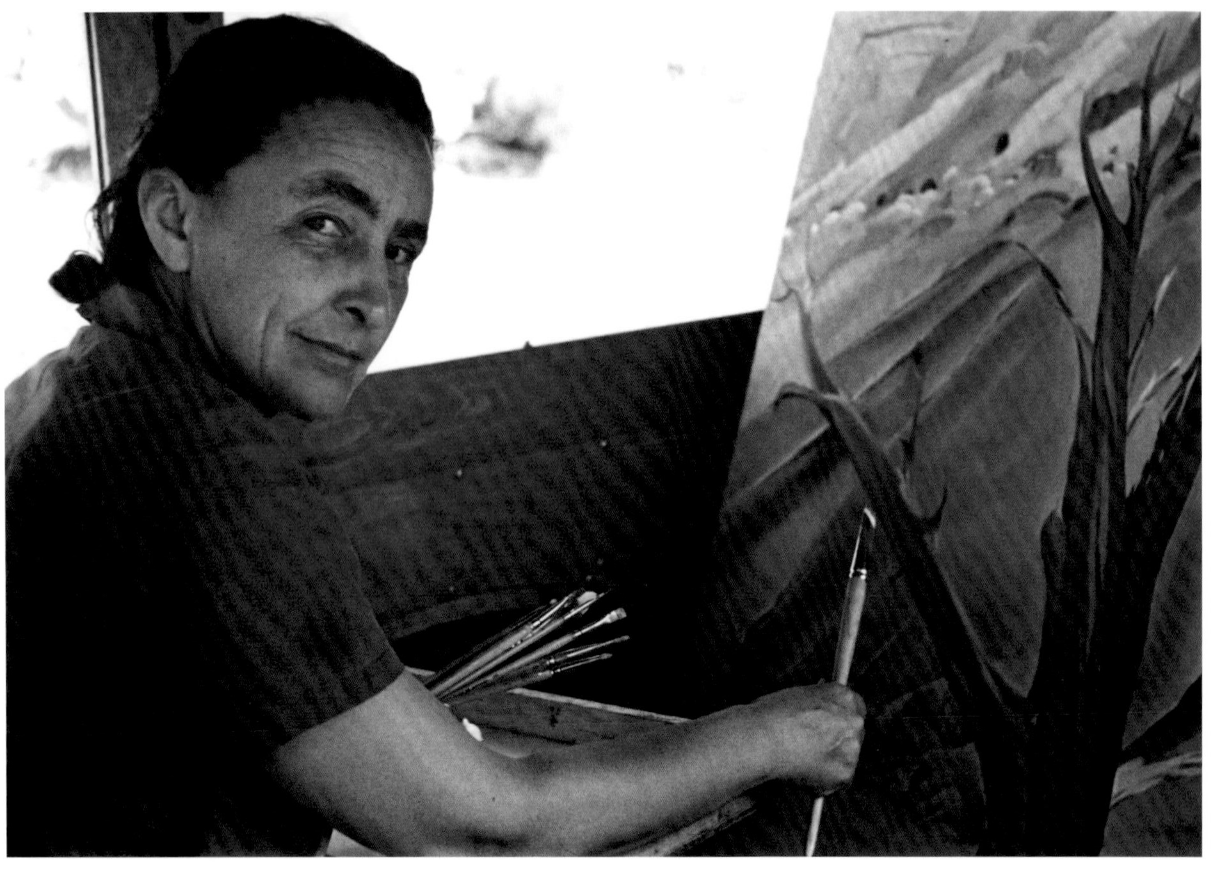

26.
Ansel Adams, *Georgia O'Keeffe Painting in Her Car, Ghost Ranch, New Mexico*, 1937

27.
Georgia O'Keeffe, *Gerald's Tree II*, 1937

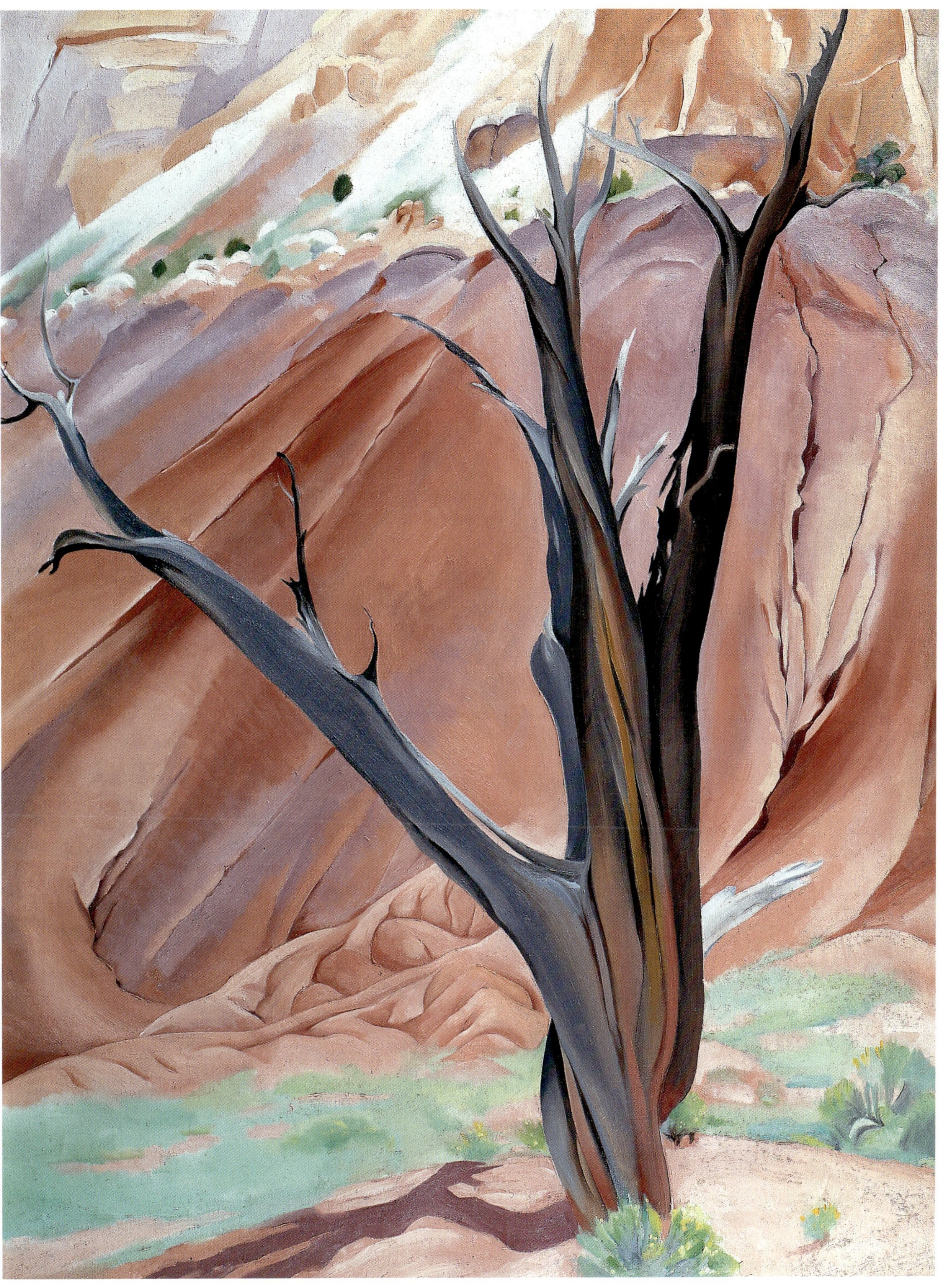

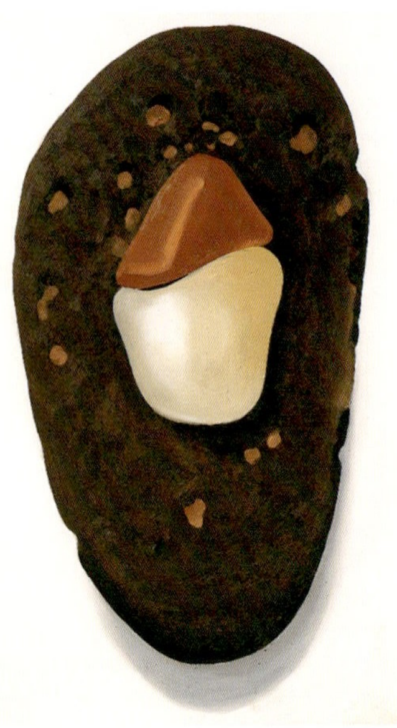

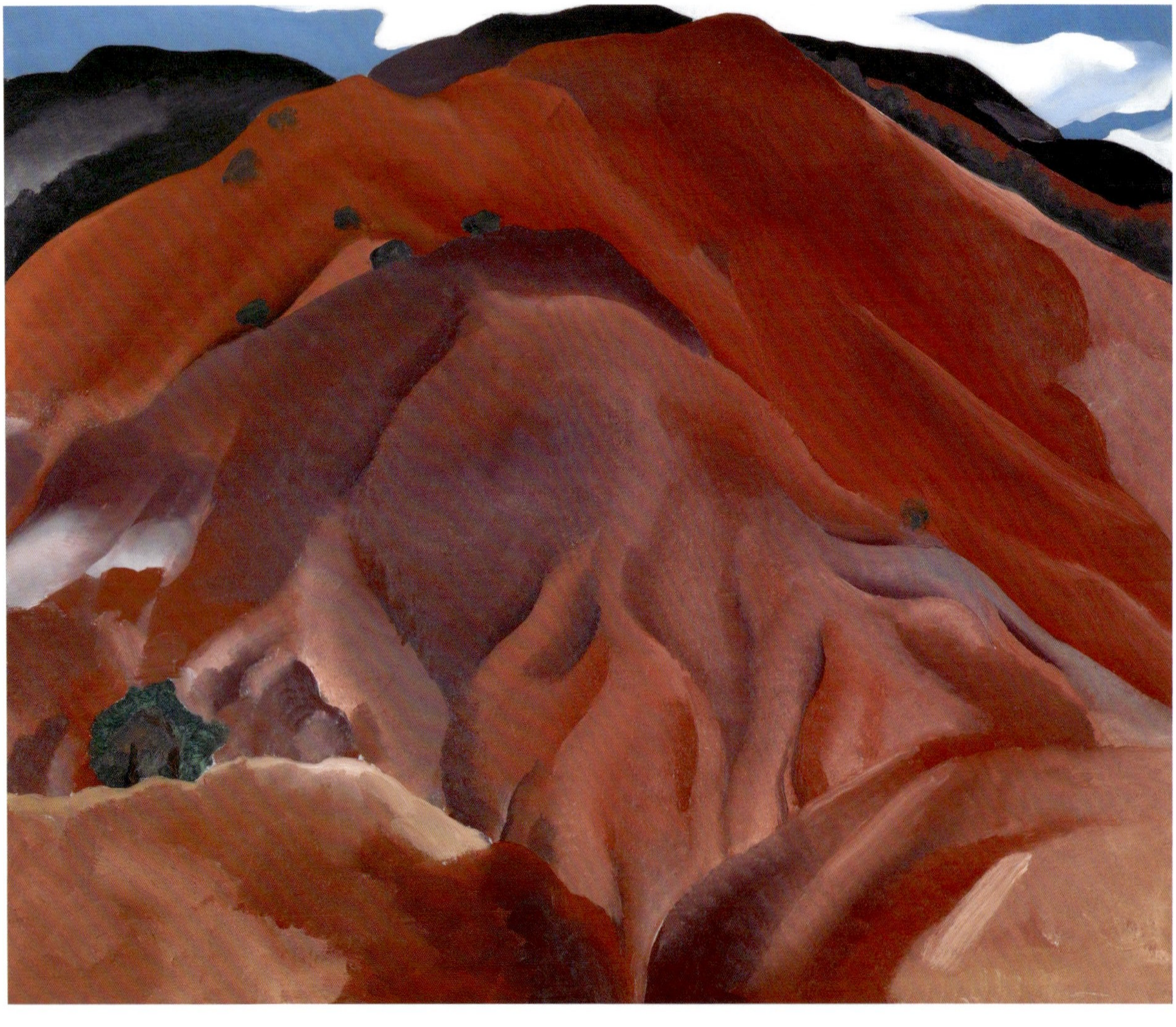

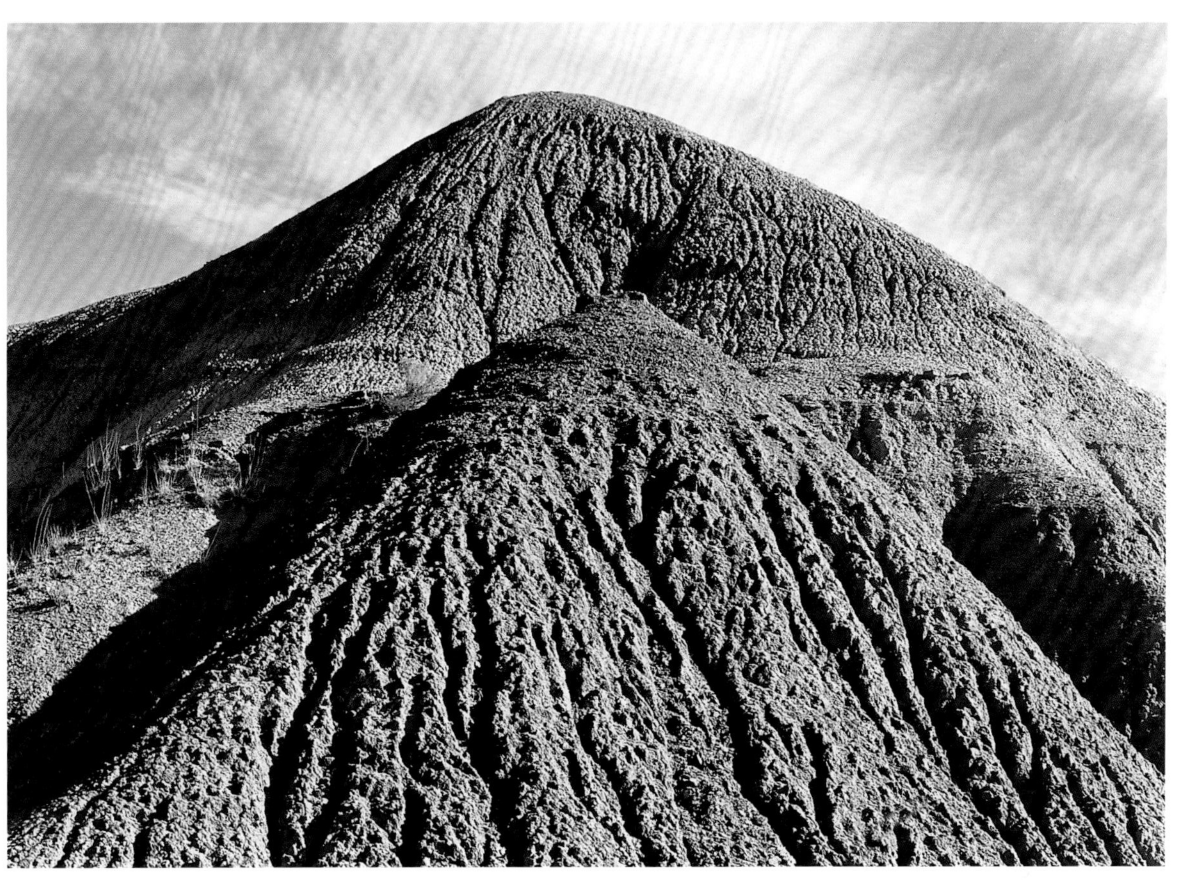

28.
Georgia O'Keeffe,
*Three Small Rocks
Big*, 1937

29.
Georgia O'Keeffe,
*Red Hills
beyond Abiquiu*,
1930

30.
Ansel Adams,
*Mud Hills—Ghost
Ranch, New
Mexico*, 1937

31.
Eliot Porter,
Ghost Ranch,
1940

32.
Eliot Porter,
Georgia O'Keeffe,
Ghost Ranch,
New Mexico, 1945

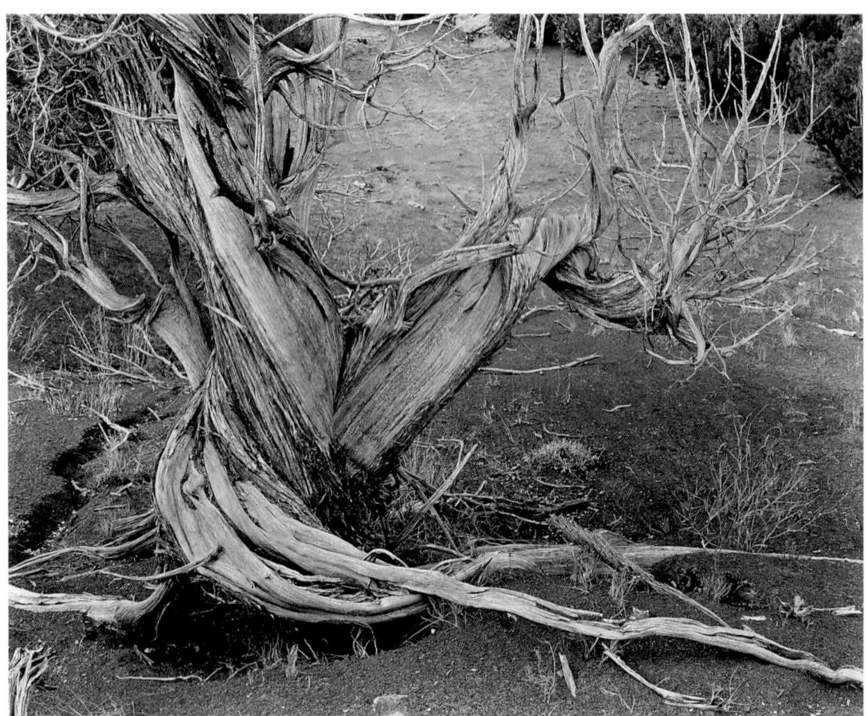

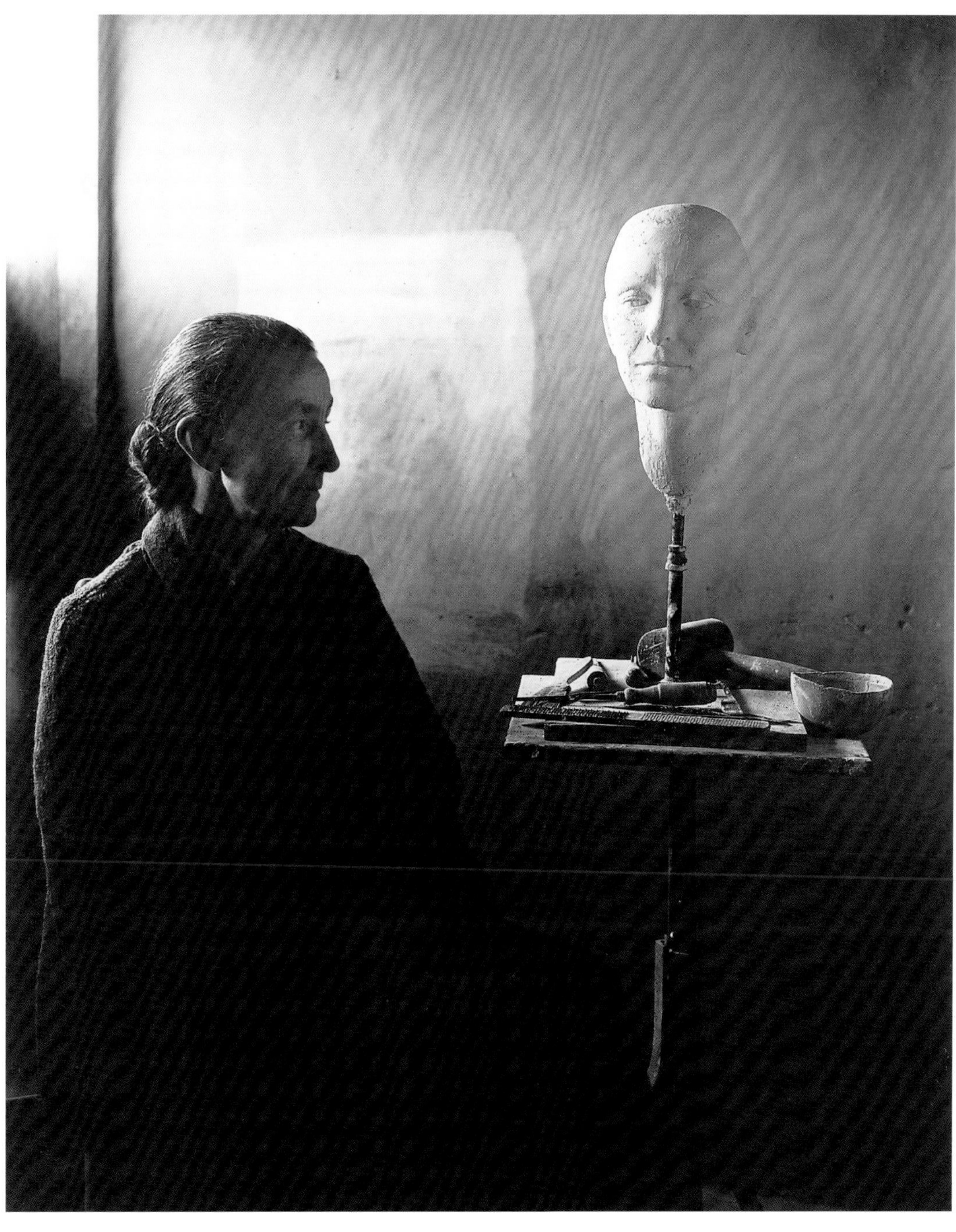

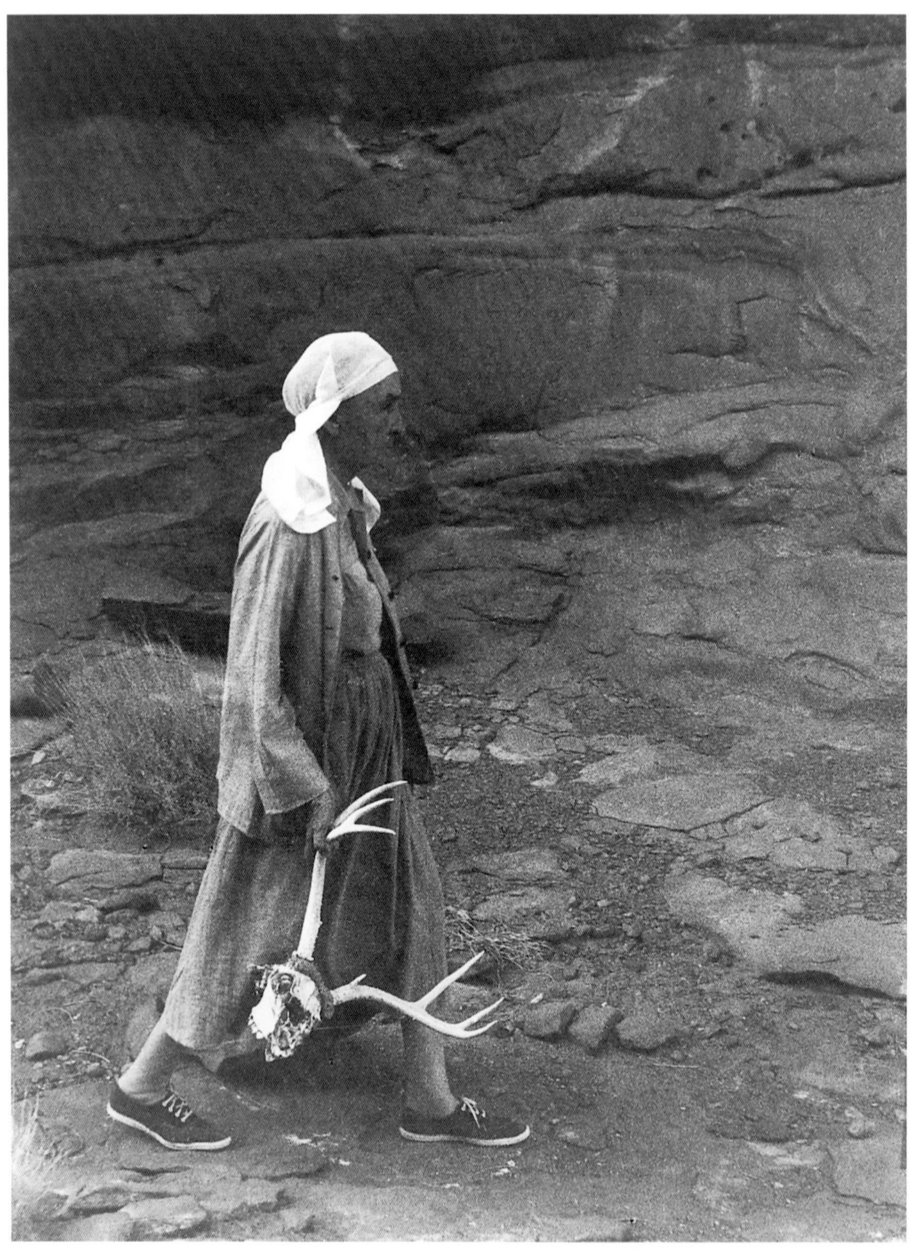

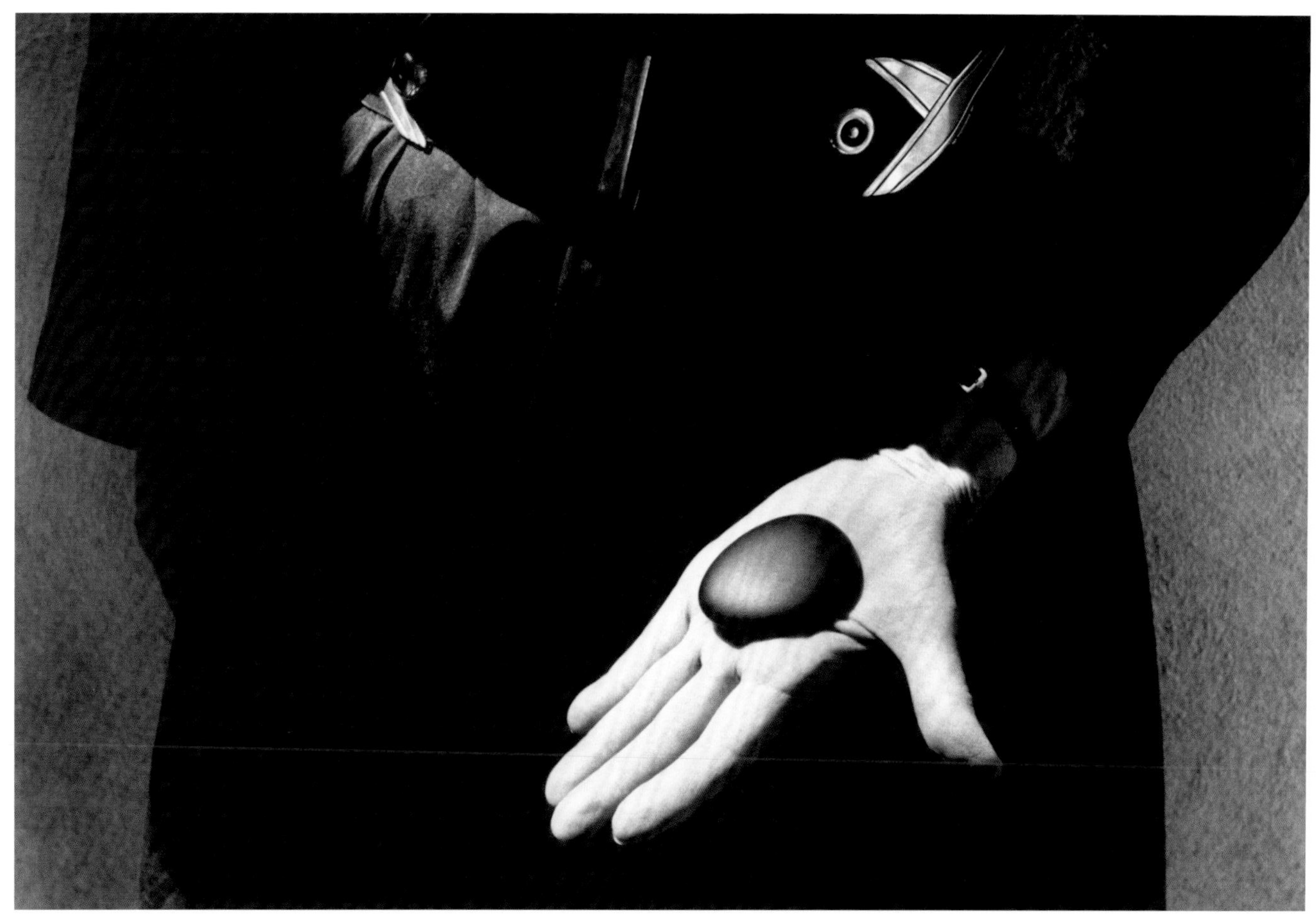

33.
Todd Webb,
*Georgia O'Keeffe
in Glen Canyon,
New Mexico*, 1961

34.
John Loengard,
*The Rock from
Eliot Porter, Abiquiu*,
1966 (printed later)

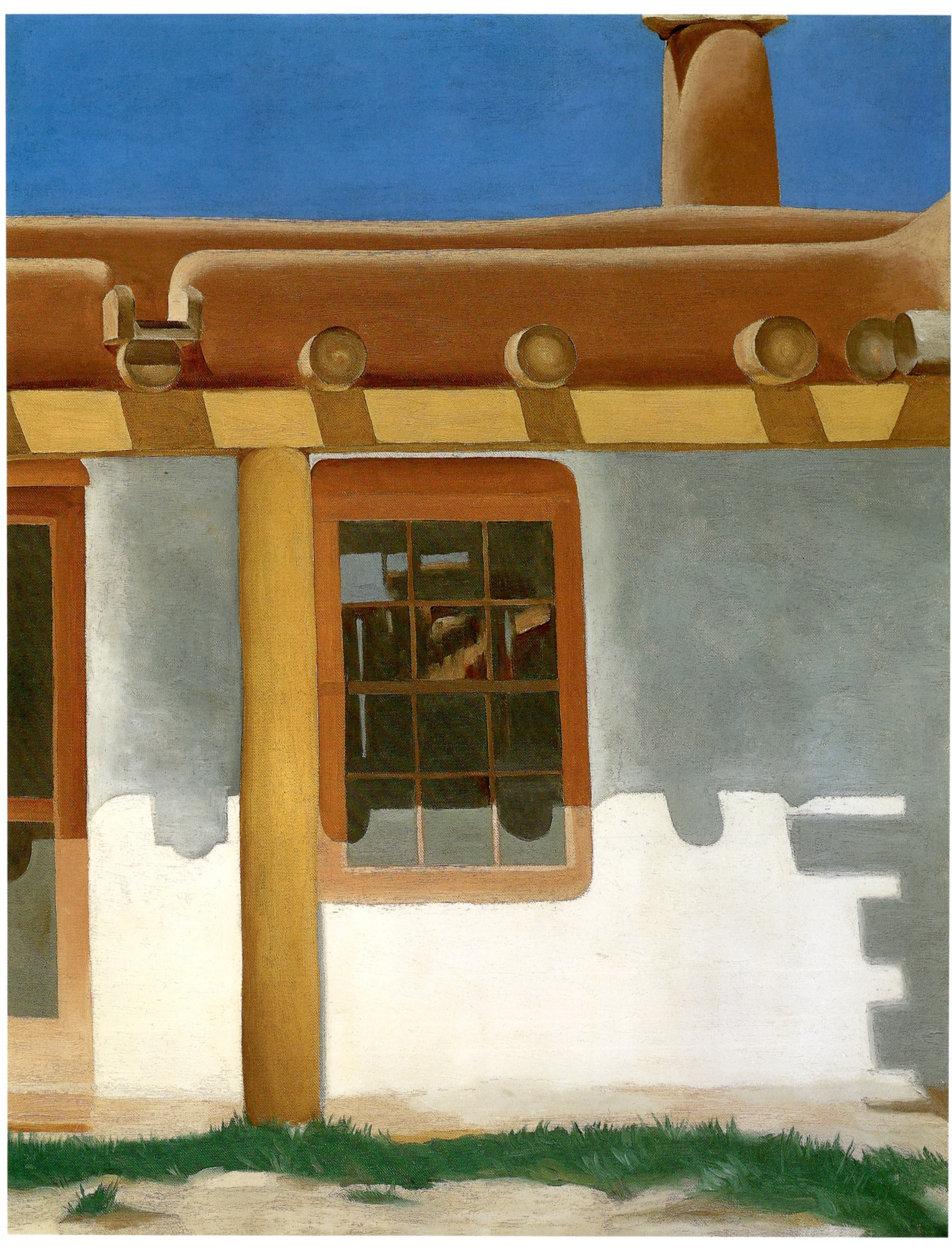

35.
Georgia O'Keeffe,
The Patio—No. 1,
1940

36.
Eliot Porter,
*Georgia O'Keeffe's
Entrance Door,
Abiquiu,
New Mexico,*
1949

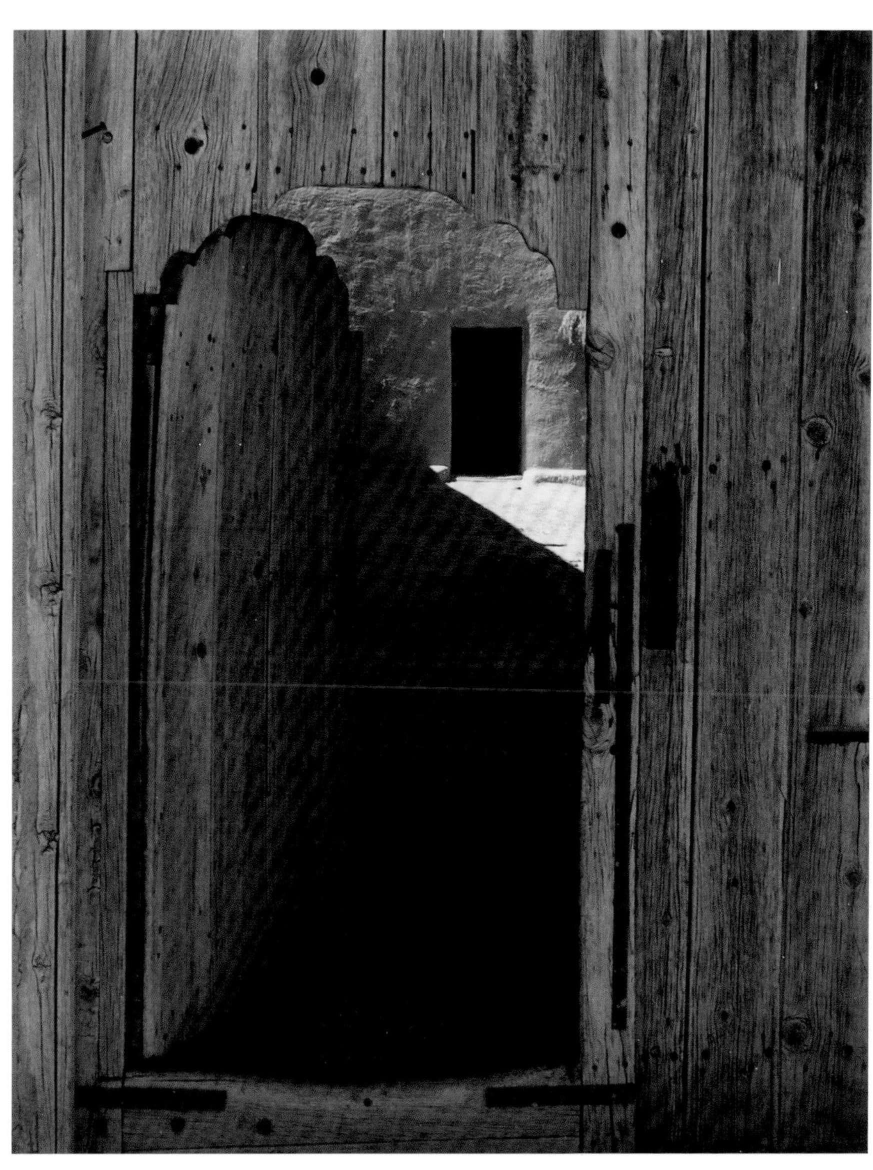

37.
Todd Webb,
*Ladder and Adobe
Wall, O'Keeffe's
Abiquiu House,
New Mexico,*
1957

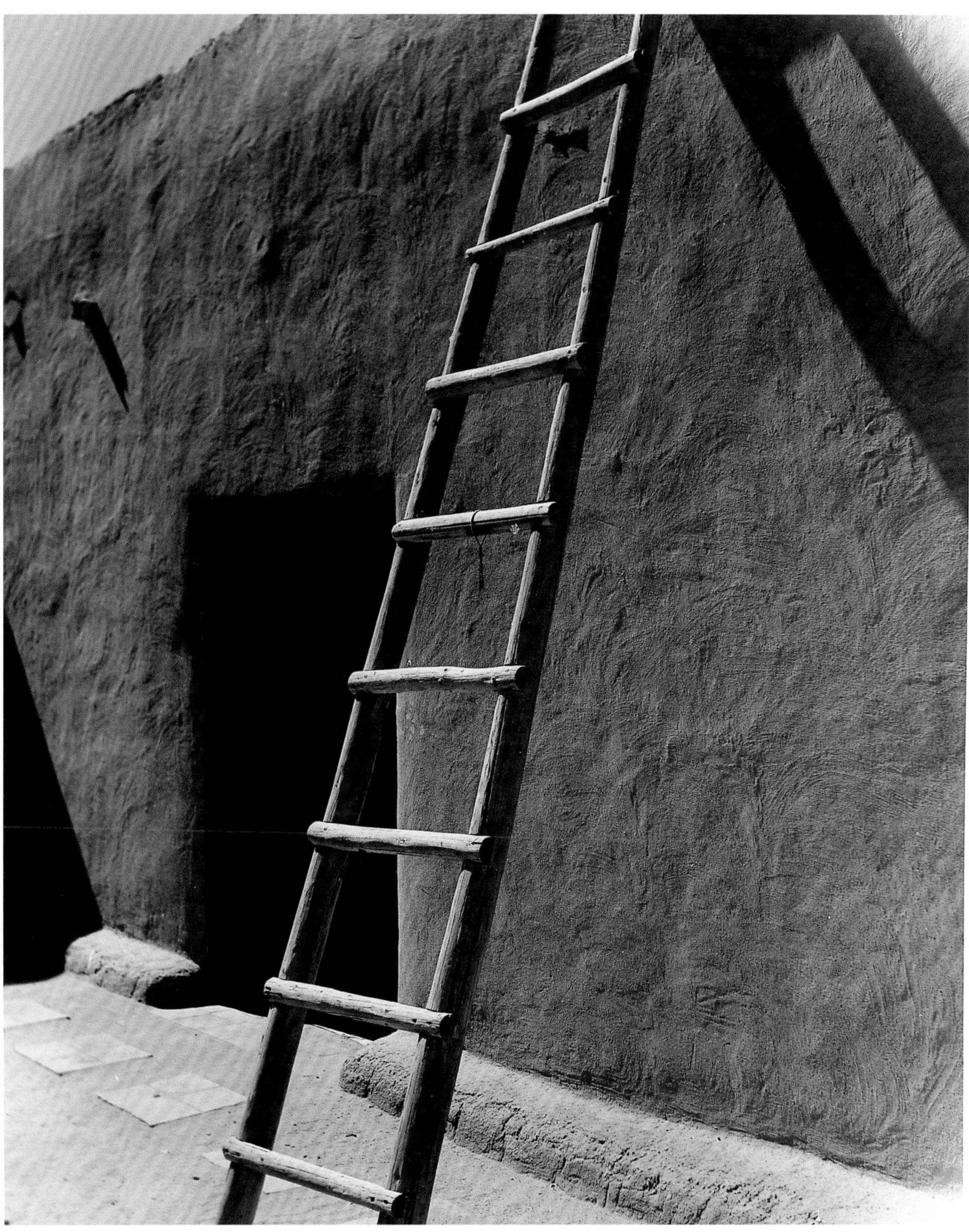

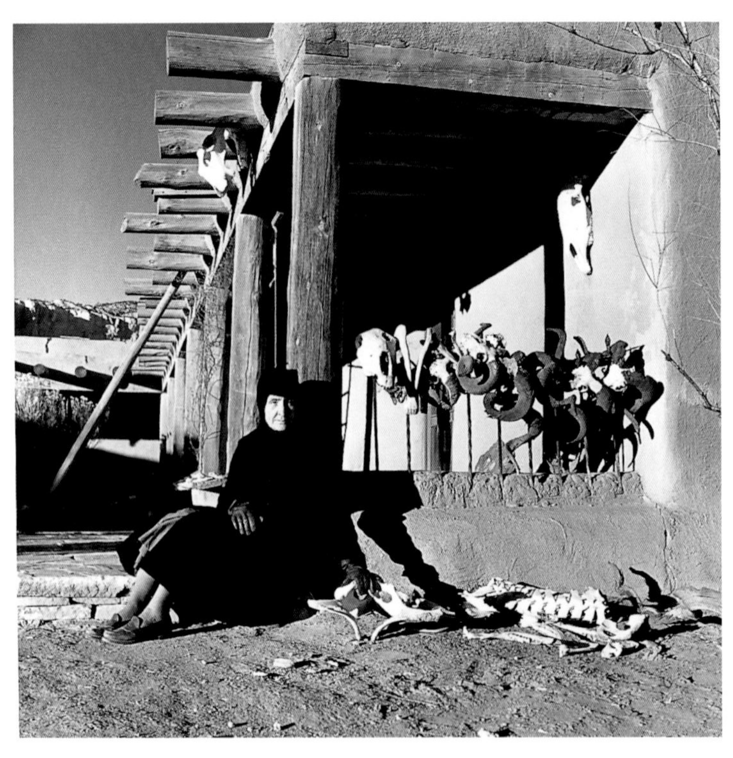

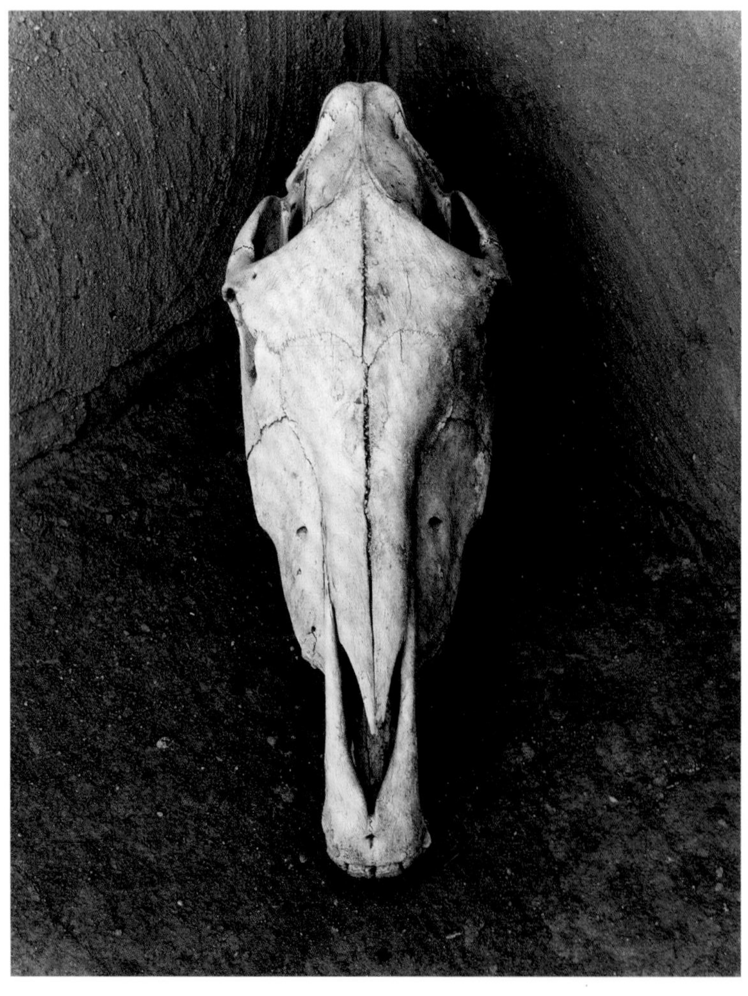

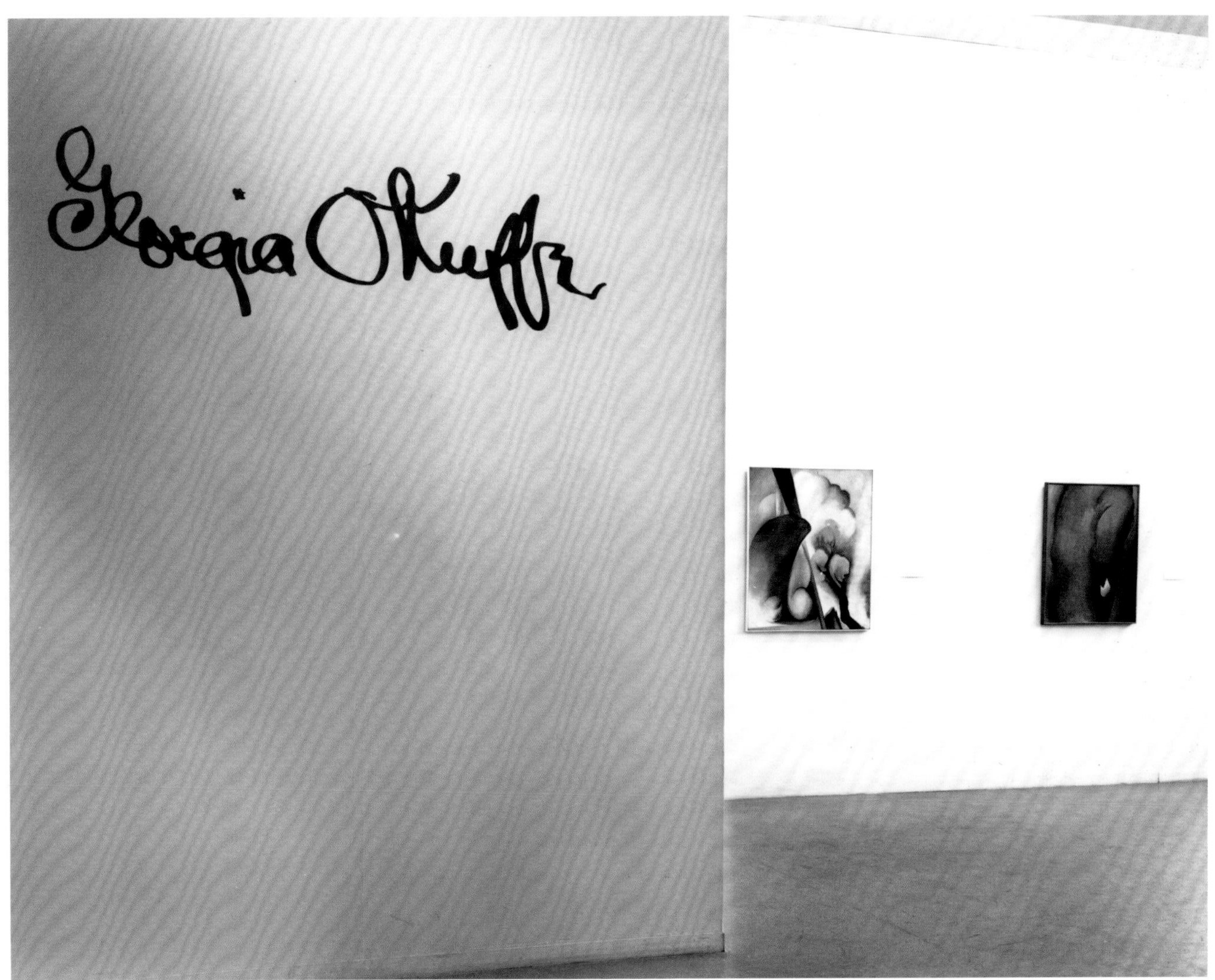

38.
George Daniell,
*Georgia O'Keeffe
Seated among
Her Props*, 1952

39.
Eliot Porter,
*Horse Skull, O'Keeffe's
House, Abiquiu,
New Mexico*, 1952

40.
Todd Webb,
*[Installation View
of O'Keeffe Exhibition
at the Museum of
Modern Art]*, 1946

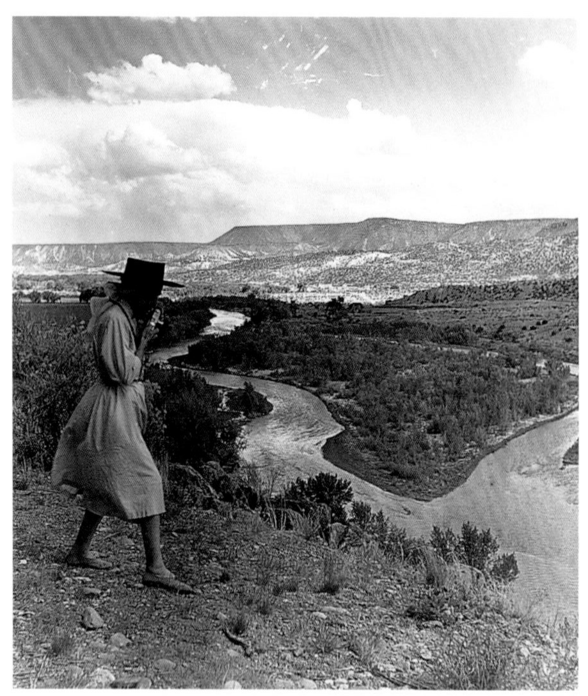

41.
Todd Webb,
O'Keeffe Photographing
the Chama River,
New Mexico, 1961

42.
Todd Webb,
Georgia O'Keeffe
in Twilight Canyon,
1964

43.
Todd Webb,
O'Keeffe's Ghost
Ranch House,
1962

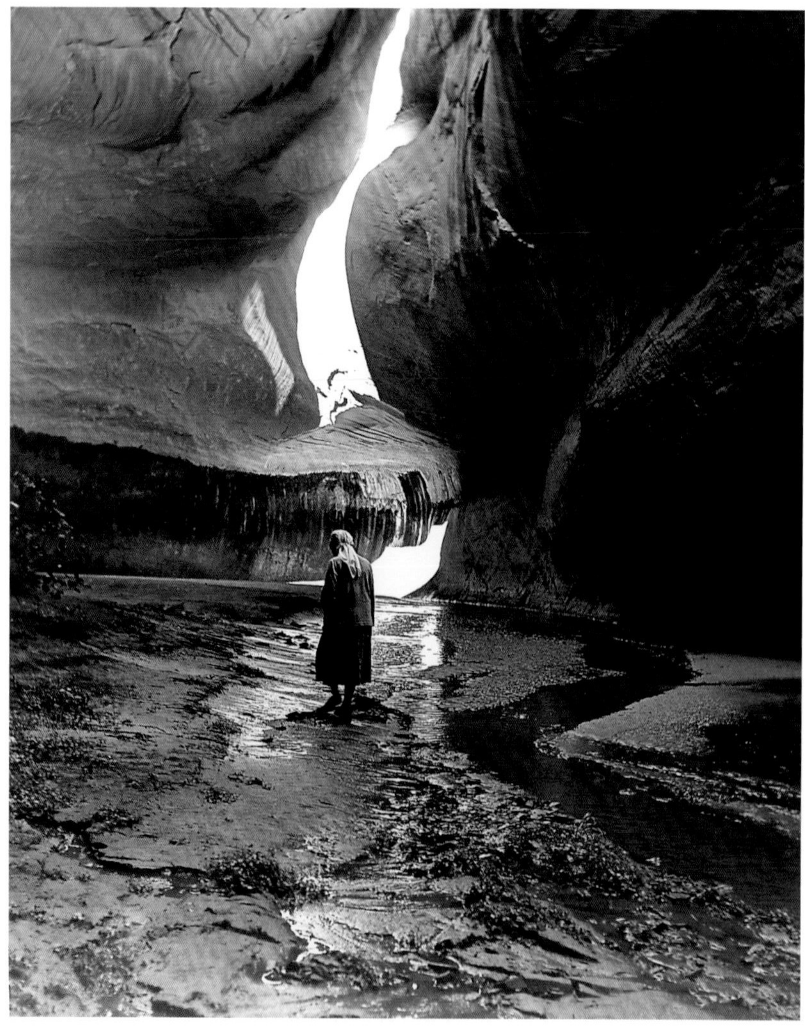

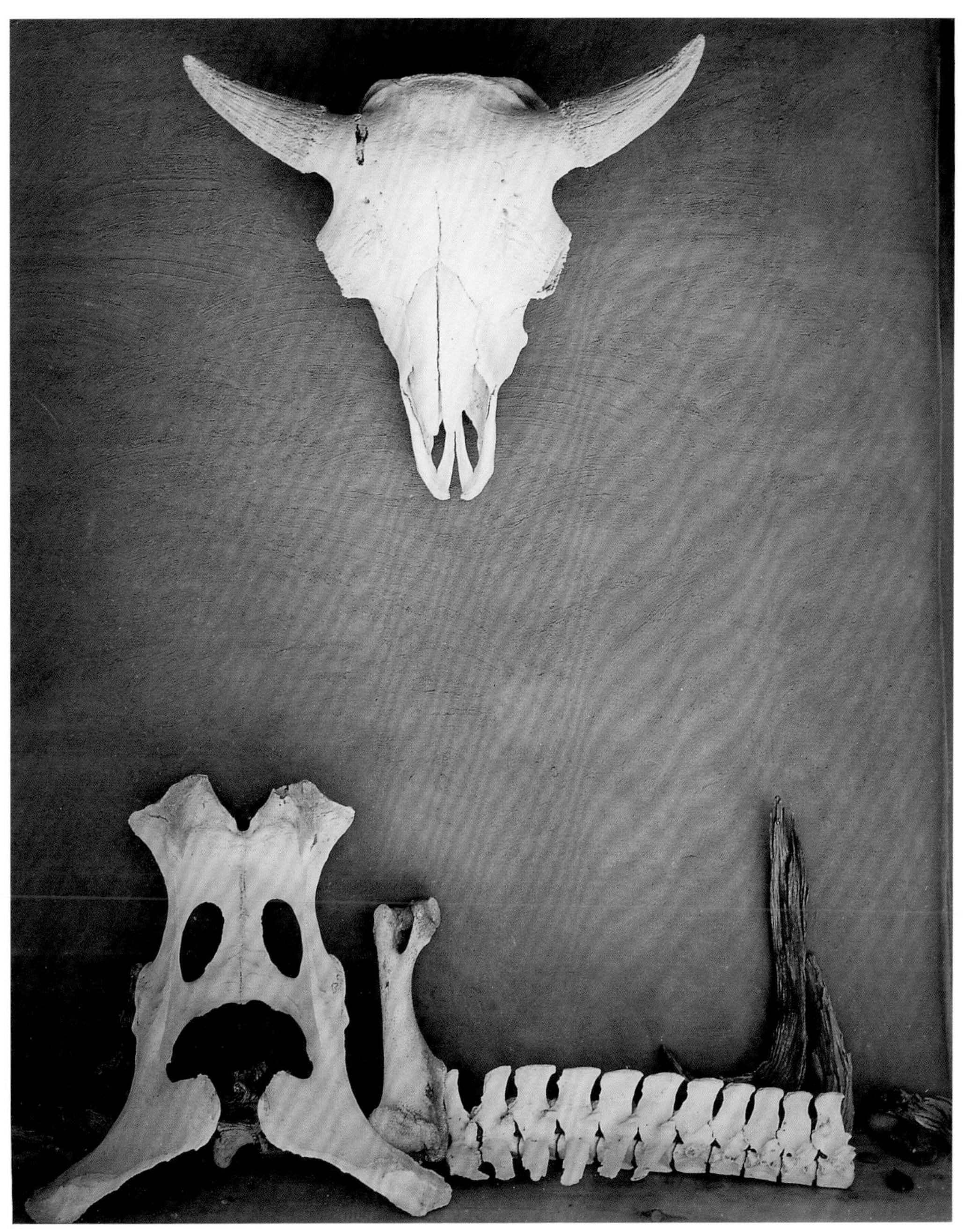

44.
Todd Webb,
*Doorway to Patio,
O'Keeffe's Abiquiu
House, New
Mexico, 1977*

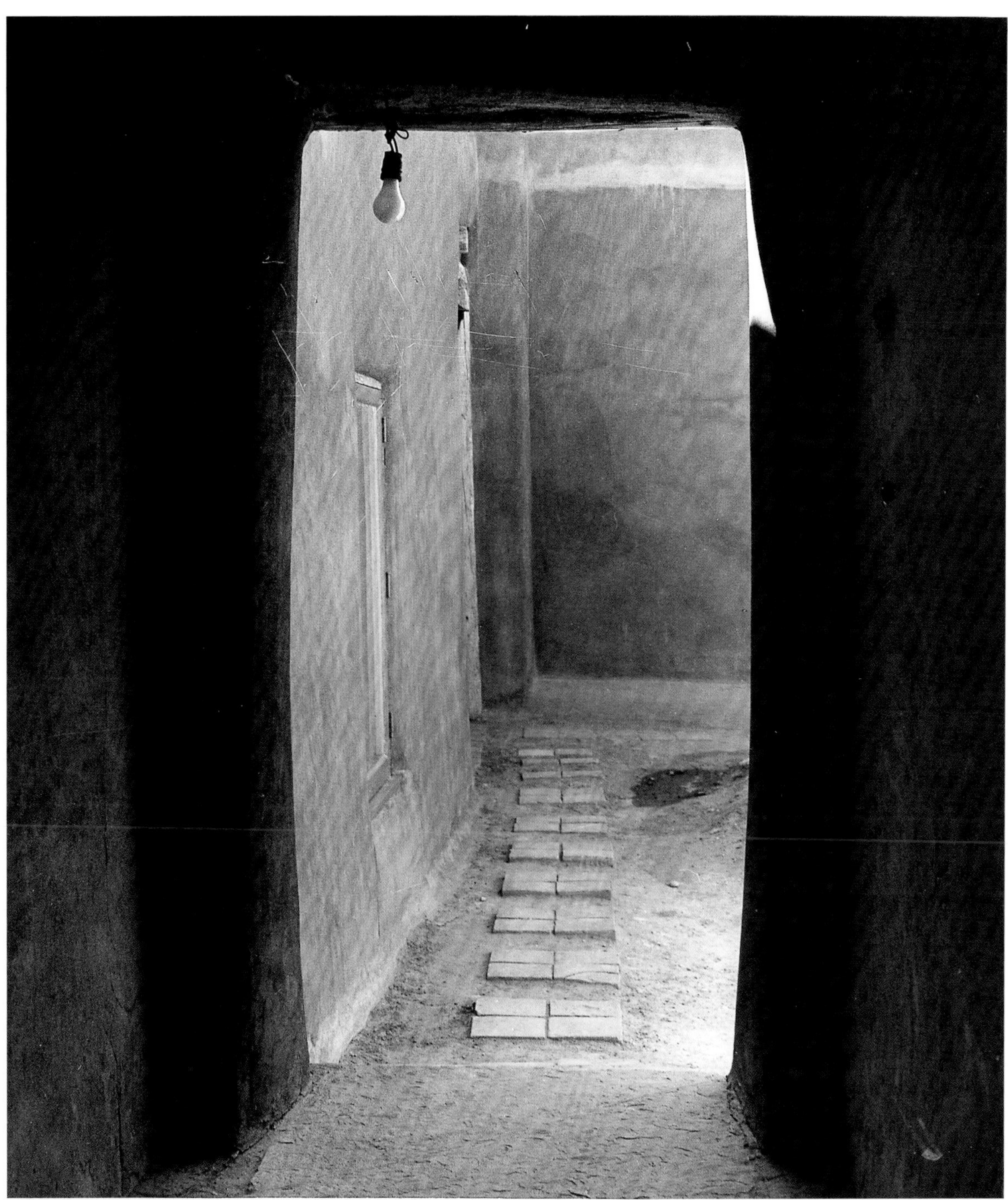

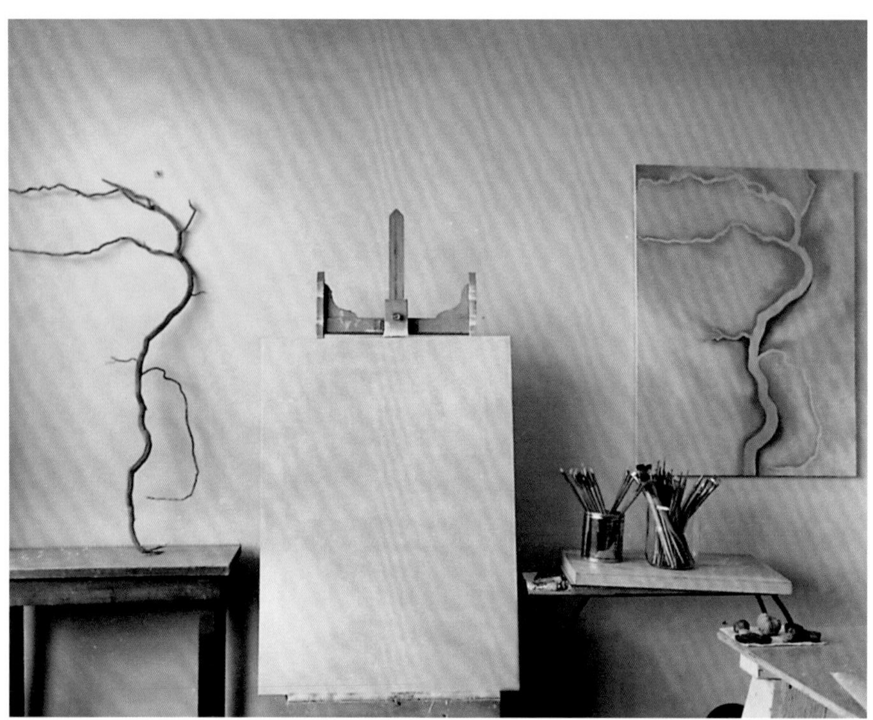

45.
Todd Webb,
*Georgia O'Keeffe's
Studio, the Abiquiu
House, New Mexico,*
1977

46.
Georgia O'Keeffe,
*From the River—
Pale,* 1959

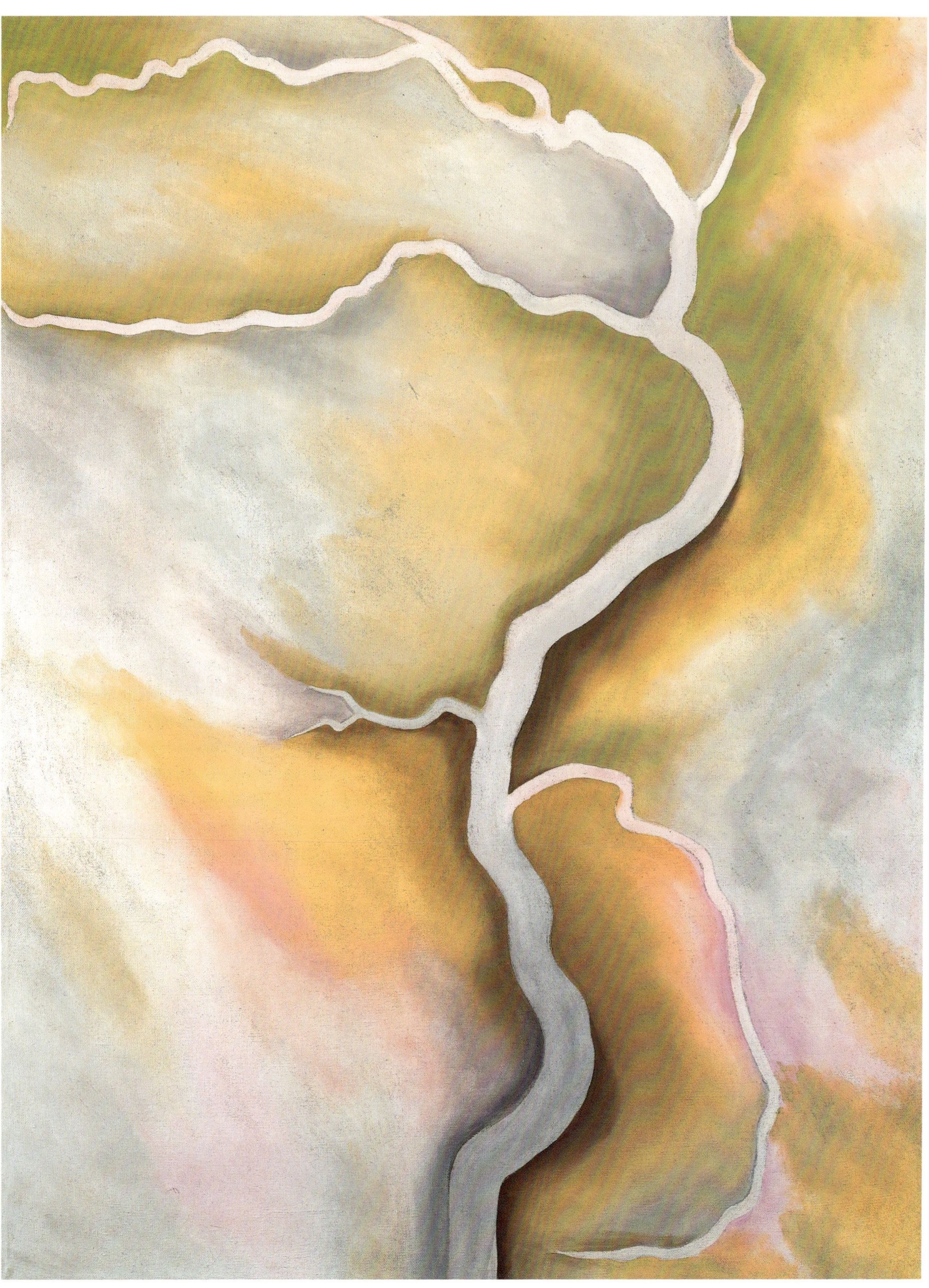

47.
Todd Webb,
O'Keeffe's Studio,
Ghost Ranch,
New Mexico, 1965

48.
Georgia O'Keeffe,
Blue Black and Grey,
1960

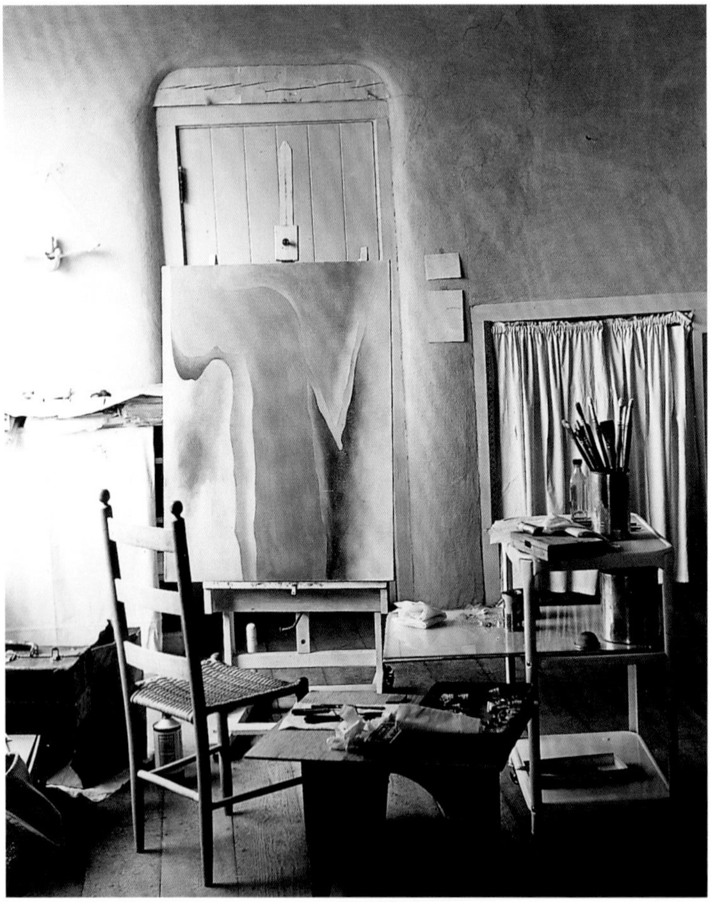

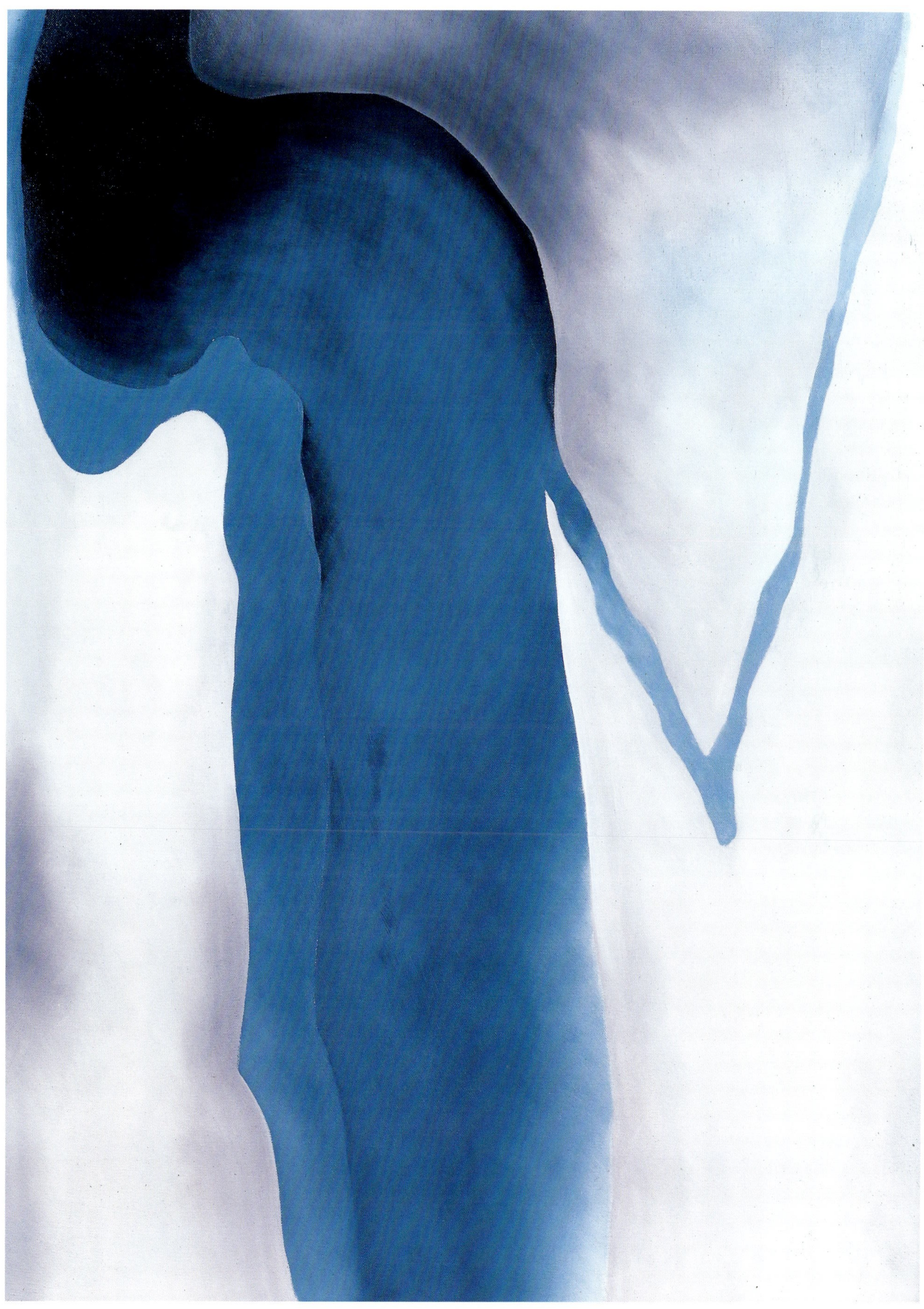

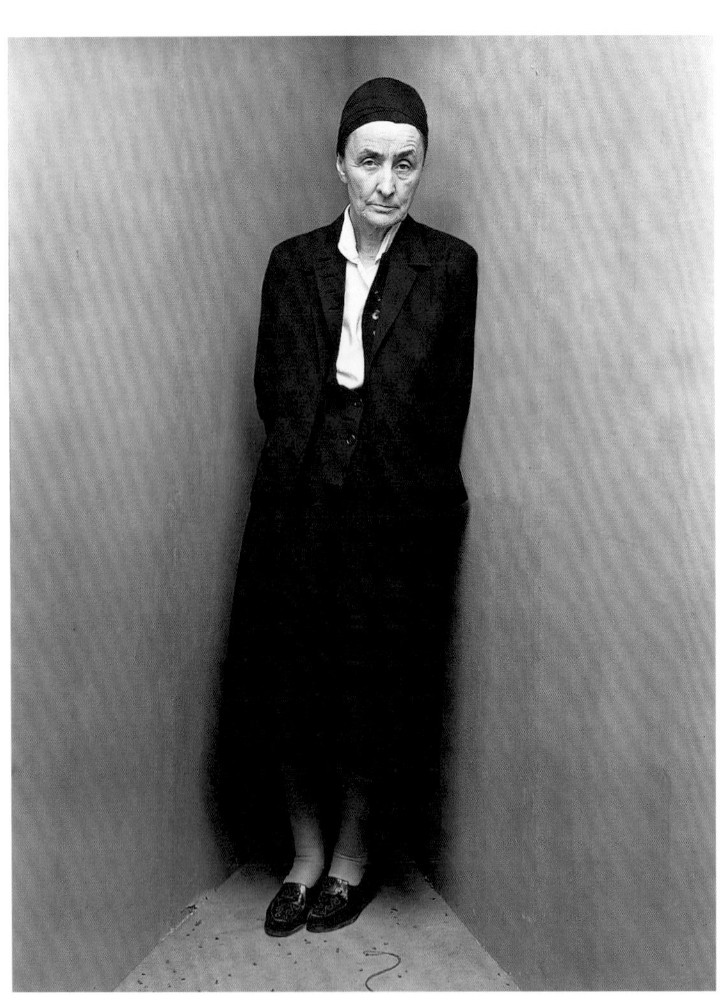

49.
Irving Penn,
Georgia O'Keeffe,
1948 (printed 1986)

50.
Philippe Halsman,
Georgia O'Keeffe,
1948 (printed later)

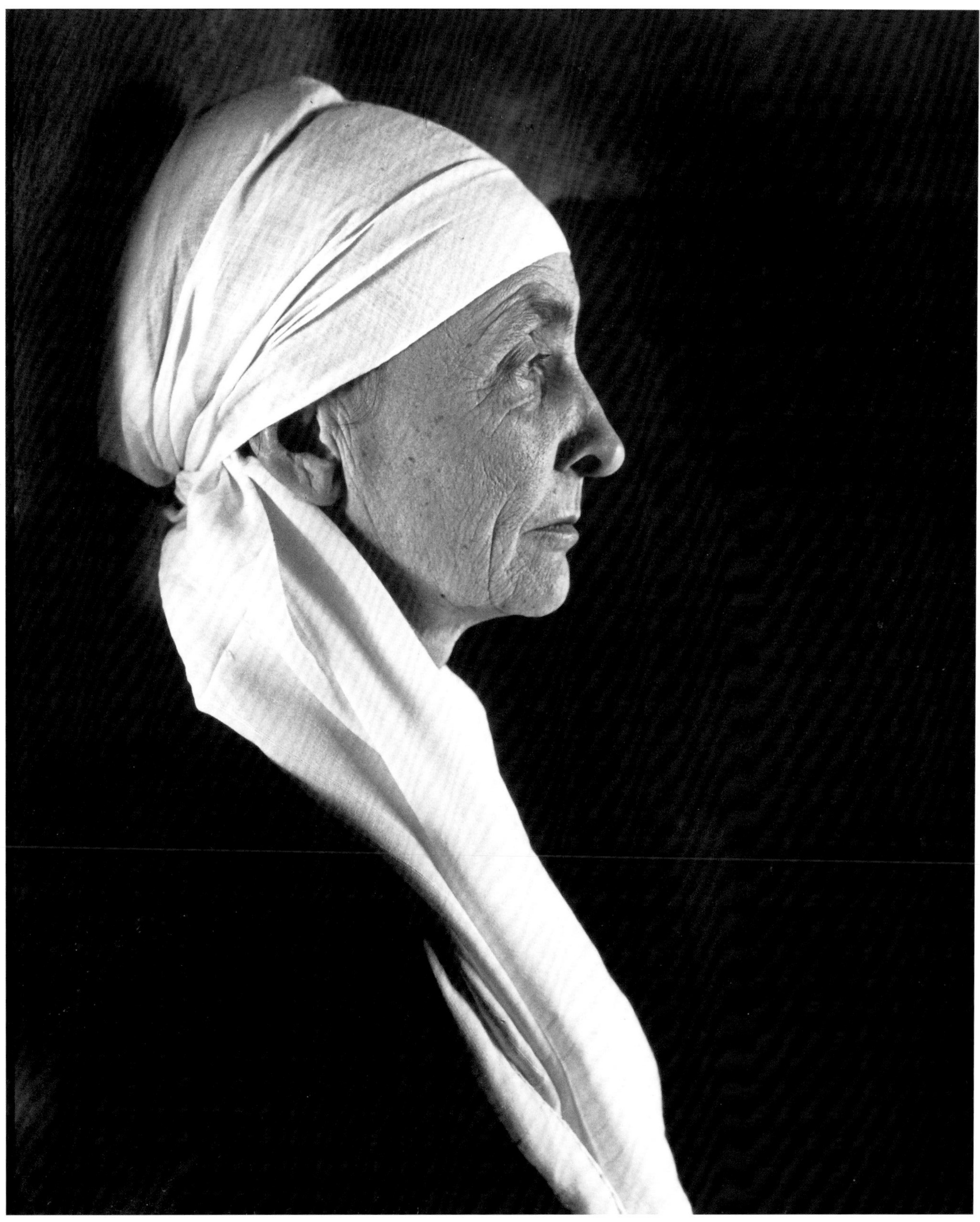

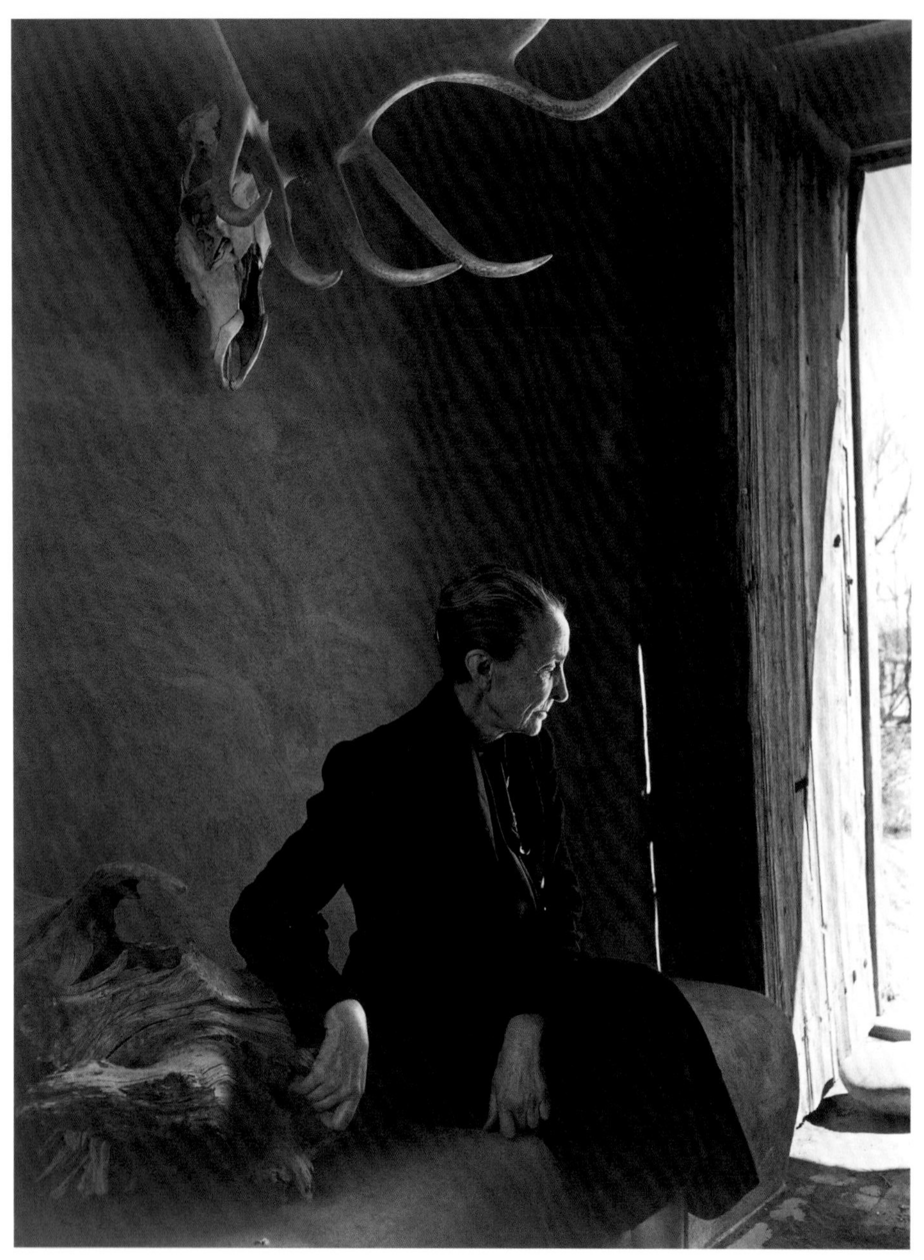

51.
Yousuf Karsh,
Georgia O'Keeffe,
1956

52.
Arnold Newman,
Georgia O'Keeffe,
Ghost Ranch,
New Mexico, 1968

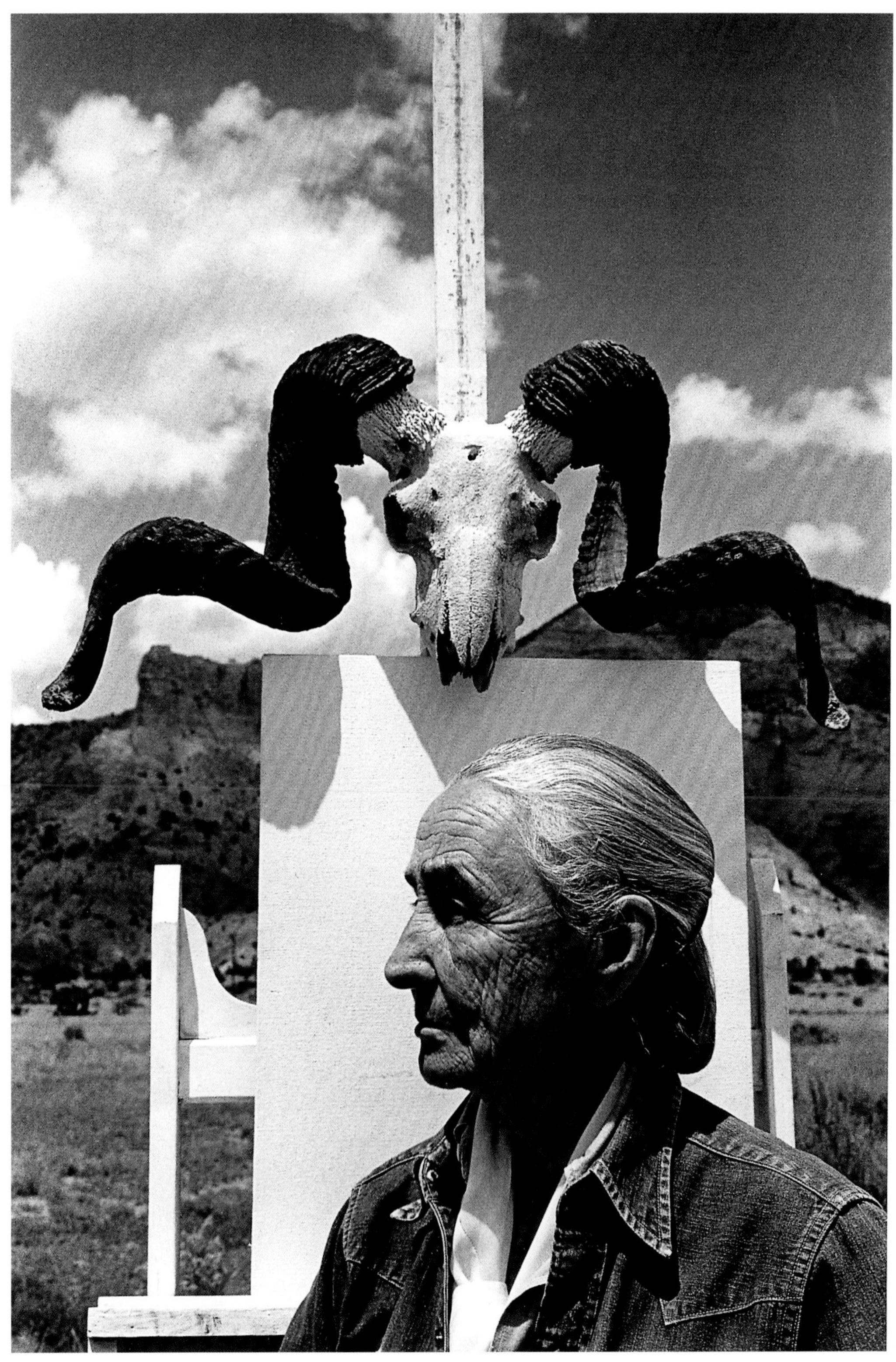

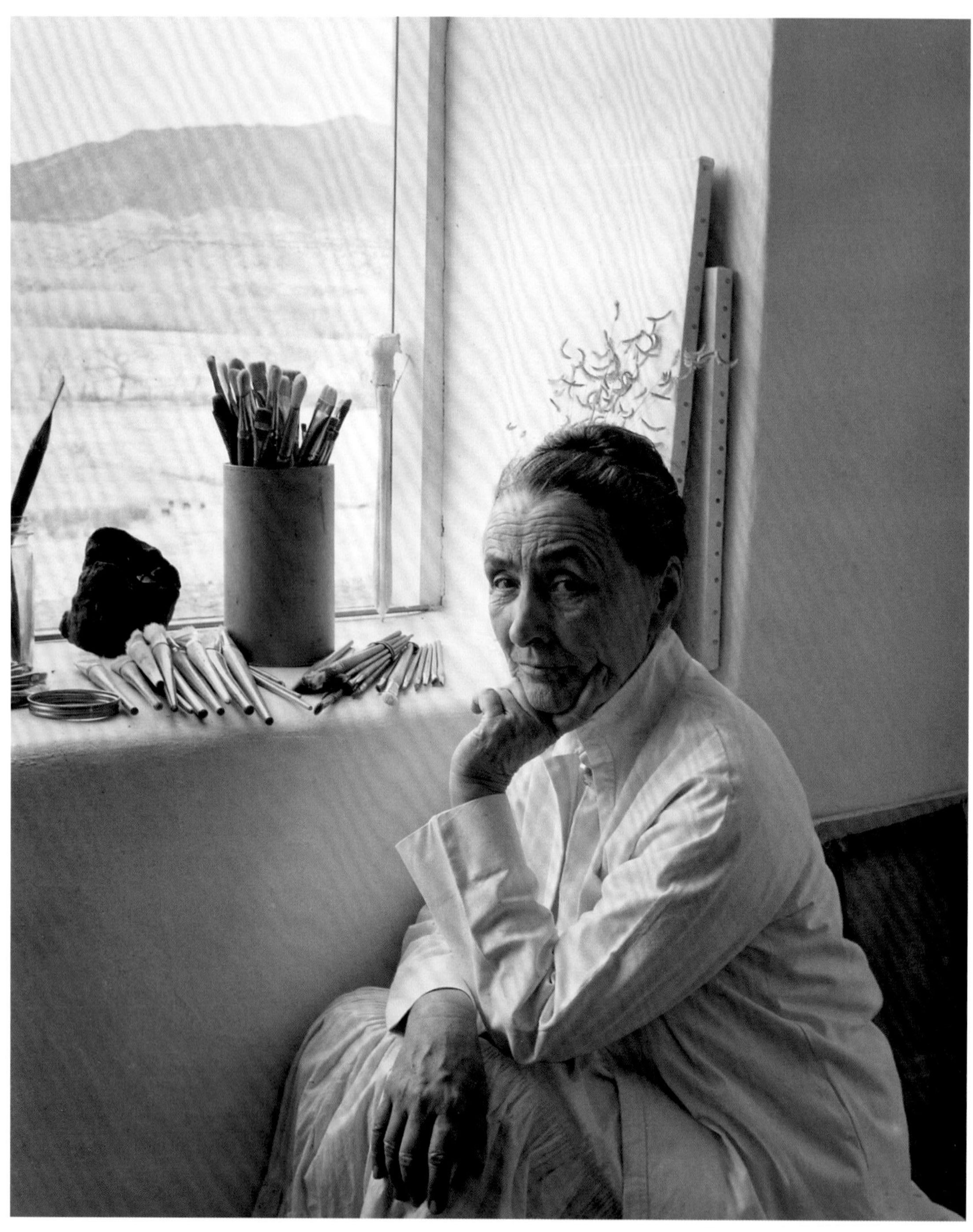

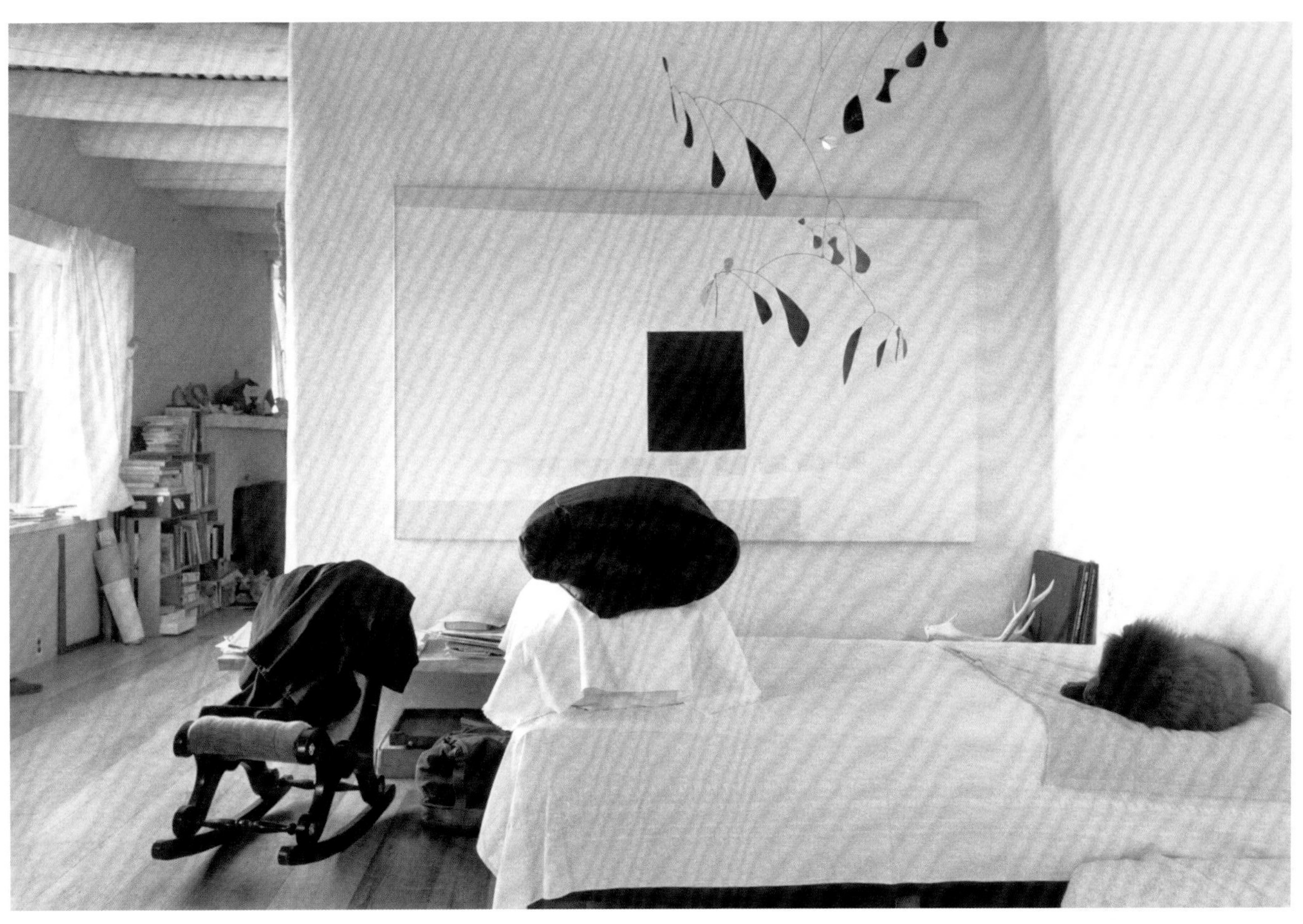

53.
Laura Gilpin,
Georgia O'Keeffe,
1953

54.
John Loengard,
*Bedroom, Ghost
Ranch*, 1967
(printed later)

55.
John Loengard,
Evening Walk,
Ghost Ranch, 1966
(printed later)

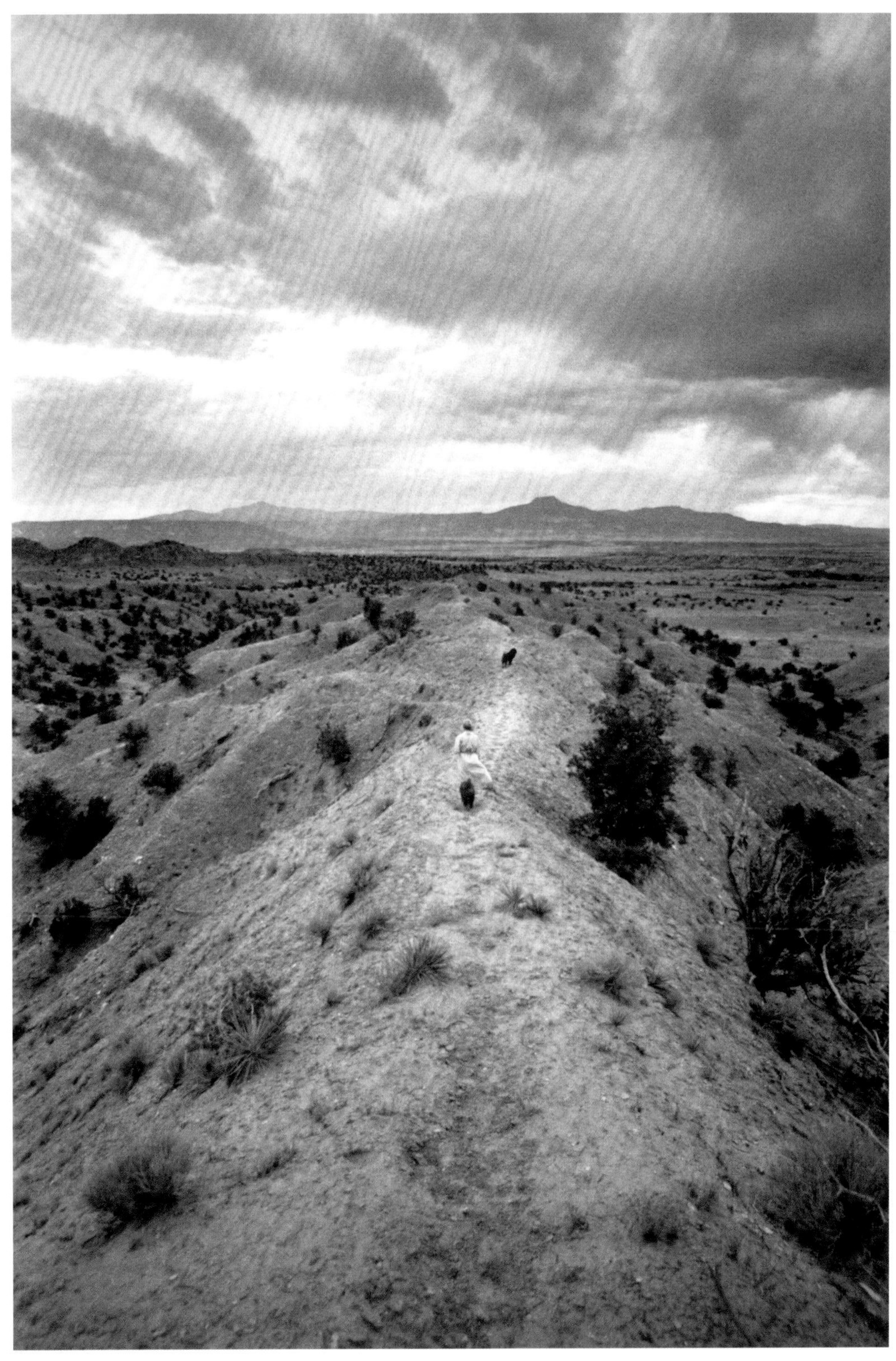

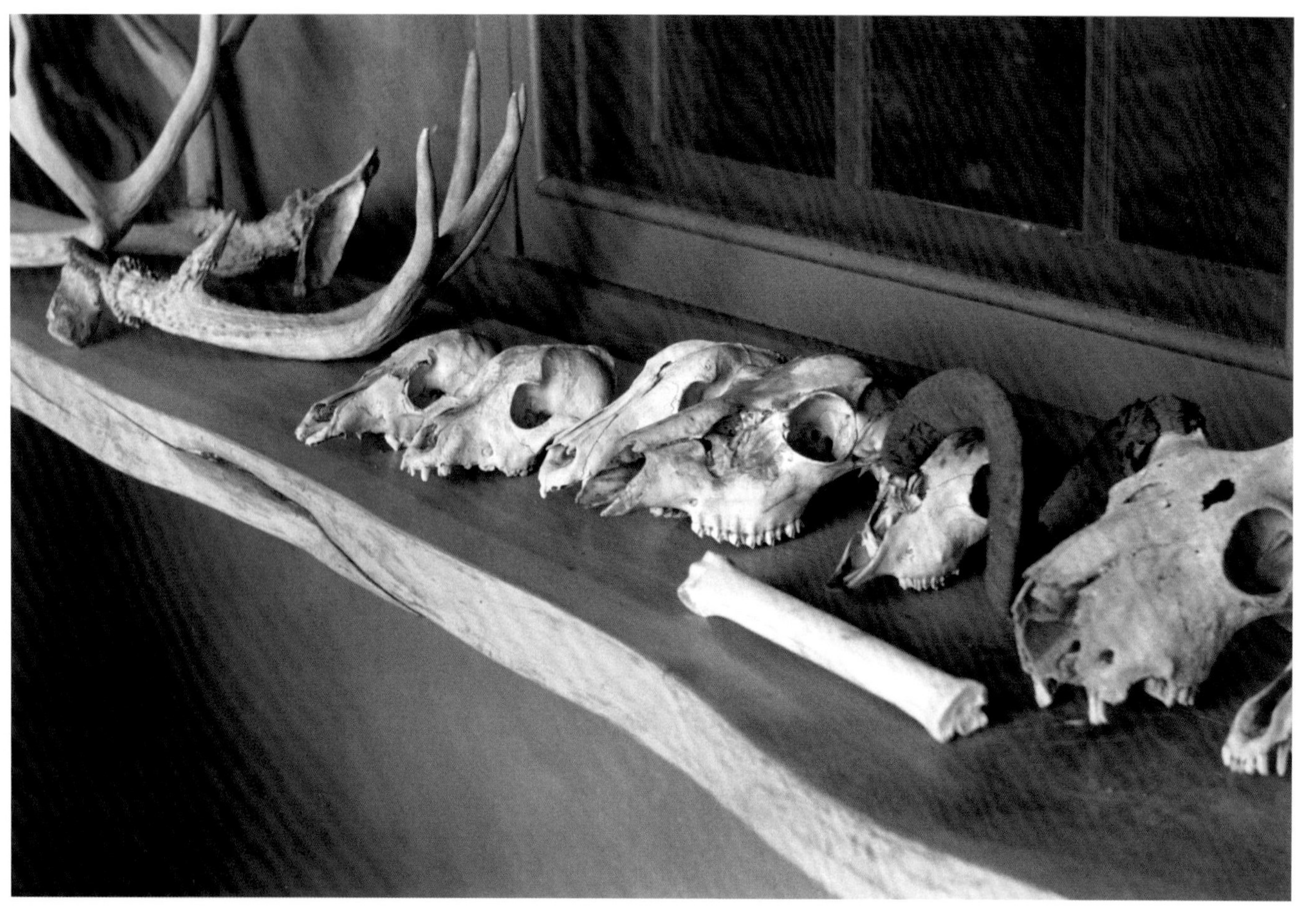

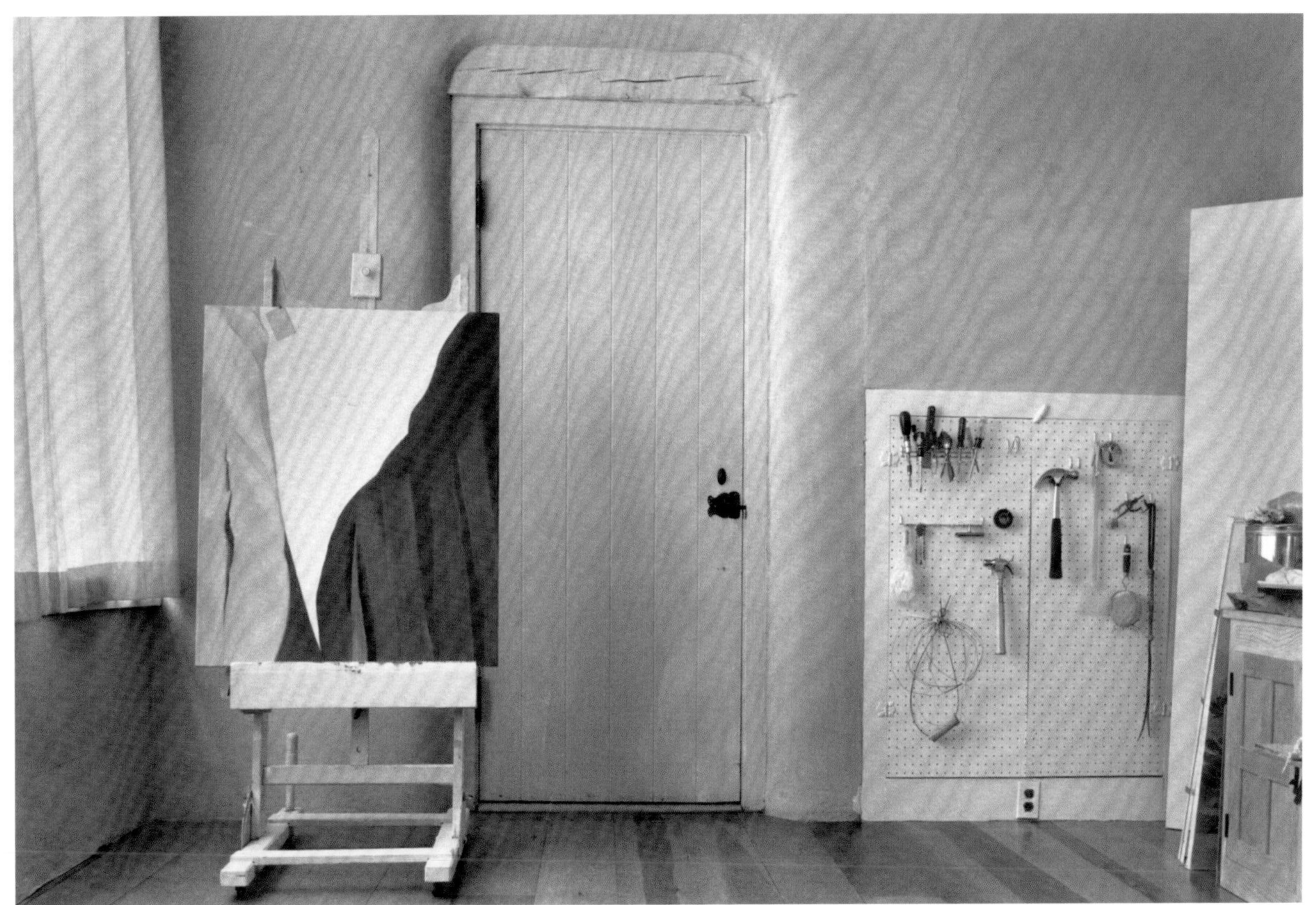

56.
John Loengard,
Ghost Ranch, 1966
(printed later)

57.
John Loengard,
Studio, Ghost Ranch,
1967 (printed later)

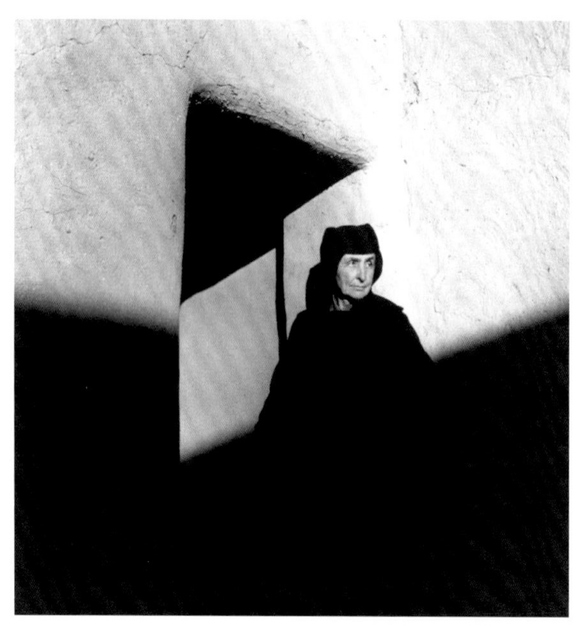

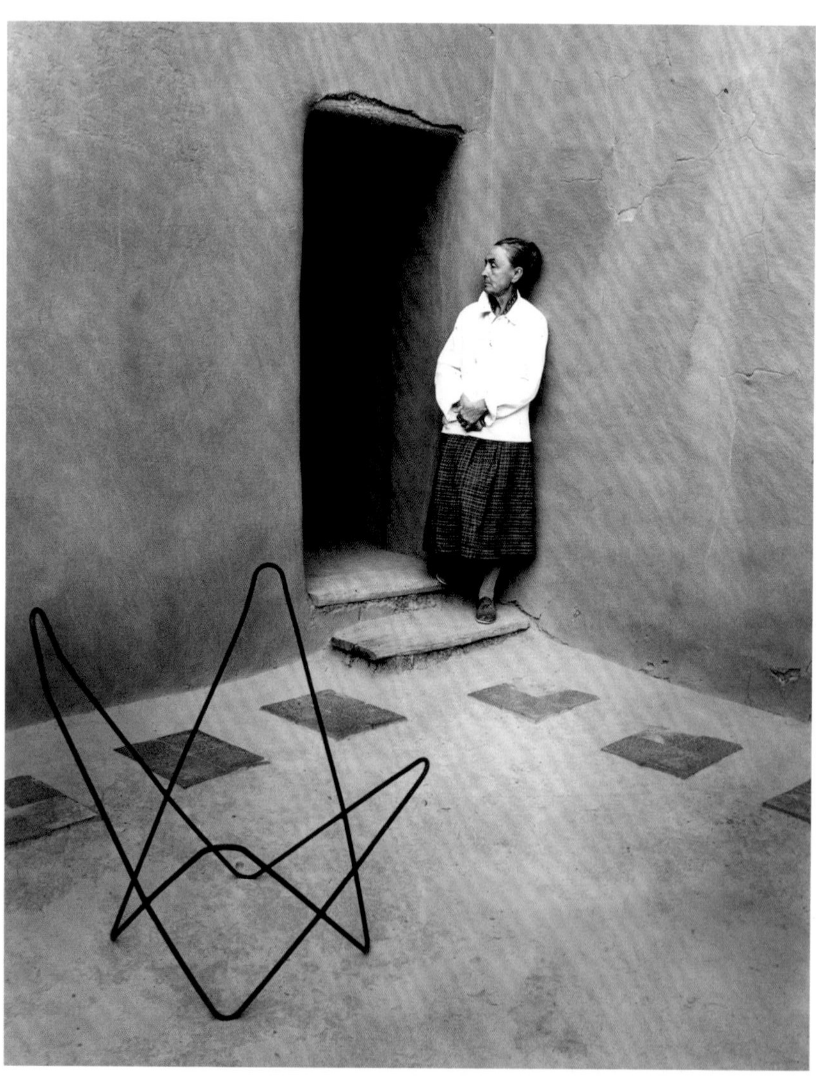

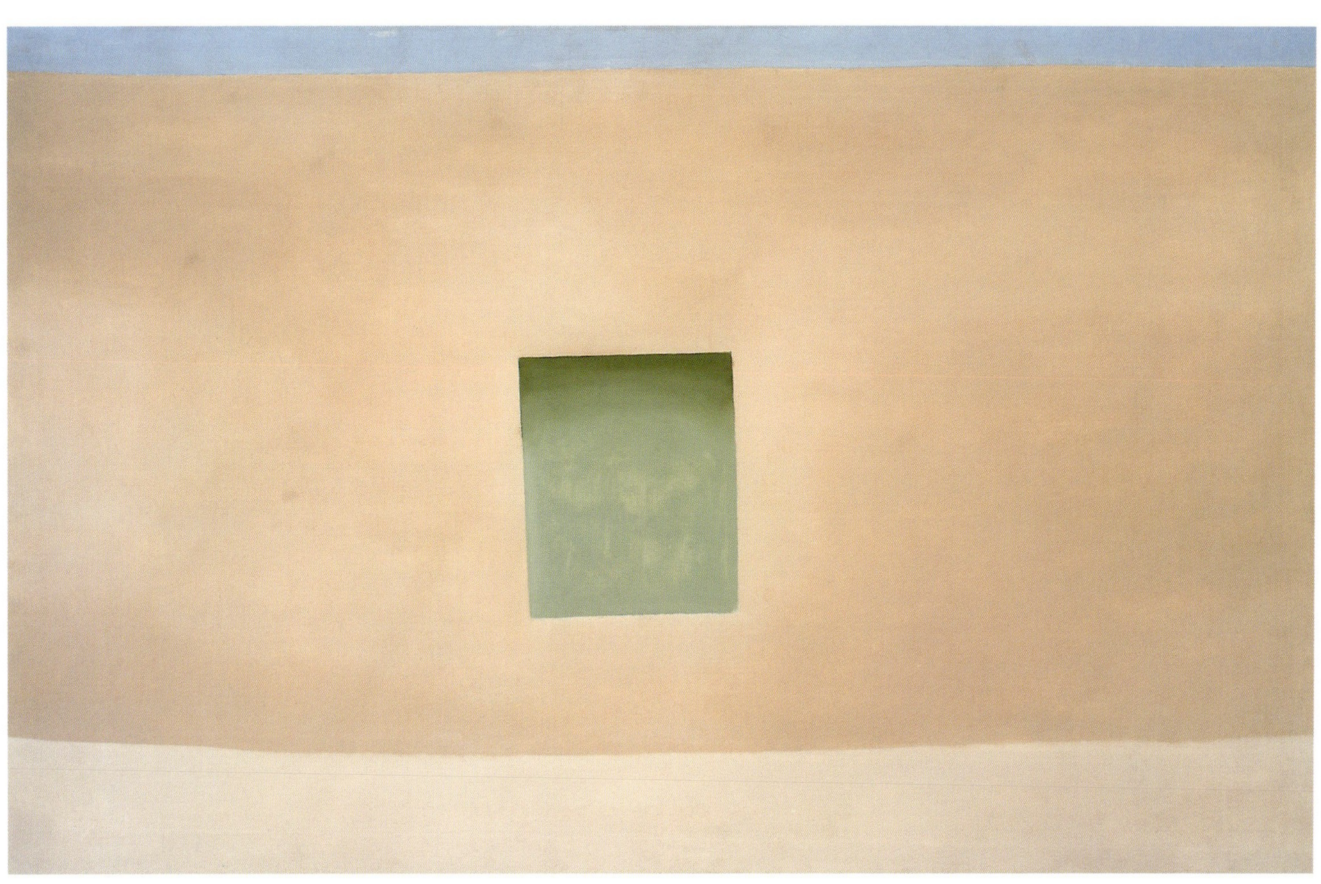

58.
George Daniell,
*Georgia O'Keeffe in
Doorway*, 1952

59.
Don Worth,
Georgia O'Keeffe,
1958

60.
Georgia O'Keeffe,
Wall with Green Door,
1952

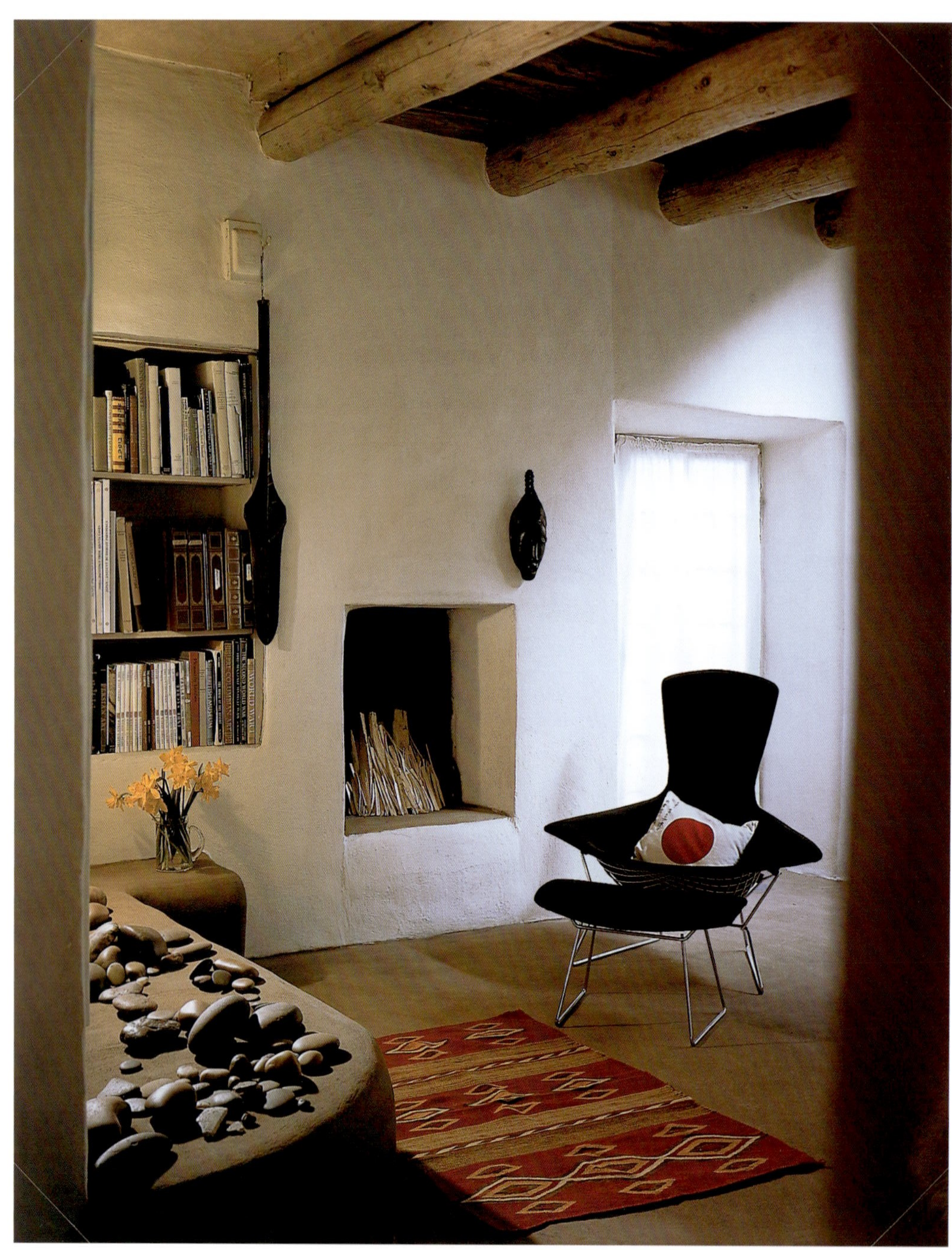

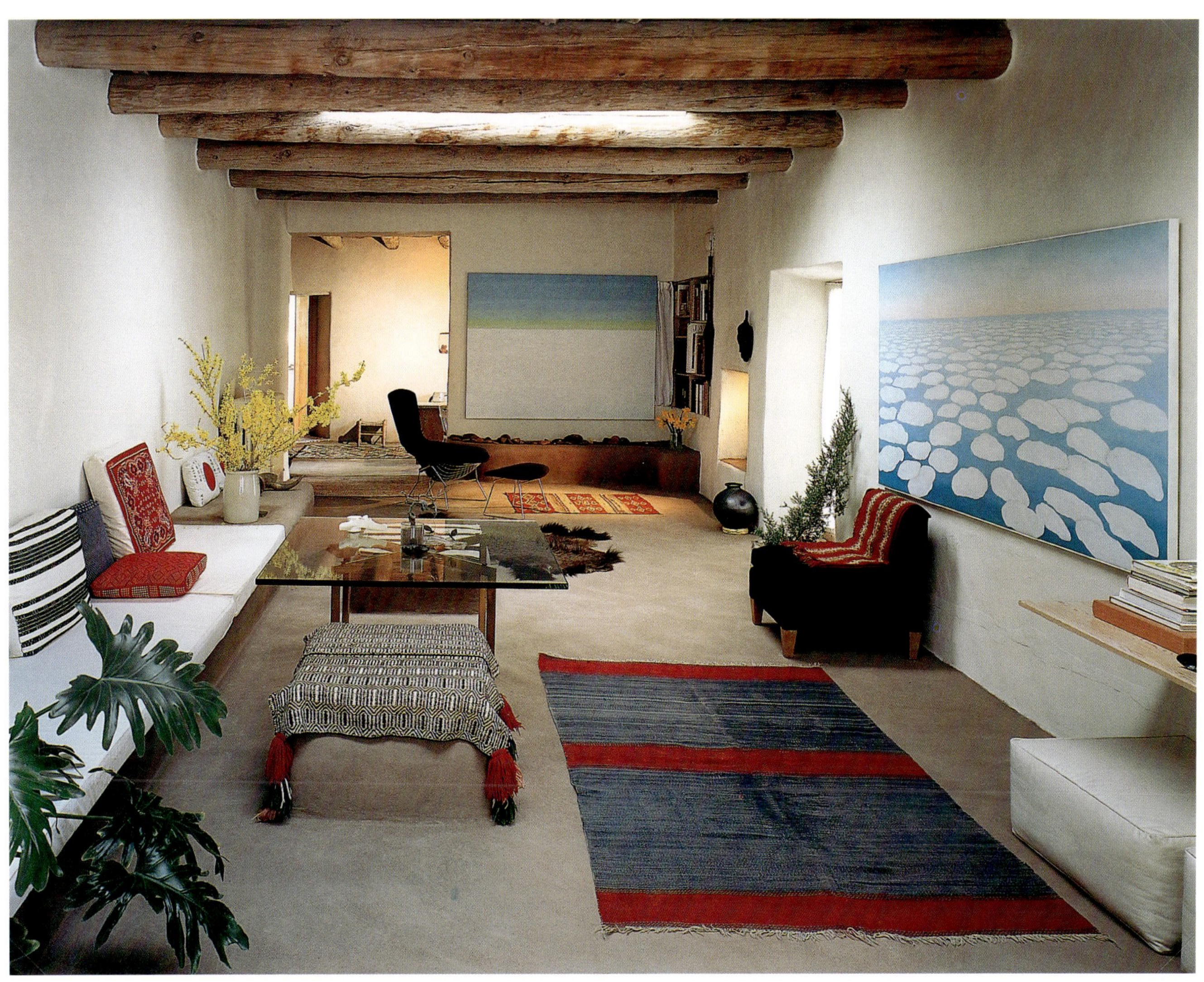

61.
Balthazar Korab,
Untitled [Living room at
Abiquiu, #27], 1965

62.
Balthazar Korab,
Untitled [Living room at
Abiquiu, #25], 1965

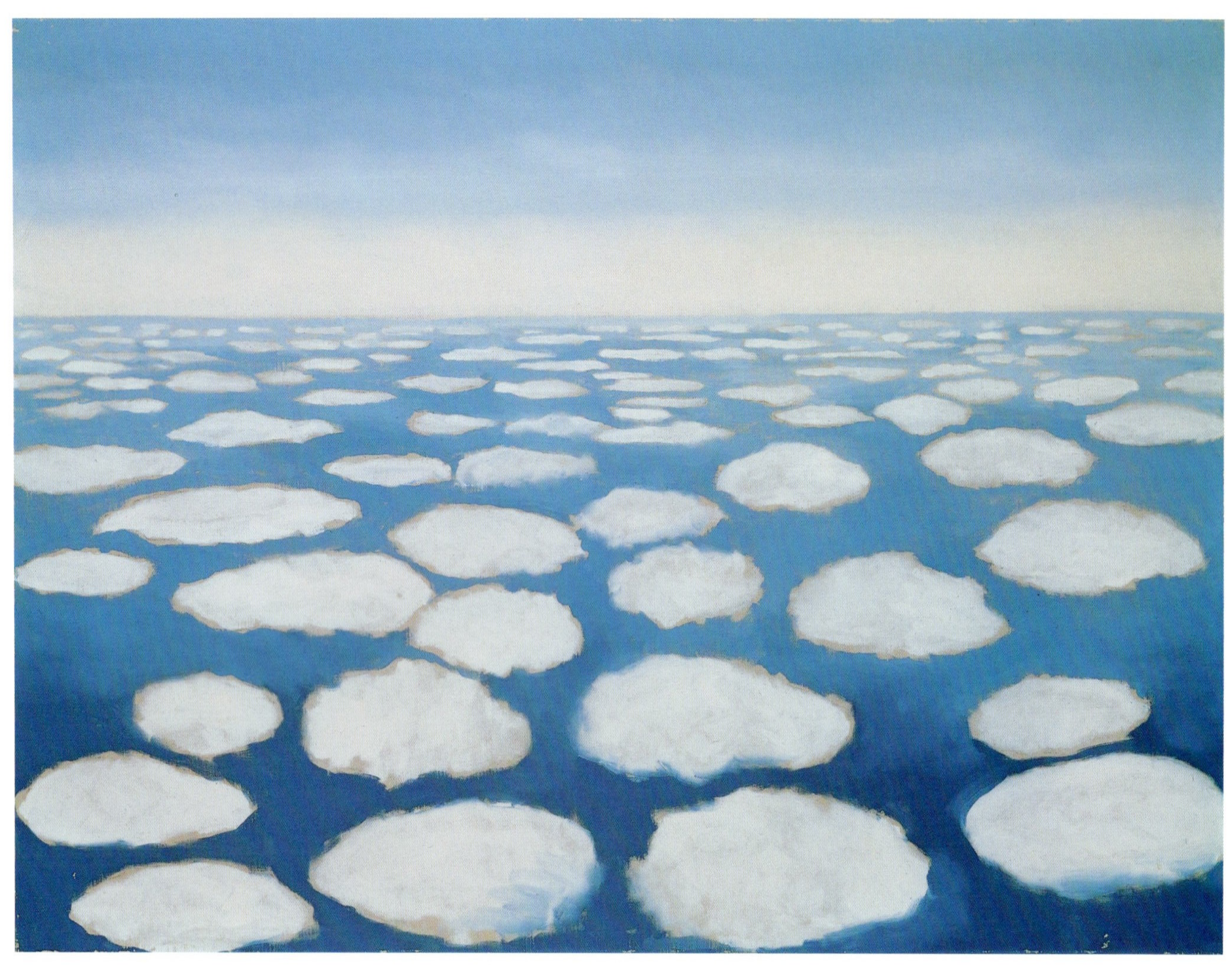

63.
Georgia O'Keeffe,
Above the Clouds I,
1962–1963

64.
Balthazar Korab,
Untitled [Georgia
O'Keeffe in her
studio, #55], 1965

65.
Balthazar Korab,
Untitled [View of
Chama River Valley
from studio, #10],
1965

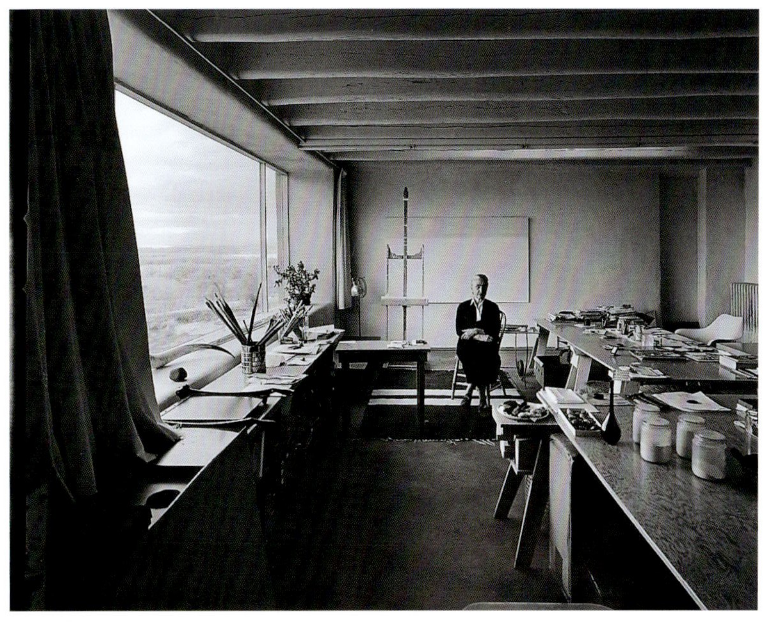

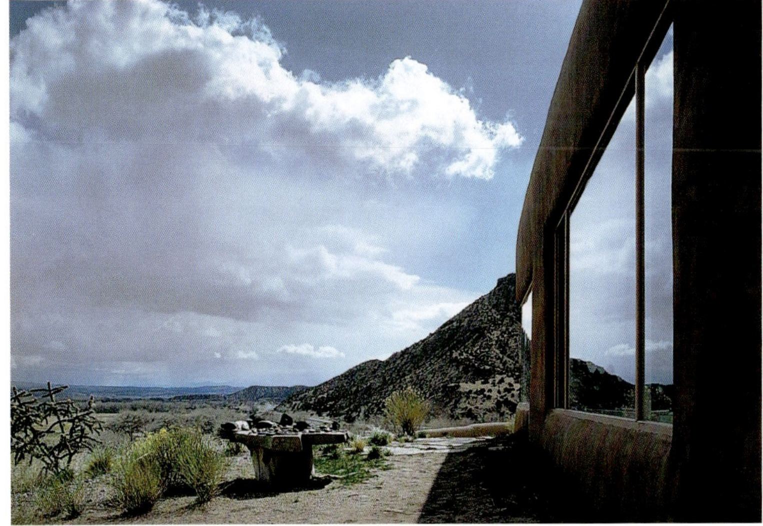

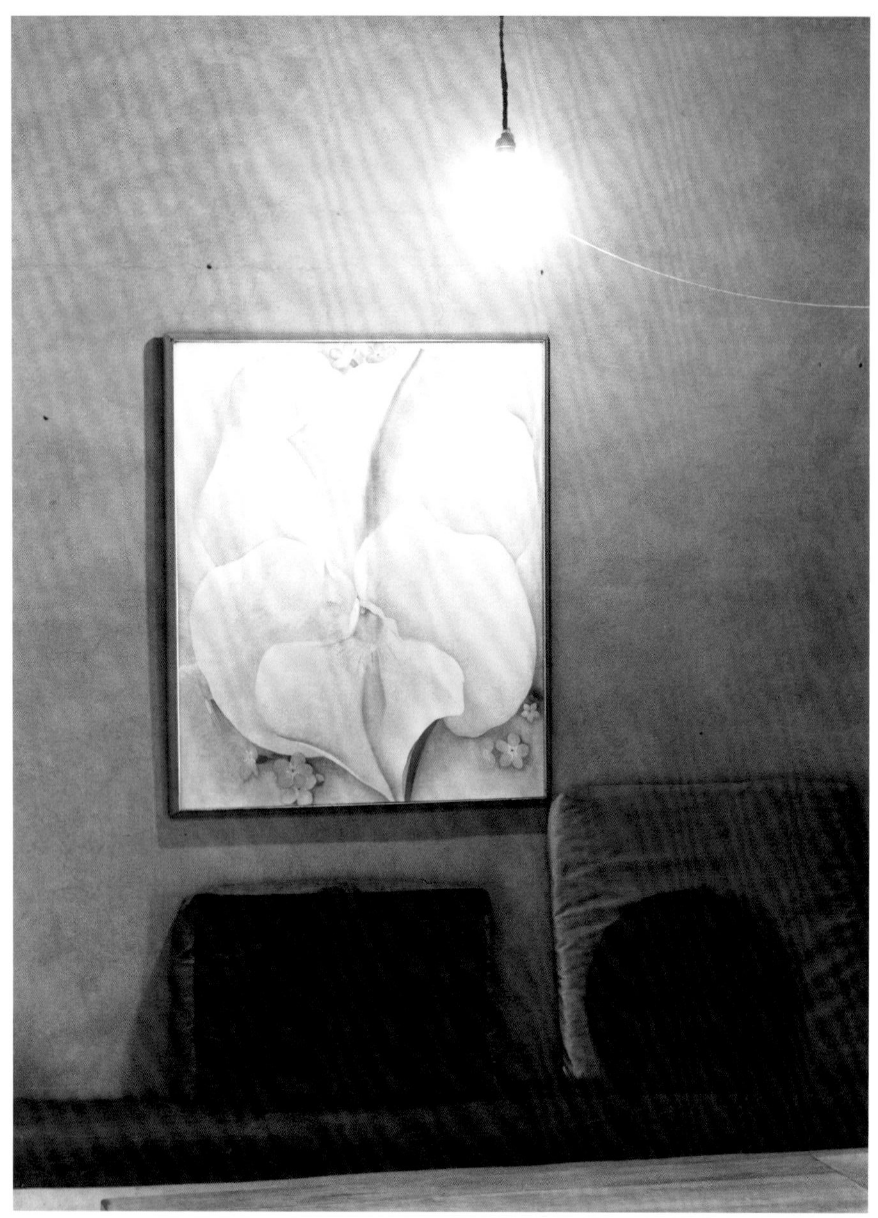

66.
Myron Wood,
*Pansies and Forget-
Me-Nots, 1927,*
1980

67.
Georgia O'Keeffe,
Coxcomb, 1931

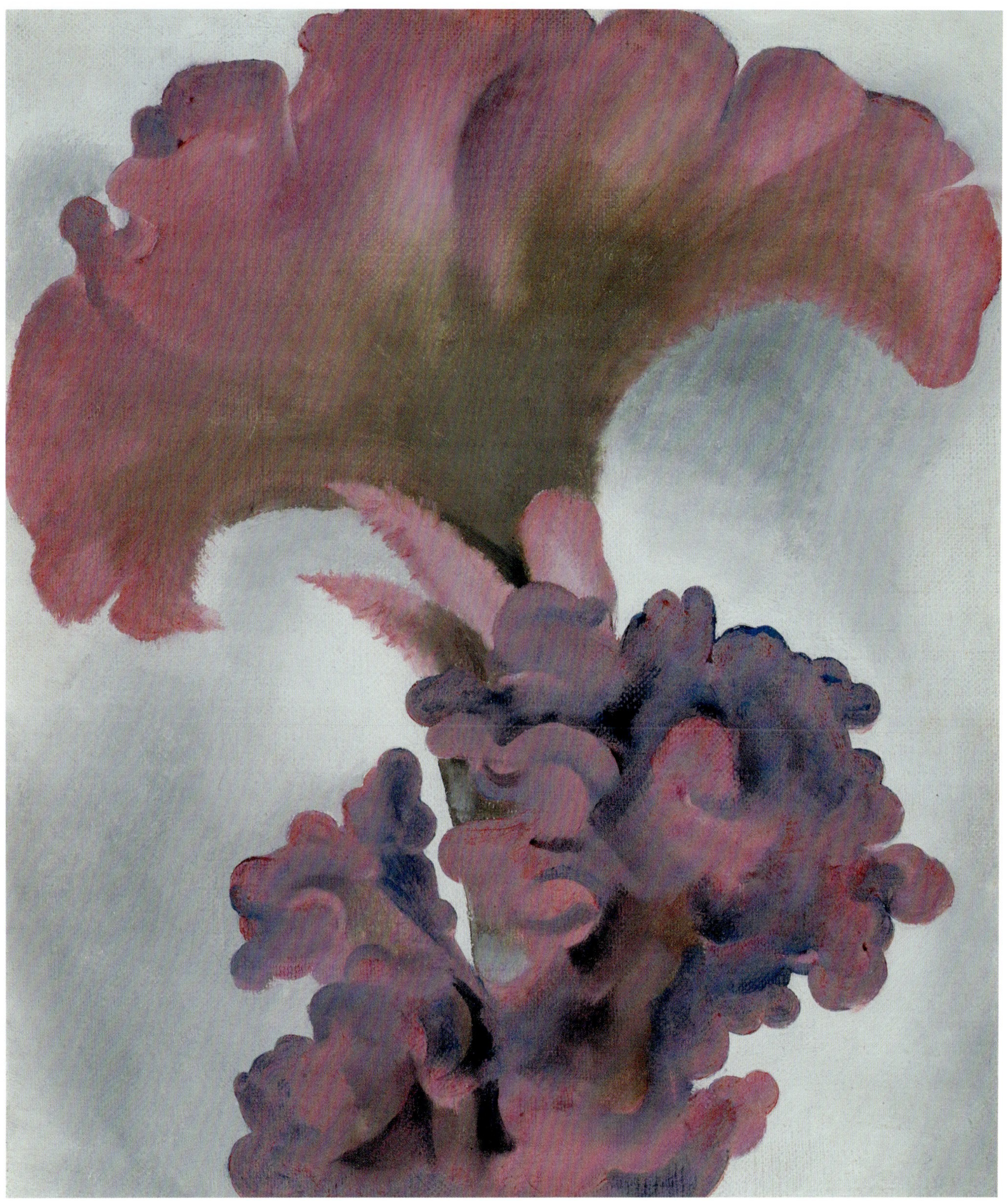

68.
Andy Warhol,
Georgia O'Keeffe,
ca. 1979

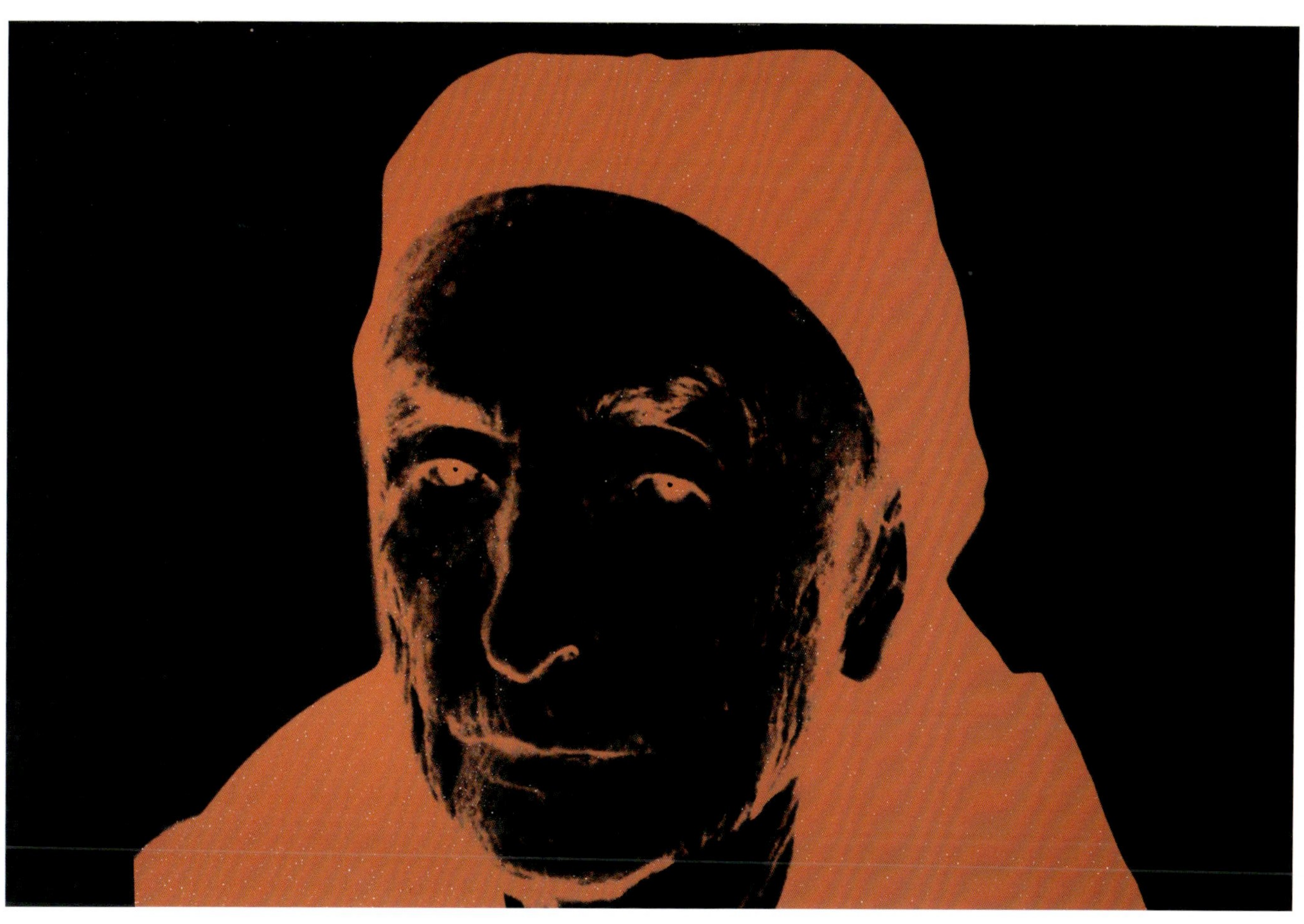

O'Keeffe
Chronology

1887

November 15: Georgia Totto O'Keeffe is born on a farm near Sun Prairie, Wisconsin.

1905–1906

Attends the School of the Art Institute of Chicago, where John Vanderpoel's classes are particularly inspirational.

1907–1908

Studies at the Art Students League, New York, with William Merritt Chase, in whose class she earns a scholarship for still life. Visits exhibitions of modern art at Alfred Stieglitz's Little Galleries of the Photo-Secession (known as 291 for its Fifth Avenue address).

1880   1890   1900

1912–1914

Is employed as an art supervisor and teacher at a public school in Amarillo, Texas, her introduction to the West.

1913–1916

Summers: Teaches art at the University of Virginia with Alon Bement.

1914–1915

Studies with Arthur Wesley Dow at Teacher's College, Columbia University, New York. Visits exhibitions of Georges Braque and Pablo Picasso, Marsden Hartley and John Marin at 291.

1915–1916

Teaches art at Columbia College, Columbia, South Carolina; begins a series of abstract charcoal drawings.

1916

May: Stieglitz opens a group show at 291 that includes works by O'Keeffe.

Fall: Accepts teaching position at West Texas State Normal College, Canyon.

1917

April: Stieglitz opens *Georgia O'Keeffe,* the first solo exhibition of her work, at 291.

May: Visits New York, meeting Paul Strand and others of Stieglitz's circle; Stieglitz photographs her for the first time.

August: Vacations in and around Ward, Colorado, and on her return to Texas spends several days in Santa Fe, New Mexico—her first visit to the state.

1918

February: Moves to south Texas.

June: Moves to New York at Stieglitz's invitation and for the next eleven years lives either in the city (winter and spring) or at the Stieglitz family summer home in Lake George, New York (summer and fall), with occasional excursions to, among other places, Maine, Washington, D.C., and Wisconsin.

1921

February: Stieglitz's photographs of O'Keeffe are exhibited in public for the first time at Anderson Galleries, New York. Marsden Hartley publishes an early appreciation of her work, an essay wrought with sexual interpretations.

1923

January: Stieglitz opens *Alfred Stieglitz Presents One Hundred Pictures: Oils, Watercolors, Pastels, Drawings, by Georgia O'Keeffe, American,* at the Anderson Galleries. This is followed shortly by the presentation of 116 new Stieglitz photographs, including numerous portraits of O'Keeffe. He subsequently organizes annual exhibitions of her work until his death in 1946.

1924

December 11: Marries Alfred Stieglitz in Cliffside Park, New Jersey, with John Marin as witness.

1928

May: Stieglitz announces sale of six O'Keeffe calla lily paintings for a record price ($25,000). Travels to Wisconsin to visit her family and childhood home.

1929

April–August: Travels to Santa Fe with Rebecca Strand; after her arrival, moves to Taos at the insistence of Mabel Dodge Luhan, who provides O'Keeffe with a studio.

June–December: The Intimate Gallery closes and Stieglitz opens An American Place gallery.

1910

1920

1930

February–March: Exhibition at An American Place includes first New Mexican subjects. O'Keeffe continues to present work there annually through 1950.

Late April–August: In New Mexico.

1933

February–March: Hospitalized in New York, suffering from a nervous breakdown. Recuperates in Bermuda and at Lake George.

1934

January: Begins painting after a thirteen-month hiatus.

June–September: Returns to New Mexico for the first time in three years.

August: Makes her first visit to Ghost Ranch, a dude ranch owned by Arthur Pack, located north of the village of Abiquiu, to which she returns frequently thereafter.

1935

July–November: In New Mexico at Ghost Ranch.

1936

June–September: In New Mexico; spends her first summer living at Rancho de los Burros, the house at Ghost Ranch that she buys in 1940. She subsequently lives there almost every summer until 1949, when she moves permanently to New Mexico.

1937

July–October: In New Mexico; takes trip through Southwest with Ansel Adams and David McAlpin.

Winter: Failing health forces Stieglitz to give up photography.

1938

August–November: In New Mexico.

1939

Late January–April: Travels to Hawaii to paint as a guest of Dole Pineapple Company.

1940

June–November: In New Mexico; buys Rancho de los Burros at Ghost Ranch.

October: Meets Maria Chabot, an aspiring writer, who lives summers with O'Keeffe until 1945, managing the house at Ghost Ranch.

1941

May–November: In New Mexico.

1942

June–November: In New Mexico.

1943

January–February: First full-scale retrospective at the Art Institute of Chicago, with catalogue by curator Daniel Catton Rich.

April–October: In New Mexico.

1944

April–October: In New Mexico.

1945

May–November: In New Mexico.

December: After return to New York, purchases a ruined hacienda on three acres in Abiquiu.

1946

May–August: Retrospective at the Museum of Modern Art, organized by James Johnson Sweeney; this is the first show there devoted to the art of a woman.

June: In New Mexico; Chabot begins renovating the Abiquiu hacienda, which she completes in 1949.

July 10: Returns to stricken Stieglitz in New York; he dies July 13.

Fall: Employs Doris Bry to organize Stieglitz papers; returns to Abiquiu.

1947

January–early summer: In New York, working to settle the Stieglitz estate.

August–December: In New Mexico.

1948

April–October: In New Mexico.

1949

Spring: Moves to New Mexico permanently, dividing time between Abiquiu (winter and spring) and Ghost Ranch (summer and autumn). Is elected to the National Institute of Arts and Letters.

1930   1940

1951

February: First trip to Mexico, beginning international travels.

1953

February: Retrospective at the Dallas Museum of Art.

Spring: First trip to Europe (France and Spain).

1956

Spring: Visits Peru for three months.

1959

Travels around the world for three months, including seven weeks in India.

1960

October–December: Retrospective at the Worcester Art Museum, Massachusetts, with Daniel Catton Rich as curator and catalogue author.

Autumn: Six-week trip to Japan, Taiwan, Philippines, Hong Kong, Southeast Asia, and the Pacific Islands.

1961

Summer: First of several trips down the Colorado River with Eliot Porter and Todd Webb.

1966

March–May: Retrospective organized by the Amon Carter Museum of Western Art, Fort Worth.

1970

October–November: Major retrospective organized by Lloyd Goodrich and O'Keeffe with help from Doris Bry for the Whitney Museum of American Art; the show later travels to Chicago and San Francisco.

1973

Autumn: Meets artist Juan Hamilton, who teachers her to work with clay; he becomes her assistant, close friend, and, later, representative.

1974

January: Visits Morocco with Hamilton: over the next decade travels with him often, visiting Central America, the Caribbean, Hawaii, and cities in the continental United States. Publishes *Some Memories of Drawings,* a portfolio of reproductions with comments by the artist.

1976

Publishes *Georgia O'Keeffe,* a best-selling book of fine reproductions with distinctive text by the artist.

1980

Laurie Lisle publishes *Portrait of an Artist: A Biography of Georgia O'Keeffe,* the first full-length study of the artist's life.

1984

In failing health, moves to Santa Fe.

1986

March 6: Dies at St. Vincent's Hospital, Santa Fe, aged ninety-nine.

1987

November: Centennial celebrated by major retrospective at the National Gallery of Art, with Jack Cowart, Juan Hamilton, and Sarah Greenough as co-curators; the show later travels to the Art Institute of Chicago, the Dallas Museum of Art, The Metropolitan Museum of Art, New York, and the Los Angeles County Museum of Art.

1950   1960   1970   1980

Exhibition Checklist

Abstraction
1916 (cast 1979–1980),
White-lacquered bronze,
10 × 10 × 1 ½ in.
(25.4 × 25.4 × 3.81 cm)
Georgia O'Keeffe Museum,
Santa Fe. Gift of
The Georgia O'Keeffe
Foundation

Nude Series VII
1917, Watercolor on
paper, 17 ¾ × 13 ½ in.
(45.1 × 34.3 cm)
Georgia O'Keeffe Museum,
Santa Fe. Gift of The
Burnett Foundation and
The Georgia O'Keeffe
Foundation

No. 17 — Special
1919, Charcoal on laid
paper, 19 ¾ × 12 ¾ in.
(50.2 × 32.4 cm)
Georgia O'Keeffe Museum,
Santa Fe. Gift of The
Burnett Foundation and
The Georgia O'Keeffe
Foundation

Green Lines and Pink
1919, Oil on canvas,
18 × 10 in. (45.7 × 25.4 cm)
Georgia O'Keeffe Museum,
Santa Fe. Gift of The
Burnett Foundation and
The Georgia O'Keeffe
Foundation

Blue Line
1919, Oil on canvas,
20 ⅛ × 17 ⅛ in.
(51.1 × 43.5 cm)
Georgia O'Keeffe Museum,
Santa Fe. Gift of The
Burnett Foundation and
The Georgia O'Keeffe
Foundation

** Portland Museum of Art
venue only*

Corn, No. 2
1924, Oil on canvas,
27 ¼ × 10 in.
(69.2 × 25.4 cm)
Georgia O'Keeffe Museum,
Santa Fe. Gift of The
Burnett Foundation and
The Georgia O'Keeffe
Foundation

*Red Hills beyond Abiquiu**
1930, Oil on canvas,
30 × 36 in. (76.2 × 91.4 cm)
Courtesy of the Eiteljorg
Museum of American
Indians and Western Art,
Indianapolis

*Horse's Skull with
White Rose*
1931, Oil on canvas,
30 × 16 ⅛ in. (76.2 × 41 cm)
Georgia O'Keeffe Museum,
Santa Fe. Extended loan,
private collection

*Coxcomb**
1931, Oil on canvas,
20 × 17 in. (50.8 × 43.2 cm)
Courtesy of the Penn-
sylvania Academy of the
Fine Arts, Philadelphia.
Partial gift and bequest of
Mrs. Bernice McIlhenny
Wintersteen

*Gerald's Tree II**
1937, Oil on canvas,
40 × 30 in.
(101.6 × 76.2 cm)
Stark Museum of Art,
Orange, Texas

*The House I Live In**
1937, Oil on canvas,
14 × 30 in. (35.5 × 76.2 cm)
Yale Collection of American
Literature, Beinecke Rare
Book and Manuscript
Library, Yale University

Three Small Rocks Big
1937, Oil on canvas,
20 × 12 in. (50.8 × 30.5 cm)
Philadelphia Museum of Art.
Gift of George Howe,
1949

*The Patio — No. 1**
1940, Oil on canvas,
24 ½ × 18 ½ in.
(62.2 × 47 cm)
Private Collection,
San Francisco

Wall with Green Door
1952, Oil on canvas,
30 ¼ × 47 ⅞ in.
(76.2 × 121.6 cm)
Corcoran Gallery of Art,
Washington, D.C. Gift of
the Woodward Foundation

From the River — Pale
1959, Oil on canvas,
41 ½ × 31 ⅜ in.
(105.4 × 79.7 cm)
Georgia O'Keeffe
Museum, Santa Fe. Gift
of The Georgia O'Keeffe
Foundation

Blue Black and Grey
1960, Oil on canvas,
40 × 30 in.
(101.6 × 76.2 cm)
Georgia O'Keeffe Museum,
Santa Fe. Gift of
The Burnett Foundation

Above the Clouds I
1962–1963, Oil on canvas,
36 ⅛ × 48 ¼ in.
(91.8 × 122.6 cm)
Georgia O'Keeffe Museum,
Santa Fe. Gift of The
Burnett Foundation and
The Georgia O'Keeffe
Foundation

*Canyon Country,
White and Brown Cliffs*
1965, Oil on canvas,
36 × 30 in. (91.4 × 76.2 cm)
Georgia O'Keeffe Museum,
Santa Fe. Gift of
The Georgia O'Keeffe
Foundation

ANSEL ADAMS
(United States, 1902–1984)

Taos Pueblo
1930 (1st edition),
Book containing twelve
gelatin silver prints,
17 5/16 × 13 1/16 × 13/16 in.
(44 × 33.2 × 2.1 cm) (book);
6 5/16 × 8 21/32 in. (16 × 22 cm)
(each image), ed. 11/100
Center for Creative Photography, University of
Arizona: Ansel Adams
Archive/Purchase

*Georgia O'Keeffe and
Orville Cox, Canyon de
Chelly National Park*
1937, Gelatin silver print,
7 3/4 × 11 in. (19.7 × 28 cm)
The Georgia O'Keeffe
Museum, Santa Fe. Gift
of The Georgia O'Keeffe
Foundation

*Georgia O'Keeffe
in the Southwest*
1937, Gelatin silver
print, 11 1/16 × 7 3/8 in.
(29.7 × 18.7 cm)
Center for Creative
Photography, University
of Arizona: Ansel
Adams Archive

*Georgia O'Keeffe
Painting in Her Car, Ghost
Ranch, New Mexico*
1937, Gelatin silver
print, 8 5/16 × 12 1/8 in.
(21.1 × 30.8 cm)
Center for Creative
Photography, University
of Arizona: Ansel
Adams Archive

*Ghost Ranch Hills,
New Mexico*
ca. 1937, Gelatin silver
print, 8 7/8 × 12 13/16 in.
(22.5 × 30.9 cm)
Center for Creative
Photography, University
of Arizona: Ansel
Adams Archive

*Mud Hills — Ghost
Ranch, New Mexico*
1937, Gelatin silver
print, 4 1/2 × 6 3/8 in.
(11.4 × 16.2 cm)
Princeton University Art
Museum. Gift of David H.
McAlpin, Class of 1920

Palomino, Ghost Ranch
1937, Gelatin silver
print, 6 5/8 × 10 5/32 in.
(16.8 × 25.8 cm)
Princeton University Art
Museum. Gift of David H.
McAlpin, Class of 1920

*St. Francis Church,
Ranchos de Taos,
New Mexico*
ca. 1937, Gelatin silver
print, 15 1/8 × 18 15/16 in.
(38.4 × 48.1 cm)
Center for Creative
Photography, University
of Arizona: Ansel
Adams Archive

*Thunderstorm, Ghost
Ranch, Chama Valley,
Northern New Mexico*
1937, Gelatin silver
print, 14 15/16 × 19 21/32 in.
(36.7 × 49.9 cm)
Center for Creative
Photography, University
of Arizona: Ansel Adams
Archive/Purchase

*Detail of O'Keeffe Painting
and Reflections, An
American Place, Gallery
of Alfred Stieglitz*
1939, Gelatin silver print,
7 1/8 × 8 7/8 in.
(18.1 × 22.5 cm)
Princeton University Art
Museum. Gift of David H.
McAlpin, Class of 1920

An American Place
1944, Gelatin silver print,
8 × 10 in. (20.3 × 25.4 cm)
Georgia O'Keeffe
Museum, Santa Fe. Gift
of The Georgia O'Keeffe
Foundation

GEORGE DANIELL
(United States, 1911–2002)

*Georgia O'Keeffe
in Doorway*
1952, Gelatin silver print,
11 3/4 × 11 3/4 in.
(29.8 × 29.8 cm)
Georgia O'Keeffe Museum,
Santa Fe. Gift of Mariann
Wells

*Georgia O'Keeffe Seated
among Her Props*
1952, Gelatin silver print,
10 1/2 × 10 1/2 in.
(26.7 × 26.7 cm)
Portland Museum of Art.
Museum purchase with
support from the Barbara
Goodbody Photography
Fund

LAURA GILPIN
(United States, 1891–1979)

Georgia O'Keeffe
1953, Gelatin silver print,
9 3/8 × 7 7/16 in.
(23.8 × 18.9 cm)
Amon Carter Museum,
Forth Worth, Texas, Bequest
of the artist. P1979.130.6

*Studio of Georgia O'Keeffe
Overlooking Chama Valley*
1960, Gelatin silver print,
7 5/8 × 9 5/8 in.
(19.4 × 24.4 cm)
Amon Carter Museum,
Forth Worth, Texas, Bequest
of the artist. P1979.108.469

PHILIPPE HALSMAN
(United States, b. Latvia,
1906–1979)

Georgia O'Keeffe
1948 (printed later),
Gelatin silver print,
24 × 20 in. (61 × 50.8 cm)
Georgia O'Keeffe
Museum, Santa Fe

YOUSUF KARSH
(Canada, b. Armenia,
1908–2002)

Georgia O'Keeffe
1956, Gelatin silver print,
39 × 29 in. (99.1 × 99.1 cm)
Georgia O'Keeffe
Museum, Santa Fe

BALTHAZAR KORAB
(United States,
b. Hungary, 1926)

Untitled [Georgia O'Keeffe
in her studio, #55]
1965, Gelatin silver print,
10 × 12 ⅞ in.
(25.4 × 32.7 cm)
Courtesy of Balthazar
Korab Ltd.

Untitled [Living room at
Abiquiu, #25]
1965, Color print,
10 ⅞ × 13 ¹⁵⁄₁₆ in.
(27.6 × 35.4 cm)
Courtesy of Balthazar
Korab Ltd.

Untitled [Living room at
Abiquiu, #27]
1965, Color print,
14 × 10 ⅞ in.
(35.6 × 27.6 cm)
Courtesy of Balthazar
Korab Ltd.

Untitled [View of
Chama River Valley from
studio, #10]
1965, Color print,
9 ⅜ × 14 in.
(23.8 × 35.6 cm)
Courtesy of Balthazar
Korab Ltd.

JOHN LOENGARD
(United States, b. 1934)

Evening Walk, Ghost Ranch
1966 (printed later),
Gelatin silver print,
15 × 10 ³⁄₁₆ in.
(38.1 × 25.8 cm)
National Portrait Gallery,
Smithsonian Institution;
acquired through the
generosity of Pat and John
Rosenwald, NPG.2004.107

Ghost Ranch
1966 (printed later),
Gelatin silver print,
10 × 14 ¹⁵⁄₁₆ in.
(25.4 × 37.9 cm)
National Portrait Gallery,
Smithsonian Institution;
acquired through the
generosity of Pat and John
Rosenwald, NPG.2004.94

Rock Collection, Abiquiu
1966 (printed later),
Gelatin silver print,
14 ¹⁵⁄₁₆ × 10 ¹⁄₁₆ in.
(37.9 × 25.5 cm)
National Portrait Gallery,
Smithsonian Institution;
acquired through the
generosity of Pat and John
Rosenwald, NPG.2004.81

*The Rock from
Eliot Porter, Abiquiu*
1966 (printed later),
Gelatin silver print,
10 ¹⁄₁₆ × 14 ¹⁵⁄₁₆ in.
(25.5 × 37.9 cm)
National Portrait Gallery,
Smithsonian Institution;
acquired through the
generosity of Pat and John
Rosenwald, NPG.2004.83

Bedroom, Ghost Ranch
1967 (printed later),
Gelatin silver print,
10 ¹⁄₁₆ × 14 ¹⁵⁄₁₆ in.
(25.6 × 37.9 cm)
National Portrait Gallery,
Smithsonian Institution;
acquired through the
generosity of Pat and John
Rosenwald, NPG.2004.75

On the Roof, Ghost Ranch
1967 (printed later),
Gelatin silver print,
10 ³⁄₁₆ × 15 ¹⁄₁₆ in.
(25.8 × 38.2 cm)
National Portrait Gallery,
Smithsonian Institution;
acquired through the
generosity of Pat and John
Rosenwald, NPG.2004.84

Studio, Ghost Ranch
1967 (printed later),
Gelatin silver print,
10 ¹⁄₁₆ × 14 ¹⁵⁄₁₆ in.
(25.5 × 37.9 cm)
National Portrait Gallery,
Smithsonian Institution;
acquired through the
generosity of Pat and John
Rosenwald, NPG.2004.78

Life
March 1, 1968,
13 ¹¹⁄₁₆ × 10 ½ in.
(34.8 × 26.7 cm)
National Portrait Gallery,
Smithsonian Institution,
acquired through
the generosity of Pat
and John Rosenwald,
AD/NPG.2004.1

ARNOLD NEWMAN
(United States, 1918–2006)

*Alfred Stieglitz and
Georgia O'Keeffe, An
American Place*
1944, Gelatin silver print,
10 × 8 in. (25.4 × 20.3 cm)
Private Collection

*Georgia O'Keeffe, Ghost
Ranch, New Mexico*
1968, Gelatin silver print,
14 × 11 in. (27.9 × 35.6 cm)
Portland Museum of
Art. Gift of the artist for
the Ernst Haas Memorial
Collection

IRVING PENN
(United States, b. 1917)

Georgia O'Keeffe
1948 (printed 1986),
Platinum-palladium print,
22 ⅞ × 17 ⁵⁄₁₆ in.
(58.1 × 44 cm)
National Portrait Gallery,
Smithsonian Institution,
Gift of Irving Penn

ELIOT PORTER
(United States, 1901–1990)

Ghost Ranch
1940, Gelatin silver print,
7 ³⁄₃₂ × 9 ⁷⁄₁₆ in.
(18.8 × 24 cm)
Princeton University Art
Museum. Gift of David H.
McAlpin, Class of 1920

*Georgia O'Keeffe, Ghost
Ranch, New Mexico*
1945, Gelatin silver print,
9 ¼ × 7 ¹⁷⁄₃₂ in.
(23.5 × 19.1 cm)
Princeton University Art
Museum. Gift of David H.
McAlpin, Class of 1920

*Georgia O'Keeffe's
Entrance Door, Abiquiu,
New Mexico*
1949, Gelatin silver
print, 9 ½ × 7 ½ in.
(24.1 × 19.1 cm)
Amon Carter Museum,
Forth Worth, Texas,
Bequest of the artist.
P1990.54.649.2

*Horse Skull, O'Keeffe's
House, Abiquiu,
New Mexico*
1952, Gelatin silver print,
9 ½ × 7 ⁷⁄₁₆ in.
(24.1 × 18.9 cm)
Amon Carter Museum,
Forth Worth, Texas,
Bequest of the artist.
P1990.54.667.1

ALFRED STIEGLITZ
(United States, 1864–1946)

Georgia O'Keeffe
1917, Platinum print,
9 ⁹⁄₁₆ × 7 ⅝ in.
(24.3 × 19.4 cm)
Georgia O'Keeffe
Museum, Santa Fe. Gift
of The Georgia O'Keeffe
Foundation

*O'Keeffe Exhibition,
April 7, 1917*
1917, Eight gelatin silver
prints bound in album,
7 ⁷⁄₁₆ × 8 ⅞ in.
(17.9 × 22.6 cm)(each
image); 11 ⅞ × 8 ¼ in.
(30.2 × 21 cm) (album)
The J. Paul Getty
Museum, Los Angeles

Georgia O'Keeffe
1918, Platinum print,
9 ¼ × 7 ¼ in.
(23.5 × 18.4 cm)
Georgia O'Keeffe
Museum, Santa Fe. Gift
of The Georgia
O'Keeffe Foundation

*Georgia O'Keeffe
in Chemise*
1918, Gelatin silver print,
10 × 8 in. (25.4 × 20.3 cm)
Georgia O'Keeffe
Museum, Santa Fe. Gift
of The Georgia O'Keeffe
Foundation

Georgia O'Keeffe
1919, Palladium print,
7 ⁵⁄₁₆ × 9 ⅛ in.
(18.6 × 23.2 cm)
The Metropolitan Museum
of Art. Gift of Georgia
O'Keeffe through the gen-
erosity of The Georgia
O'Keeffe Foundation and
Jennifer and Joseph Duke,
1997 (1997.61.56)

Georgia O'Keeffe—Hands
ca. 1919 (printed 1920s/
1930s), Gelatin silver print,
9 ⁷⁄₁₆ × 7 ½ in. (24 × 19.1 cm)
Georgia O'Keeffe
Museum, Santa Fe. Gift
of The Georgia O'Keeffe
Foundation

Interpretation
1919, Gelatin silver print,
5 ¼ × 3 ⅜ in. (13.3 × 8.6 cm)
Georgia O'Keeffe
Museum, Santa Fe. Gift
of The Georgia O'Keeffe
Foundation

*O'Keeffe Exhibition at
Anderson Gallery*
1923, Gelatin silver print,
8 × 10 in. (20.3 × 25.4 cm)
Georgia O'Keeffe
Museum, Santa Fe. Gift
of The Georgia O'Keeffe
Foundation

*Georgia O'Keeffe—
After Return from
New Mexico*
1929, Gelatin silver print,
3 ¹⁄₁₆ × 4 ⅝ in.
(7.8 × 11.7 cm)
Georgia O'Keeffe
Museum, Santa Fe. Gift
of The Georgia O'Keeffe
Foundation

Georgia O'Keeffe
1930, Gelatin silver print,
9 ⅜ × 7 ½ in.
(23.8 × 19.1 cm)
Georgia O'Keeffe
Museum, Santa Fe. Gift
of The Georgia O'Keeffe
Foundation

Georgia O'Keeffe
1931, Gelatin silver print,
7 9/16 × 9 7/16 in.
(19.2 × 24 cm)
The Metropolitan Museum
of Art. Gift of Georgia
O'Keeffe through the
generosity of The Georgia
O'Keeffe Foundation
and Jennifer and Joseph
Duke, 1997 (1997.61.37)

Georgia O'Keeffe
1933, Gelatin silver print,
9 7/16 × 7 7/16 in.
(23.9 × 18.9 cm)
The Metropolitan Museum
of Art. Gift of Georgia
O'Keeffe through the
generosity of The Georgia
O'Keeffe Foundation
and Jennifer and Joseph
Duke, 1997 (1997.61.40)

ANDY WARHOL
(United States, 1928–1987)

Georgia O'Keeffe
ca. 1979, Screenprint with
diamond dust on Arches
Aquarelle (Cold Pressed)
paper, 40 1/4 × 59 3/4 in.
(102.2 × 151.8 cm)
Andy Warhol Museum,
Pittsburgh; Founding
Collection, Contribution
The Andy Warhol Foun-
dation for the Visual
Arts, Inc.

TODD WEBB
(United States, 1905–2000)

*[Installation View of
O'Keeffe Exhibition at the
Museum of Modern Art]*
1946, Gelatin silver print,
8 × 10 in. (20.3 × 25.4 cm)
Georgia O'Keeffe Museum,
Santa Fe. Maria Chabot
Archive

*Ladder and Adobe Wall,
O'Keeffe's Abiquiu House,
New Mexico*
1957, Gelatin silver print,
12 3/8 × 10 in.
(31.4 × 25.4 cm)
Courtesy of Evans Gallery,
Portland, Maine

*Georgia O'Keeffe in Glen
Canyon, New Mexico*
1961, Gelatin silver print,
10 3/4 × 8 in. (27.3 × 20.3 cm)
Courtesy of Evans Gallery,
Portland, Maine

*O'Keeffe Photographing
the Chama River,
New Mexico*
1961, Gelatin silver
print, 11 1/4 × 9 5/8 in.
(28.6 × 24.4 cm)
Courtesy of Evans Gallery,
Portland, Maine

*O'Keeffe's Ghost
Ranch House*
1962, Gelatin silver print,
12 3/8 × 9 7/8 in.
(31.4 × 25.1 cm)
Courtesy of Evans Gallery,
Portland, Maine

*Georgia O'Keeffe at
Ghost Ranch*
1963, Gelatin silver print,
4 1/2 × 4 1/2 in.
(11.4 × 11.4 cm)
Portland Museum of Art.
Gift of the Evans
Gallery and Todd and
Lucille Webb

*Georgia O'Keeffe
in Twilight Canyon*
1964, Gelatin silver print,
12 × 9 1/2 in. (30.5 × 24.1 cm)
Courtesy of Evans Gallery,
Portland, Maine

*O'Keeffe's Studio, Ghost
Ranch, New Mexico*
1965, Gelatin silver print,
9 5/16 × 7 1/2 in.
(23.7 × 19.1 cm)
Courtesy of Evans Gallery,
Portland, Maine

*Doorway to Patio,
O'Keeffe's Abiquiu House,
New Mexico*
1977, Gelatin silver print,
8 1/2 × 7 3/8 in.
(21.6 × 18.7 cm)
Courtesy of Evans Gallery,
Portland, Maine

*Georgia O'Keeffe's
Studio, the Abiquiu House,
New Mexico*
1977, Gelatin silver print,
6 1/2 × 8 3/8 in.
(16.5 × 21.3 cm)
Courtesy of Evans Gallery,
Portland, Maine

MYRON WOOD
(United States, b. 1921)

In the Living Room
1979, Gelatin silver print,
6 1/4 × 8 1/2 in.
(15.9 × 21.6 cm)
Private Collection

DON WORTH
(United States, b. 1924)

Georgia O'Keeffe
1958, Gelatin silver print,
16 × 20 in.
(40.6 × 50.8 cm)
Georgia O'Keeffe Museum,
Santa Fe. Gift of Andrew
Smith and Claire Lozier

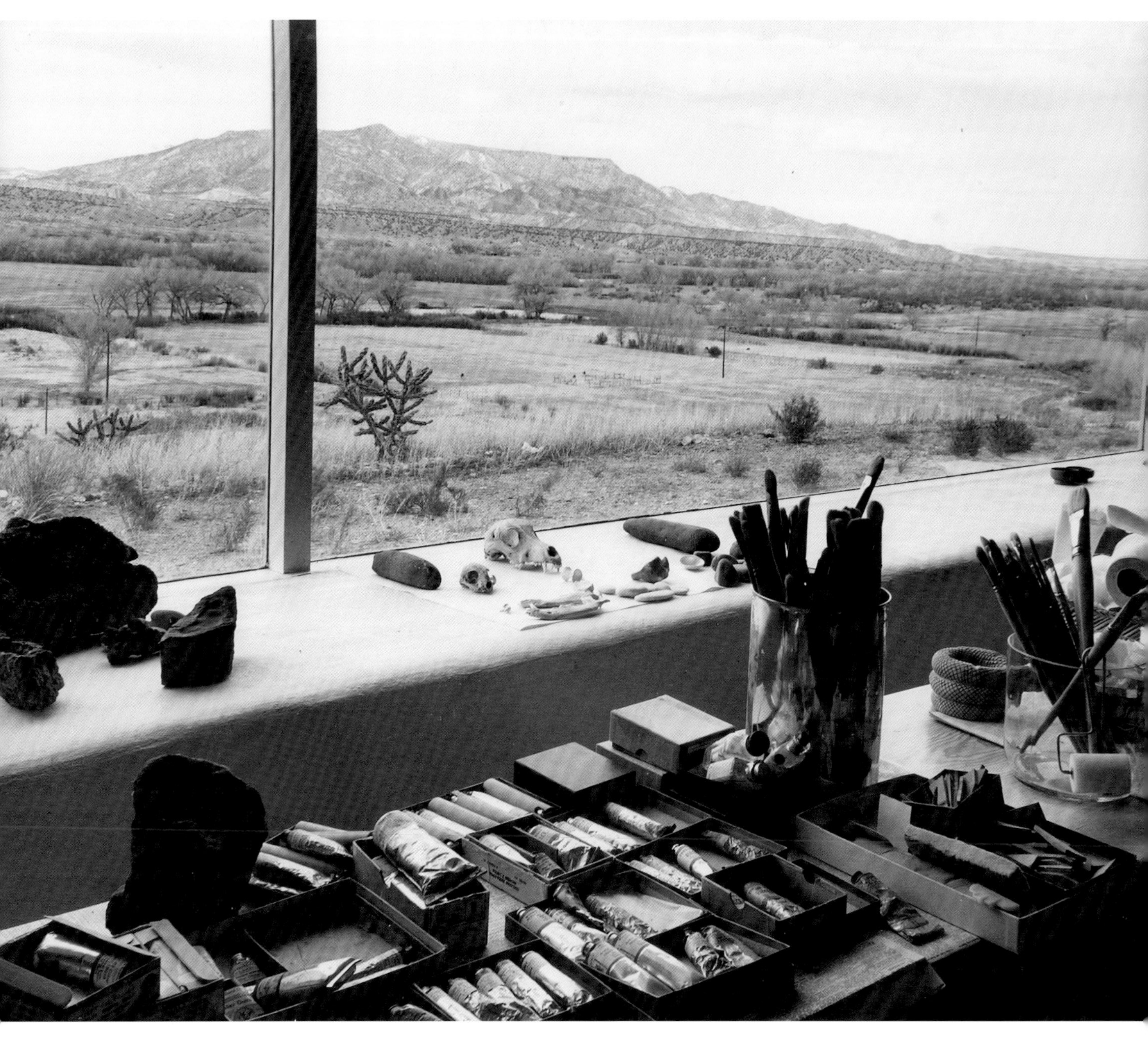

Laura Gilpin, *Studio of Georgia O'Keeffe Overlooking Chama Valley,* 1953, Gelatin silver print, 7 ⅝ × 9 ⅝ in. (19.4 × 24.4 cm), Amon Carter Museum, Forth Worth, Texas, Bequest of the artist. P1979.108.469

Selected Bibliography

GEORGIA O'KEEFFE

Brennan, Marcia. *Painting Gender, Constructing Theory: The Alfred Stieglitz Circle and American Formalist Aesthetics.* Cambridge, Mass.: MIT Press, 2001.

Bry, Doris, and Nicholas Callaway, eds. Georgia *O'Keeffe — In the West.* New York: Alfred A. Knopf, 1989.

Cowart, Jack, Juan Hamilton, and Sarah Greenough. *Georgia O'Keeffe, Art and Letters.* Washington, D.C.: National Gallery of Art in association with New York Graphic Society Books; Boston: Little, Brown, 1987.

Dijkstra, Bram. *Georgia O'Keeffe and the Eros of Place.* Princeton, N.J.: Princeton University Press, 1998.

Drohojowska-Philp, Hunter. *Full Bloom: The Art and Life of Georgia O'Keeffe.* New York: W. W. Norton, 2004.

Eldredge, Charles C. *Georgia O'Keeffe.* New York: Harry N. Abrams in association with the National Museum of American Art, Smithsonian Institution, 1991.

Goodrich, Lloyd, and Doris Bry. *Georgia O'Keeffe.* New York: Whitney Museum of American Art, 1970.

Hammond, Anne. *Georgia O'Keeffe and Ansel Adams: Natural Affinities.* Boston: Little, Brown, 2008.

Lisle, Laurie. *Portrait of an Artist: A Biography of Georgia O'Keeffe.* New York: Seaview Books, 1980. Reprinted with additions, New York: Washington Square Press, 1987.

Lynes, Barbara Buhler. *O'Keeffe, Stieglitz, and the Critics, 1916–1929.* Ann Arbor: University of Michigan Press, 1989. 2nd ed., Chicago: University of Chicago Press, 1991.

———. *Georgia O'Keeffe Catalogue Raisonné.* 2 vols. New Haven and London: Yale University Press in association with the National Gallery of Art, Washington, D.C., and the Georgia O'Keeffe Foundation, Abiquiu, N.Mex., 1999.

Lynes, Barbara Buhler, Lesley Poling-Kempes, and Frederick W. Turner. *Georgia O'Keeffe and New Mexico: A Sense of Place.* Princeton, N.J.: Princeton University Press, 2004.

Merrill, Christopher, and Ellen Bradbury, eds. *From the Faraway Nearby: Georgia O'Keeffe as Icon.* Albuquerque: University of New Mexico Press, 1998.

O'Keeffe, Georgia. *Georgia O'Keeffe.* New York: Viking Press, 1976; New York: Penguin Books, 1985.

Rich, Daniel Catton. *Georgia O'Keeffe.* Chicago: Art Institute of Chicago, 1943.

———. *Georgia O'Keeffe — Forty Years of Her Art.* Worcester, Mass.: Worcester Art Museum, 1960.

Robinson, Roxana. *Georgia O'Keeffe: A Life.* New York: Harper and Row, 1989.

Stieglitz, Alfred. *Georgia O'Keeffe: A Portrait.* New York: The Metropolitan Museum of Art, 1978. Reprinted with additions, New York: The Metropolitan Museum of Art, 1997.

Wagner, Anne Middleton. *Three Artists (Three Women): Modernism and the Art of Hesse, Krasner, and O'Keeffe.* Berkeley: University of California Press, 1996.

Wilder, Mitchell A., ed. *Georgia O'Keeffe.* Fort Worth, Tex.: Amon Carter Museum, 1966.

Photographers

ANSEL ADAMS

Adams, Ansel. *Photographs of the Southwest.* Boston: Little, Brown, 1976.

Adams, Ansel, and Mary Street Alinder. *Ansel Adams: An Autobiography.* Boston: Little, Brown, 1985.

Alinder, James, and John Szarkowski. *Ansel Adams: Classic Images.* Boston: Little, Brown, 1985.

Alinder, Mary Street. *Ansel Adams: A Biography.* New York: Henry Holt, 1996.

Haas, Karen E., and Rebecca A. Senf. *Ansel Adams in the Lane Collection.* Boston: MFA Publications, 2005.

LAURA GILPIN

Sandweiss, Martha A. *Laura Gilpin: An Enduring Grace*. Fort Worth, Tex.: Amon Carter Museum, 1986.

PHILIPPE HALSMAN

Bello, Jane Halsman, and Steve Bello, eds. *Philippe Halsman: A Retrospective; Photographs from the Halsman Family Collection*. Boston: Little, Brown, 1998.

YOUSUF KARSH

Borcoman, James, Estelle Jussim, Philip J. Pocock, and Lilly Koltun. *Karsh: The Art of the Portrait*. Ottawa: National Gallery of Canada, 1989.

Karsh, Yousuf. *Faces of Our Time*. Toronto: University of Toronto Press, 1971.

———. *Karsh: A Sixty-Year Retrospective*. Boston: Little, Brown, 1996.

JOHN LOENGARD

Loengard, John. *Georgia O'Keeffe at Ghost Ranch: A Photo Essay*. New York: teNeues, 1994.

———. *Image and Imagination: Georgia O'Keeffe*. San Francisco: Chronicle Books, 2007.

O'Keeffe, Georgia, John Loengard, and Lothar Schirmer. *Georgia O'Keeffe/ John Loengard: Paintings and Photographs; A Visit to Abiquiu and Ghost Ranch*. Munich: Schirmer Mosel, 2006.

ARNOLD NEWMAN

Fern, Alan, and Arnold Newman. *Arnold Newman's Americans*. Washington, D.C.: National Portrait Gallery, Smithsonian Institution, in association with Bulfinch/Little, Brown, 1992.

IRVING PENN

Foresta, Merry A., and William F. Stapp. *Irving Penn: Master Images*. Washington, D.C.: Smithsonian Institution Press, 1990.

MacGill, Peter. *Irving Penn: New and Unseen*. New York: Pace Wildenstein, 1999.

Westerbeck, Colin, ed. *Irving Penn: A Career in Photography*. Chicago: Art Institute of Chicago in association with Bulfinch/Little, Brown, 1997.

ELIOT PORTER

Rohrbach, John, Rebecca Solnit, and Jonathan Porter. *Eliot Porter: The Color of Wildness*. New York: Aperture Foundation, in association with the Amon Carter Museum, 2001.

ALFRED STIEGLITZ

Greenough, Sarah. *Alfred Stieglitz: The Key Set*. Vol. 1, *1886–1922*. Vol. 2, *1923–1937*. Washington, D.C.: National Gallery of Art and New York: Harry N. Abrams, 2002.

ANDY WARHOL

Feldman, Frayda, and Jorg Schellmann. *Andy Warhol Prints: A Catalogue Raisonné, 1962–1987*. 3rd ed. New York D.A.P./ Distributed Art Publishers in association with R. Feldman Fine Arts, 1997.

Warhol, Andy. *Andy Warhol: Photography*. New York: Edition Stemmle, 1999.

TODD WEBB

Webb, Todd. *Georgia O'Keeffe: The Artist's Landscape*. Pasadena, Calif.: Twelvetrees Press, 1984.

———. *Looking Back: Memoirs and Photographs*. Albuquerque: University of New Mexico Press, 1991.

MYRON WOOD

Wood, Myron, and Christine Taylor Patten. *O'Keeffe at Abiquiu*. New York: Harry N. Abrams, 1995.

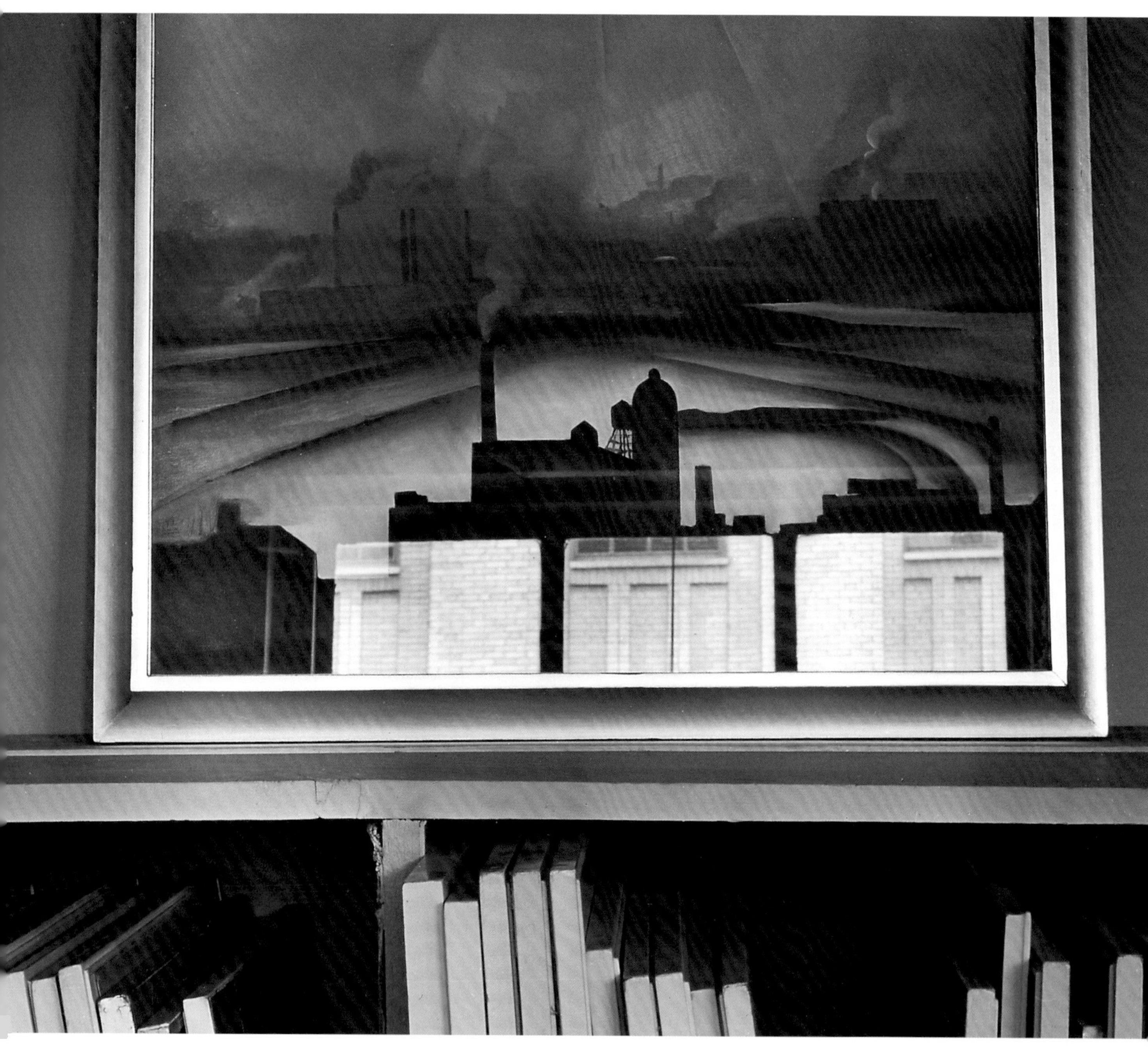

Ansel Adams, *Detail of O'Keeffe Painting and Reflections, An American Place, Gallery of Alfred Stieglitz* 1939, Gelatin silver print, 7 ⅛ × 8 ⅞ in. (18.1 × 22.5 cm) Princeton University Art Museum. Gift of David H. McAlpin, Class of 1920

Index

Page numbers in italics indicate illustrations

A

Abiquiu: Maria Chabot restoration of, 19, 20, 108; courtyard entryway at, 19–20; furniture in, 28–29, 96, 98; *Horse Skull, O'Keeffe's House, Abiquiu, New Mexico* (1952, Porter), 76; Yousuf Karsh portrait of O'Keeffe at, 23–24, 88; magazine pieces on, 28–29, 33, 98, 99, 101; modernist aesthetic at, 28, 29; patios at, 19, 21, 28, 72, 81; studio at, 25, 26, 29, 64, 82, 90, 101; in Todd Webb's photographs, 20, 21, 75, 81; Myron Wood at, 29–30; Don Worth photographs of, 28, 96

Above the Clouds I (1962–1963, O'Keeffe), 29, 99, 100

Abstraction (1916, O'Keeffe), 8–9, 37n4, 50

abstraction in art of O'Keeffe, 8–10, 21, 22, 28, 37n4, 50, 84, 85, 96

Adams, Ansel: canyon landscapes of, 15–16; at Ghost Ranch, 14, 16, 17, 64, 66; influence on O'Keeffe, 14; David McAlpin and, 14, 17–18, 39n39; on O'Keeffe's life in New Mexico, 17; portraits of O'Keeffe by, 14, 15, 16, 17, 48, 63, 64, 67; Alfred Stieglitz and, 14, 17

After a Walk Back of Mabel's (1930, O'Keeffe), 12

Alfred Stieglitz and Georgia O'Keeffe, An American Place (1944, Newman), 24–25, 47

Alfred Stieglitz Presents One Hundred Pictures: Oils, Watercolors, Pastels, Drawings by Georgia O'Keeffe, 10, 57, 107

An American Place (Stieglitz gallery): Ansel Adams exhibition at, 14; *Alfred Stieglitz and Georgia O'Keeffe, An American Place* (1944, Newman), 24–25, 47; *Details of O'Keeffe Painting and Reflections, An American Place, Gallery of Alfred Stieglitz* (1939, Adams), 17, 67; O'Keeffe exhibition at, 12, 16, 107; opening of, 107; Eliot Porter exhibition at, 18

Anderson Gallery (New York), 9, 10, 12, 16, 57, 107

architecture: adobe walls, 20, 28, 75; in church paintings, 13–14; O'Keeffe's interest in Santa Fe architecture, 25–26; patios, 19, 21, 28, 72, 81; in photographs of Ansel Adams, 13–14; vernacular architecture, 14, 38n28

Arden, Elizabeth, 32, 35

art (O'Keeffe): abstraction in, 8–10, 21, 22, 28, 37n4, 50, 84, 85, 96; architectural idioms in, 14, 25–26; charcoal drawings by, 8, 9–10, 41–78, 54, 107; color in, 10, 14, 22, 35, 44, 85; critics on, 10–11, 22; exhibitions of, 20, 32, 77; Freudian interpretations of, 3, 4, 9, 44; health of O'Keeffe and, 10–11; Japanese influences in O'Keeffe's art, 29; minimalist paintings, 28, 97; personality reflected in, 23–24; purchased by David McAlpin, 17; Radio City Music Hall commission, 11; sexualized interpretations of, 3–4, 44, 107; space used in, 25–26; watercolors, 10. *See also* exhibitions (O'Keeffe)

Austin, Mary, 13

automobiles, 11–12, 16, 38n21, 46, 59, 64

B

Beaton, Cecil, 33

Bedroom, Ghost Ranch (1967, Loengard), 26, 27, 91

Bertoia, Harry, 28, 29, 98

bird chair and ottoman (Bertoia), 28, 29, 98

black-and-white photography, 18, 68

Blue Black and Grey (1960, O'Keeffe), 22, 85

Blue Line (1919, Georgia O'Keeffe), 10, 44

bone collection: at Abiquiu, 29; antlers, 23–24, 61, 88, 94; at Ghost Ranch, 20, 23–24, 49, 76, 94; horse skulls, 12–13, 20, 60, 61, 76; O'Keeffe on, 26; in O'Keeffe paintings, 12–13, 61; in Stieglitz photographs of O'Keeffe, 13, 60; still-life arrangements by Loengard, 26, 27, 94; in Webb's photography, 21, 79

butterfly chair (Ferrari-Hardoy), 28, 96

C

Calder, Alexander, 23, 26, 27, 53

Callery, Mary, 18, 39–44, 69

Camera Work, 8

cars, 11–12, 16, 38n21, 46, 59, 64

celebrity photography. *See individual photographers*

Chabot, Maria, 19, 20, 108

Chama River and Chama River Valley, 19, 26, 78, 115

charcoal drawings (O'Keeffe), 8, 9–10, 41n78, 54, 107

church of San Francisco de Asis, 13

church paintings (O'Keeffe), 13–14

cloud paintings (O'Keeffe), 29, 99, 100

color used by O'Keeffe, 10, 14, 22, 35, 44, 85

Corn, No. 2 (1924, O'Keeffe), 3, 45

Cowart, Jack, 109

Cox, Orville, 15, 63

Coxcomb (1931, O'Keeffe), 31, 103

critics: on abstract art of O'Keeffe art, 22; on 1978 portrait exhibition at Metropolitan Museum of Art, 2–3; Freudian interpretations of O'Keeffe's art, 3–4; on nudity in Stieglitz portraits of O'Keeffe, 9; sexual interpretations of O'Keeffe art, 10, 107

Cromwell, Georgia Engelhard, 2

Crowninshield, Frank, 31–32

D

Daniell, George, 27–28, 76, 96

Detail of O'Keeffe Painting and Reflections, An American Place, Gallery of Alfred Stieglitz (1939, Adams), 17, 118

Doorway to Patio, O'Keeffe's Abiquiu House, New Mexico (1977, Webb), 21, 81

Dove, Arthur, 22

Dow, Arthur Wesley, 29, 107

dress style (O'Keeffe): black in, 12, 22, 28, 86, 96; head coverings, 23, 70, 87; jewelry, 12, 23, 53, 59

E

Eames, Ray, 29

Evening Walk, Ghost Ranch (1966, Loengard), 26, 27, 93

F

exhibitions (O'Keeffe): at Anderson Gallery, 9, 10, 12, 16, 57, 107; Museum of Modern Art (MoMA), 20, 32, 77; photographs of, 8–9, 10, 12, 16, 20, 57, 77, 107; retrospective exhibitions of, 32, 109; at 291, 8

Ferrari-Hardoy, Jorge, 28

flowers, 3–4, 17, 32, 44, 45, 107

Freudian interpretations of O'Keeffe's art, 3, 4, 9, 44

From the River—Pale (1959, O'Keeffe), 21, 22, 82, 83

furniture, 28, 29, 96, 98

G

Georgia O'Keeffe, Ghost Ranch, New Mexico (1945, Porter), 18, 69

Georgia O'Keeffe, Ghost Ranch, New Mexico (1968, Newman), 25, 89

Georgia O'Keeffe: The Artist's Landscape (Webb's book, 1984), 21, 79

Georgia O'Keeffe (1917, Stieglitz), 1, 42

Georgia O'Keeffe (1918, Stieglitz), 2, 43

Georgia O'Keeffe (1918, Stieglitz), 53

Georgia O'Keeffe (1919, Stieglitz), 9, 51

Georgia O'Keeffe (1930, Stieglitz), 12, 58

Georgia O'Keeffe (1931, Stieglitz), 13, 60

Georgia O'Keeffe (1933, Stieglitz), 12, 59

Georgia O'Keeffe (1948, Halsman), 23, 87

Georgia O'Keeffe (1948, Penn), 22–23, 86

Georgia O'Keeffe (1953, Gilpin), 25, 26, 90

Georgia O'Keeffe (1956, Karsh), 23–24, 88

Georgia O'Keeffe (1958, Worth), 28, 96

Georgia O'Keeffe (1979, Warhol), 35, 105

Georgia O'Keeffe—After Return from New Mexico (1929, Stieglitz), 4, 12, 31, 46

Georgia O'Keeffe and Orville Cox, Canyon de Chelly National Park (1937, Adams), 15, 63

*Georgia O'Keeffe at Ghost
   Ranch* (1963, Webb), 49
Georgia O'Keeffe—Hands
   (1919, Stieglitz), 9, *55*
Georgia O'Keeffe in Doorway
   (1952, Daniell), 28, *96*
*Georgia O'Keeffe in Glen
   Canyon, New Mexico*
   (1961, Webb), *70*
*Georgia O'Keeffe in the
   Southwest* (1937, Adams),
   14, *48*
*Georgia O'Keeffe in Twilight
   Canyon* (1961, Webb), *78*
*Georgia O'Keeffe Painting in
   Her Car, Ghost Ranch,
   New Mexico* (1937, Adams),
   16, *64*
*Georgia O'Keeffe Seated
   among Her Props* (1952,
   Daniell), *76*
*Georgia O'Keeffe's Entrance
   Door, Abiquiu, New
   Mexico* (1949, Porter), 19,
   73
*Georgia O'Keeffe's Studio,
   the Abiquiu House, New
   Mexico* (1977, Webb),
   21, *82*
Gerald's Tree, 16
Gerald's Tree II (1937,
   O'Keeffe), *65*
Ghost Ranch, 7; *Bedroom,
   Ghost Ranch* (1967,
   Loengard), 26, *91*; bone
   collection at, 20, 23–24, 49,
   76, 94; daily life at, 15–17,
   26–27, 38n35; *Georgia
   O'Keeffe, Ghost Ranch,
   New Mexico* (1968, New-
   man), 25, *89*; John Loen-
   gard photographs at, 26–27,
   47, 94; *Mud Hills—Ghost
   Ranch, New Mexico* (1937,
   Adams), *66*; O'Keeffe's
   painting of, 15, 16, 62;
   Eliot Porter, 18, *69*;
   Rancho de los Burros, 15,
   108; *On the Roof, Ghost
   Ranch* (1967, Loengard),
   26–27, 47; studios at, 21,
   27, *84*, *95*; visitors at, 15,
   38n35; in *Vogue* (magazine),
   33; Todd Webb at, 21,
   49, *79*, *84*; Myron Wood
   photographs of, 30
Ghost Ranch (1940, Porter),
   18, *68*, *69*
Ghost Ranch (1966, Loengard),
   26, *94*
Gilpin, Laura, 25, 26, *90*, *115*
Glen Canyon, 18–19, 20
gnarled trees and tree stumps,
   24
Green Lines and Pink (1919,
   O'Keeffe), 10, *56*
Greenough, Sarah, 109

H

Halsman, Philippe, 23, *87*
Hamilton, Juan, 30, 34, 109
hands in photographs of
   O'Keeffe, 9–10, 13, 24,
   55, 60, 71, *88*
Hartley, Marsden, 107
Heard, Gerald, 16, 38n35
homes of O'Keeffe:
   architecture of, 29;
   furniture in, 28, 29, 98;
   modernist aesthetic in,
   29, 30; personality reflected
   in, 30–31; Rancho de los
   Burros, 15, 108;
   southwestern elements in,
   28–29. *See also* Abiquiu;
   Ghost Ranch
horseback riding, 16
*Horse Skull, O'Keeffe's House,
   Abiquiu, New Mexico*
   (1952, Porter), *76*
horse skulls, 13, 20, 60, 61, 76
Horse's Skull with White Rose
   (1931, O'Keeffe), 13, *61*
House Beautiful (magazine),
   25–26, 28
The House I Live In (1937,
   O'Keeffe), 15, 16, *62*
Hughes, Robert, 32

I

*Installation View at O'Keeffe
   Exhibition at the Museum
   of Modern Art* (1946,
   Webb), 20, *77*
Interpretation (1919, Stieglitz),
   8–9, 37n4, *51*
interview with Andy Warhol,
   32, 34, 35, 41–89
Intimate Gallery (Stieglitz), 107

J

Japanese influences in
   O'Keeffe's art, 29
Jareckie, Stephen, 39n39
Jimson Weed (O'Keeffe), 32
Johnson, Philip, 35
Johnson, Robert Wood, 16
Johnson, Spud, 18
Jussim, Estelle, 24

K

Karsh, Yousuf, 23–24, *88*
Klein, Calvin, 35
Korab, Balthazar, 28–29, 98,
   99, 101

L

*Ladder and Adobe Wall,
   O'Keeffe's Abiquiu House,
   New Mexico* (1957, Webb),
   20, *75*
Lake George, New York, 11,
   107, 108
*Life and Death—Hands and
   Skull* (1930, Stieglitz), 13,
   60
Life (magazine), 13, 15, 20, 23,
   26–27, 32, 47
Lisle, Laurie, 109
Little Galleries of the Photo-
   Secession. *See* 291 (Stieglitz
   gallery)
Loengard, John, 19; *Ghost
   Ranch* (1966, Loengard),
   26, *94*; at Ghost Ranch,
   26, 91, 94; O'Keeffe's art
   in photographs of, 27;
   on O'Keeffe's persona in
   consumer culture, 36;
   photographs of O'Keeffe
   houses in *Life* (magazine),
   26; *On the Roof, Ghost
   Ranch* (1967, Loengard),
   26–27, 47; still-life
   arrangements of bones,
   26, 27, 94; *Studio, Ghost
   Ranch* (1967, Loengard),
   95
Luhan, Mabel Dodge, 11,
   13, 107

M

magazines: homes of O'Keeffe
   portrayed in, 26–29, 33, 47,
   98, 99, 101; persona of
   O'Keeffe in, 15, 20, 32–34;
   women's magazines on
   Georgia O'Keeffe, 22,
   31–32, 33–34, 36
Makos, Christopher, 35
Marin, John, 22, 107
McAlpin, David Hunter, 14,
   15, 16, 17, 39–39
McBride, Henry, 3
Meem, John Gaw, 19, 25,
   40–62
Metropolitan Museum of Art,
   2–3, 17
Mexico, travel to, 18
minimalist paintings of
   O'Keeffe, 28, 97
modernism, 27–28, 29–30,
   96, 97
Ms. (magazine), 36
*Mud Hills—Ghost Ranch,
   New Mexico* (1937, Adams),
   17, *67*
Museum of Modern Art
   (MoMA), 14, 17, 20, 31–32,
   77, 108
Music—Pink and Blue No. 1
   (1918, O'Keeffe), 9
My Last Door (1952–1954,
   O'Keeffe), 27, *91*
Myth series (Warhol), 35

N

National Institute of Arts and
   Letters, 108
Navajo art, 12, 38–21, 59
Newhall, Beaumont, 17
Newman, Arnold, 1, 24–25,
   47, *89*
Norman, Dorothy, 11
New Yorker (magazine), 33
No. 15—Special (1916–1917,
   O'Keeffe), 9, 41n78
No. 17—Special (1919,
   O'Keeffe), 9–10, 54, *55*
Nude Series VII (1917,
   O'Keeffe), *57*
nudity, 2, 9, 10, 57

O

O'Keeffe, Georgia:
   architectural subjects of,
   13–14, 25–26; beauty
   associated with, 32; cars of,
   11–12, 16, 38n21, 46, 59,
   64; death of Stieglitz, 22,
   86; dependence on Stieglitz,
   3–4, 13–14, 15; education
   of, 7–8, 29, 106, 107;
   eyesight of, 30, 35; hands in
   photographs of, 9–10, 13,
   24, 55, 60, 71, 88; health of,
   10–11, 35, 107, 108, 109;
   interview with Andy
   Warhol, 32, 34, 35, 41n89;
   and modernism, 27–30,
   96, 97; on moving to New
   Mexico, 26; nudity in
   Stieglitz portraits of, 9–10;
   as older woman, 23, 30–31,
   35, 41n89, 49, 87; photography of, 21, 78; publications of, 32–33, 109;
   rafting trips, 18–19, 21,
   39–39, 109; relations with
   Stieglitz, 1–4, 7, 11, 13–17,
   24–25, 47, 107; sculpture
   of, 8–9, 37n4, 51; Stieglitz's
   involvement in career of,
   9, 10, 57, 107; teaching
   positions of, 8, 107; travels
   of, 17, 18, 108, 109; works:
   Above the Clouds I (1962–
   1963), 29, 99, 100; *Abstraction* (1916), 8–9, 37n4,
   50; *After a Walk Back of
   Mabel's* (1930), 12; *Blue
   Black and Grey* (1960), 22,
   85; *Blue Line* (1919), 44;
   Corn, No. 2 (1924), 45;
   Coxcomb (1931), 31, 103;
   Gerald's Tree II (1937), 65;

Green Lines and Pink (1919), 10, *56; Horse's Skull with White Rose* (1931), 13, *61; The House I Live In* (1937), 15, 16, *62; Jimson Weed, 32; Music—Pink and Blue No. 1* (1918), 9; *My Last Door* (1952–1954), 27, *91; No. 15—Special* (1916–1917), 9, 41n78; *No. 17—Special* (1919), 9–10, 54, 55; *Nude Series VII* (1917), 57; *The Patio—No. 1* (1940), 19, *72; Red Hills beyond Abiquiu* (1930), 16, *67; From the River—Pale* (1959), 21, 22, 82, *83; Three Small Rocks Big* (1937), 16, *66; Wall with Green Door* (1952), 28, *97;* on Frank Lloyd Wright, 29, 40n72. *See also* Abiquiu; art (O'Keeffe); bone collection; dress style (O'Keeffe); exhibitions (O'Keeffe); persona (O'Keeffe); Ghost Ranch; *headings for specific photographers;* Stieglitz, Alfred

O'Keeffe Exhibition, April 17, 1917 (1917, Stieglitz), 8, *50*

O'Keeffe Exhibit at Anderson Gallery (1923, Stieglitz), 10, 12, 16, 57, 107

O'Keeffe Photographing the Chama River, New Mexico (1961, Webb), *78*

O'Keeffe's Ghost Ranch House (1962, Webb), 21, *79*

O'Keeffe's Studio, Ghost Ranch, New Mexico (1965, Webb), 21, *84*

On the Roof, Ghost Ranch (1967, Loengard), 26–27, *47*

P

Pansies and Forget-Me-Nots (1927, 1980, Wood), 30, *102*

The Patio—No. 1 (1940, O'Keeffe), 19, *72*

Penn, Irving, 22–23, *86*

Polaroid camera, 21, 35, *78*

Pollitzer, Anita, 8

Porter, Eliot: Colorado River rafting trips, 18–19, 21, 109; exhibition at An American Place, 18; *Georgia O'Keeffe, Ghost Ranch, New Mexico* (1945, Porter), *69; Georgia O'Keeffe's Entrance Door, Abiquiu, New Mexico* (1949, Porter), 19, *73; Ghost Ranch* (1940, Porter), 68; *Horse Skull, O'Keeffe's House, Abiquiu, New Mexico* (1952, Porter), *76;* Mexican churches photographed by, 18; *The Rock from Eliot Porter, Abiquiu* (1966, Loengard), 19, 26–27, *71*

Portrait of an Artist: A Biography of Georgia O'Keeffe (Lisle, 1980), 109

Pueblo, Colorado, public library project, 29–30

pueblo revival, 30

R

Radio City Music Hall commission, 11

rafting trips, 18–19, 21, 39–39, 109

Rancho de los Burros, 15, 108

Ranchos de Taos Church, 13–14

Read, Helen Appleton, 10

Red Hills beyond Abiquiu (1930, O'Keeffe), 16, *67*

Rembrandt effect in photography, 18

Rich, Daniel Catton, 109

Roche, Mary, 28

Rockefeller, Godfrey, 14

The Rock from Eliot Porter, Abiquiu (1966, Loengard), 19, 26–27, *71*

rocks, 16, 19, 26–27, 67, 71, *98*

Rodin, Auguste, 8

Rose, Barbara, 33–34, 35–36

Rosenfeld, Paul, 9

S

San Francisco de Asis (church), 13

Santa Fe, New Mexico, 11–12, 21, 25–26

Schwartz, Sanford, 33

sculpture of O'Keeffe, 8–9, 37–4, *50, 51*

Seligmann, Herbert, 10, 22

sexuality, 2–4, 9–10, 12, 107

silk-screen prints, 35

Some Memories of Drawing (O'Keeffe's book, 1974), 109

Stieglitz, Alfred: Ansel Adams and, 14, 17; Anderson Gallery (New York), 9, 10, 12, 16, 57, 107; bones from New Mexico in photography of, 12–13; composite portraiture by, 1–2; death of, 22, 86; hands in photographs of O'Keeffe, 9–10, 55, 60; his imagining of O'Keeffe, 9–10, 31; O'Keeffe exhibitions at galleries of, 8, 10, 12, 16, 57, 107; on O'Keeffe's sculpture, 8–9, 37n4, *51;* personality of, 1–2, 11; relationship with O'Keeffe, 1–4, 7, 11, 13–17, 24–25, 47, 107; 291 (gallery), 7–8, 29, 106, 107. *See also* An American Place (Stieglitz gallery)

Strand, Paul, 11, 107

Strand, Rebecca, 11, 107

Studio, Ghost Ranch (1967, Loengard), 27, *95*

Studio of Georgia O'Keeffe Overlooking Chama Valley (1953, Gilpin), *115*

studios of O'Keeffe, 16, 22, 84; at Abiquiu, 25, 26, 29, 64, 82, 90, *101;* at Ghost Ranch, 21, 84, 95; modernist aesthetic of, 29

Sweeney, James Johnson, 108

T

Taos Pueblo (1930, Adams), 13, 14

Tesuque, New Mexico, 18, 19

"The Self, the Style and the Art of Georgia O'Keeffe" (Rose article, 1986), 34

Three Small Rocks Big (1937, O'Keeffe), 16, 66

291 (Stieglitz gallery), 7–8, 29, 106, 107

Tyrrell, Henry, 10

U

Untitled [Georgia O'Keeffe in her studio, #55] (1965, Korab), *101*

Untitled [Living room at Abiquiu, #25, #27] (1965, Korab), 99

V

Vanity Fair (magazine), 31–32

vernacular architectural forms, 14, 38n28

Vogue (magazine), 22, 33–34

W

Wall with Green Door (1952, O'Keeffe), 28, 97

Warhol, Andy, 32, 34, 35, 36, 41n89, *105*

Webb, Todd: Abiquiu in photographs of, 20, 21, 75, *81;* bone collection in works of, 21, *79;* friendship with O'Keeffe, 20–21; *Georgia O'Keeffe in Twilight Canyon* (1961, Webb), 78; Ghost Ranch photographs of, 21, 49, 79, 84; Glen Canyon photographs, 21, *70; Installation View at O'Keeffe Exhibition at the Museum of Modern Art* (1946, Webb), 20, 77; *O'Keeffe Photographing the Chama River, New Mexico* (1961), 78; photographic techniques of, 20; rafting trip with O'Keeffe and Eliot Porter, 21; studios of O'Keeffe photographed by, 21, 22, 82, 84

Westerbrook, Colin, 22

Western Interiors and Design, 29

Whitney Museum, 32

Wood, Myron, 27, 29–30, *102*

Worcester Art Museum, 32, 109

World's Fair (New York), 17

Worth, Don, 27, 28, *96*

Wright, Frank Lloyd, 29, 40n72